The Religion Matters Reader

The Religion Matters Reader

Joseph P. Laycock

Natasha L. Mikles

W. W. NORTON & COMPANY
Independent Publishers Since 1923

W. W. Norton & Company has been independent since its founding in 1923, when William Warder Norton and Mary D. Herter Norton first published lectures delivered at the People's Institute, the adult education division of New York City's Cooper Union. The firm soon expanded its program beyond the Institute, publishing books by celebrated academics from America and abroad. By midcentury, the two major pillars of Norton's publishing program—trade books and college texts—were firmly established. In the 1950s, the Norton family transferred control of the company to its employees, and today—with a staff of four hundred and a comparable number of trade, college, and professional titles published each year—W. W. Norton & Company stands as the largest and oldest publishing house owned wholly by its employees.

Editor: Roby Harrington
Project Editor: Linda Feldman
Editorial Assistant: Vincent Yu
Managing Editor, College: Marian Johnson
Managing Editor, College Digital Media: Kim Yi
Associate Director of Production, College: Benjamin Reynolds
Media Editor: Carly Fraser Doria
Media Editorial Assistant: Jessica Awad
Digital Project Editor: Cooper Wilhelm
Marketing Manager: Megan Zwilling
Design Director: Rubina Yeh
Text Design: Lissi Sigillo
Director of College Permissions: Megan Schindel
Composition: Westchester Publishing Services
Manufacturing: Maple Press

Library of Congress Cataloging-in-Publication Data

Names: Laycock, Joseph, 1980- author. | Mikles, Natasha L., 1986- author.
Title: The Religion matters reader / Joseph Laycock, Natasha Mikles.
Description: First edition. | New York, NY : W. W. Norton & Company, [2021] |
    Includes bibliographical references.
Identifiers: LCCN 2020053064 | **ISBN 9780393543209 (paperback)** |
    ISBN 9780393871449 (epub)
Subjects: LCSH: Religions—Textbooks.
Classification: LCC BL80.3 .L386 2021 | DDC 200—dc23
LC record available at https://lccn.loc.gov/2020053064

W. W. Norton & Company, Inc., 500 Fifth Avenue, New York, NY 10110-0017
wwnorton.com
W. W. Norton & Company Ltd., 15 Carlisle Street, London W1D 3BS
1234567890

For our students

Brief Contents

Contents

Introduction   1

Hinduism   16

Buddhism   53

Sikhism

Judaism

Christianity

Islam

Confucianism   161

Daoism   185

Navajo   198

Atheism 241

About the Authors

Joseph P. Laycock is an associate professor of religious studies at Texas State University. He is the coeditor for the journal *Nova Religion* and the author of multiple books on religion.

Natasha L. Mikles is a lecturer in Asian Religions in the religious studies program at Texas State University. She is the editor of the *Journal of Gods and Monsters*, as well as the author of numerous articles related to popular Buddhist literature.

Acknowledgments

We would like to thank the wonderful staff at Norton, especially Roby Harrington, Vinny Yu, Linda Feldman, Lissi Sigillo, Elizabeth Trammell, Kim Bowers, Carly Fraser Doria, and Elizabeth Pieslor.

What to Read?

by Stephen Prothero

At least since the invention of the printing press, choosing what to read has been a problem for readers, and it has become more acute with the invention of the World Wide Web. In many academic disciplines, including religious studies, it was once possible to "control" the literature in the field, or at least in subfields such as Buddhist studies or American religious history. Not anymore. The proliferation of texts, virtual and otherwise, has made the development of high school and college courses difficult, and the editing of readers like this one simultaneously foolhardy and urgent. If you are doing a film or a course or a reader on the world's religions, you have only so many minutes or days or pages.

In a brilliant TED Talk delivered by a 318-year-old hologram, the novelist, playwright, and religious studies major Monica Byrne has wisely observed that "creation needs constraint." Without the limits of a canvas of a certain size, a haiku of a certain form, or (in her case) a TED Talk of a certain length, the artist cannot really get her artistic process up and running.

Here Joseph Laycock and Natasha Mikles have followed my textbook, *Religion Matters*, in presenting an introductory religious studies course through the eyes of nine religious traditions. They have followed my four-part model by looking in each case for:

1. The problem each religion sees in human life on earth;
2. The solution it offers to that problem;
3. The techniques it employs to cure what ails us; and
4. The exemplars who chart the path from the problem to the solution.

They have also followed *Religion Matters* in concluding each chapter with a contemporary controversy. At the urging of their editor, they have further limited themselves to just five relatively short readings from each religious tradition.

Many teachers and students alike will doubtless be horrified that they have left out Gandhi or the Dalai Lama or Jesus himself. But learning, too, requires constraint. And inside their constraints Laycock and Mikles have, in my view, chosen well, attending to both classical and contemporary expressions and giving considerable space to the expressions of women and people of color. Given the patriarchal realities of religions across the millennia, finding women's voices is not always easy. Finding nonwhite voices is considerably easier, since precisely zero of the religions in this reader were founded by a white person, and every single Hindu, Buddhist, Sikh, Jewish, Christian, Islamic, Confucian, Daoist, and Navajo scripture was created by a person (or persons) of color.

But it is not the choices of editors that matter in readers like this. What matters are the choices of students who use them. What matters when it comes to the study of religious texts is the decision of readers to engage them with a combination of empathic understanding and critical thinking. The transcendentalist author and activist Henry David Thoreau once said that he had no reason to leave his hometown because he could see the world from the confines of Concord, Massachusetts. You, too, can see the worlds of Buddhism through these five Buddhist readings and the worlds of Islam through these five Islamic readings. But you can do so only if you approach them with empathy and read them with care—slowly, deeply, with a curiosity born of a desire to learn about ways of living other than your own.

Here you can come to understand how and why early Hindu thinkers came to believe that we humans are stuck in a cycle of life, death, and rebirth. And you can evaluate the strategies Hindus and Buddhists alike devised to liberate themselves (and others) from that cycle. You will encounter a Jewish activist who is fighting for equal access for women to Jerusalem's Western Wall while arguing that "well-behaved women seldom make history." You will also encounter some of those history-making women, including the Sufi poet Rabia, the Catholic activist Dorothy Day, and the atheist rebel Madalyn Murray O'Hair. If you read with care and curiosity both *The Analects* of Confucius and the contemporary take on Confucius by the Chinese media star Yu Dan, you can start to understand how scriptures are always being repurposed for new societies and new times. If you attend to the arguments made in *Navajo Nation v. US Forest Service*, about efforts by Navajos and other First Nation peoples to prevent the federal government from using treated wastewater to make snow on their sacred mountain, you can learn how law and religion are so often tied up with one another, and how nation-states often use and abuse religious people and religious symbols for their own purposes.

Religions are misunderstood when they are seen as answers to some cosmic test. More than answer banks, they are question generators, offering opportunities to reflect on what in many cases are unanswerable questions. This reader offers a similar opportunity to any student of religion willing to enter into conversation with the living and the dead about the questions we humans have been asking ourselves since before we had readers and before we had books.

Introduction

This reader provides an examination of nine major religions (as well as atheism) with the goals of featuring (1) the uniqueness of each tradition, (2) the internal diversity within each tradition, and (3) the importance of knowing about these traditions for understanding contemporary events and controversies. The pursuit of these three goals means that this reader is somewhat different from other world religion readers.

The texts selected here are not limited to "scripture"—a category that does not apply to all religions equally well. Nor are they intended to represent the "foundational" texts of the tradition. Students will note, for example, that the Hebrew Bible, the New Testament, and the Quran are all absent. This choice was made because multiple translations of these texts are readily available online. But it is also in keeping with religious studies scholar J. Z. Smith's insight that the academic study of religion is about rendering the strange familiar and the familiar strange. Texts such as court decisions, interviews, and news reports are included so that the student may look at familiar traditions with fresh eyes as well as encounter traditions with which they are unfamiliar.

Instead of emphasizing the "most important" texts of a tradition, this reader is based on a four-part model of religion, developed by Stephen Prothero, in which each tradition postulates (1) a human problem, (2) a solution to that problem, (3) techniques for achieving that solution, and (4) exemplars who serve as models for following the techniques. To be clear, this four-part model is a *model*; it is a way of thinking about things, not the thing itself. The model provides a framework for comparing religions in order to understand how each religion is unique and perceives the world in its own way. Each unit, then, contains five readings revealing different facets of the tradition.

The first reading is a text that highlights how this tradition perceives the human problem and its solution. In her book *Doubt*, philosopher Jennifer Michael Hecht wrote that believers and nonbelievers alike must reckon with what she called a "meaning-rupture." As human beings, we have a mental image of how the world should work—a world where there is love and reason and things make sense. At the same time, we experience a world that appears random, senseless, and cruel. As Hecht puts it, "We live in a meaning-rupture because we are human and the universe is not." But from where does this rupture arise? Is it because we are born to a state of original sin that separates us from God? Because existence is suffering that must be overcome through enlightenment? Or because humans have forgotten how to live in a state of social harmony with one another? And what is on the other side of this rupture? Paradise? Nirvana? The quality of harmony and beauty that the Navajo way calls *hozho*? However a tradition understands the problem and solution, they are intimately bound together: a text that emphasizes the problem implies the solution and vice versa.

The second text describes a technique for achieving the solution. The techniques of world religions include everything from the three paths of Hindu yoga to Daoist internal alchemy to Navajo Blessingway ceremonies and even Luther's insistence that "faith alone" is all that is required. Of course, most traditions have many techniques and many ways of practicing them. The selections provided here attempt to offer a sense of the range of these techniques, as well as a basis for comparing them.

The third and fourth readings describe exemplars of the tradition. Exemplars can include anything from living people to legendary saints and immortals to the Holy People of the Navajo. Most religions have a vast array of exemplars spanning centuries, traditions, and continents. Including only two seems woefully inadequate; however, the two that were chosen are meant to demonstrate some of the diversity within the tradition. They are also intended to reflect to some degree how the values and beliefs of that religion are "lived" in the real world among real people, who often do not hold the same concerns as the authoritative institutions that have traditionally defined much of the discussion in world religion classrooms.

The fifth reading outlines a "controversy" related to the tradition. The controversy is in no way an indictment of the religion or even an issue unique to that tradition. For example, all world religions have engaged in violence, but we have highlighted only Buddhist violence in Myanmar; many religions have been wielded by conservative political movements, but we have focused only on the Hindutva movement in contemporary India. What these controversies reveal is not that the tradition has some sort of imperfection in need of fixing but rather that religion matters. While there are many benefits to studying world religion, a key assumption of this reader is that the political, economic, cultural, and military controversies of our day are often intimately entangled with the world's religions and that religious literacy is necessary to adequately understand these issues.

In addition to the nine traditions featured here, this reader also contains two shorter sections: an introductory section with essays discussing methodology in religious studies and suggestions on how to analyze religious traditions in the classroom, and a section on atheism featuring the ideas of two important atheists. These sections point to further areas of exploration in religious studies.

Almost every scholar of religious studies today got their start in some form of an introduction to world religions' class. This course and this reader, therefore, are meant to be a beginning, rather than an end—something to inspire further inquiry, exploration, and contemplation. We by no means assume that everyone reading this volume will pursue graduate work in religious studies; rather, we hope that students leave with the tools to continue educating themselves and analyzing how people use religious (and nonreligious) ideas to make sense of the world around them.

Reading 1

What Is the Academic Study of Religion?

Russell T. McCutcheon

Russell McCutcheon is an important voice on methodology in the field of religious studies. In his numerous books and essays he has called on scholars of religious studies to be more self-critical and to accurately analyze what religious cultures actually do rather than make theological judgments about what they should do. McCutcheon has also called on religious studies scholars to be more critical of the term "religion" and to acknowledge that this term was created by Europeans, that it does not always accurately fit beliefs and practices of non-European cultures, and that there are political interests at stake in whether or not something is labeled a "religion." In the essay that follows, McCutcheon has distilled his most important ideas about methodology in the study of religion as an introduction to undergraduates.[1]

---

1 This short introduction was originally written in the late 1990s as a class handout for the author's own introduction to the study of religion course and shared widely with others. It appears here in a slightly updated fashion.

Anthropology or Theology?

The academic study of religion is fundamentally an *anthropological enterprise*, or what some might just describe as *anthropocentric*. That is, it is primarily focused on studying people (ἄνθρωπος [or *anthropos* in English], an ancient Greek term, means "human being" + λόγος [or *logos*], meaning "word" and often used as a suffix in English to name the rational, systematic study of some topic, such as biology, archeology, or psychology); it examines the development and variety of their claims, practices, and institutions, rather than assessing the truth of their various beliefs or actions. An anthropocentric approach to the study of religion (which, of course, is not to say that the study of religion is simply a sub-field of the academic discipline known as anthropology) is therefore to be distinguished from what we might term a confessional, a religious, or a theological approach (θεός [*theos*] is also an ancient Greek term, for "deity" or "god"), which is generally concerned with determining the nature, will, or wishes of a god or the gods, along with determining how they ought to impact human beings and the way that they live their lives. Traditionally, the term "theology" has referred to specifically Christian discourses on God (i.e., theology = systematic Christian thought on the meaning, significance, and fulfillment of the Christian witness), though the term now widely applies either to any religion's own articulate self-study or to its own study of other religions (from evangelism and missionary work to developing a theology of world religions or promoting a certain form of religious pluralism and tolerance—all of which are equally understood as theological pursuits, though different types of theology may drive each).

Descriptive or Normative?

Although the academic study of religion—sometimes also called Religious Studies, Comparative Religion, the History of Religions, or even the Science of Religion—is concerned with judging such things as *historical accuracy* (e.g., Did a person named Siddhartha Gautama, later called the Buddha by his followers, actually exist, and if so, when and where?) and *descriptive accuracy* (e.g., What does a Muslim person mean when they say that Muhammad was the "seal of the prophets"?), it is not concerned to make *normative judgments* concerning the way people *ought* to live or behave and what they *ought* to believe or say. Instead, studying such things as the variety of ways in which someone can, for example, understand themselves to be Jewish—from Orthodox to Conservative and Reformed, to name but the three more prominent sub-groups—is what occupies its attention. To phrase it another way, we could say that, whereas the anthropocentric study of religion is concerned with the descriptive "is" of the history and variety of human claims and practices, a theological study of religion is concerned with the prescriptive "ought" of the gods.

As should be clear, these two enterprises therefore have very different data (*what* it studies) and methods (*how* it studies): the academic study of religion studies people, their claims, their actions, and their social systems whereas the theological study of religion takes these into account as well but in order to eventually understand something about God/the gods and what is seen as their proper impact on people's lives.

Comparison and Theory

Like many scholarly disciplines in the modern university, the academic study of religion is a product of late nineteenth-century Europe. It is a product of Europeans encountering—through trade, exploration, and military conquest—new beliefs and behaviors, sometimes understood by our predecessors as strange and exotic though often also seen by them as surprisingly familiar and surprisingly recognizable. Early scholars of religion were therefore interested in making sense of these similarities and differences, prompting many of them to collect and compare beliefs, myths, and rituals found the world over (though rarely doing fieldwork themselves, at least in the early years of the field). After all, early explorers, soldiers, and missionaries were all writing home about their experiences or returning to Europe with their diaries and journals filled with tales that, despite their obvious exoticness to the eyes of people then living in London, Paris, or Amsterdam, also chronicled things that often bore a striking resemblance to those things that Christians at the time might have taken for granted. As such, early scholars, puzzled by both the familiarity and the novelty of other people's practices and symbols, used the *comparative method* in the cross-cultural study of people's religious beliefs, intent on determining, in the early days of the field, if "they" had religion as "we" did. That these early comparative studies are easily read today as rather problematic—such as the once common effort to rank different groups by seeing some as "primitive," "uncivilized," or derivative of those groups with which the scholars were themselves members—should not surprise us and must be recognized as we read their early writings; however, improvements, since then, in scholarly efforts to use a *nonevaluative* comparative method should also be recognized.

To compare in a nonevaluative manner means that one searches for observable, documentable, and often unexpected similarities and differences, evident once the scholar places two items beside each other for the first time or in some novel way (such as comparing two creation stories or two initiation rituals—a comparison always driven by the scholar's own curiosities or assumptions), but doing so without making normative judgments concerning which similarities or differences are good or bad, right or wrong, original or derivative, primitive or modern. To compare in a nonevaluative manner is also about more than just comparison or even recognizing the role that scholars' assumptions play in their work; for it also means that scholars then theorize as to *why* just these similarities or *why* just those differences exist. For example, many Christians would claim that the historical person named Jesus of Nazareth was "the Son of God" (a similarity within much of Christianity) yet only some of these same Christians would claim that the Pope is God's primary representative on earth (a difference within Christianity). As an anthropocentric scholar of religion, can you theorize as to *why* this difference exists despite so many other shared similarities among those who call themselves Christians? Now, a theological approach might account for this difference by suggesting that one side in this debate is simply wrong, ill-informed, or sinful (depending on which theologian you happen to ask, of course); but an anthropocentric approach would, as scholars sometimes say, "bracket out" and thereby set aside all such normative or theological judgments and, instead, theorize that the differences might have something to do with, say, the psychology of the people involved, their method of social organization, their mode of economic activity, etc., all depending on which other academic disciplines scholars draw on in their studies of religion.

In other words, the anthropocentric study of religion as practiced in the public university is a member of the cross-disciplinary human sciences and, as such, it starts its work with the presumption that religious claims, practices, and institutions are observable, historical events that can therefore be studied in the same manner as all other human behaviors and situations. If they are more than that, then scholars of religion leave it to theologians to pursue another avenue in their study.

Religion and the U.S. Supreme Court

Although the study of religion came to North American universities from Europe prior to World War I and, for a brief time, flourished at such schools as the University of Chicago, Penn, and Harvard, it was not until the 1960s that Departments of Religious Studies began to be widely established in American public universities. The success of these departments—recalling that we're speaking here specifically of public schools— is often linked to the Supreme Court's understanding of the U.S. Constitution.

The opening line to the Constitution's First Amendment famously reads as follows: "Congress shall make no law respecting an establishment of religion, or prohibiting the free exercise thereof. . . ." Legal scholars therefore distinguish between the First Amendment's "establishment clause" and its "free exercise clause." In other words, the Amendment states that the elected government must not enforce, support, or encourage (i.e., "establish") a particular religion, nor can it curtail its citizens' religious choices and practices (i.e., the "free exercise" of their religion). It may well be significant that, in the opening lines of the First Amendment, it is made explicit that all citizens of the United States have the absolute right to believe in any or even no religion whatsoever. As such, U.S. court cases involving religion will usually focus on alleged infractions of one clause or the other, with claims being made that the government had unconstitutionally regulated or limited its citizens' right to free religious expression and practice, on the one hand, or, on the other, improperly advocated for and thereby supported a certain form of religion.

In 1963 a landmark case known as the School District of Abington Township, PA, versus the Schempp family (usually just called *Abington v. Schempp*) came before the Court. In this case a family successfully sued a public school board for one of its school's daily opening exercises, in which a Bible verse was read over the school's public address system. (It was then a longstanding practice, based on an earlier Pennsylvania law that stated that "[a]t least ten verses from the Holy Bible [be] read, without comment, at the opening of each public school on each school day.") In an 8–1 decision the Court decided that, as a publicly funded institution charged to represent and thereby not exclude the members of a diverse, taxpaying citizenry, the school board was infringing on the First Amendment rights of its students, not just by supporting a specifically Christian worldview but, more importantly perhaps, a religious worldview. As the majority decision phrased it: "The fullest realization of true religious liberty requires that government neither engage in nor compel religious practices, that it effect no favoritism among sects or between religion and nonreligion, and that it work deterrence of no religious belief."

In a section of the decision often quoted over the years by U.S. scholars of religion, Justice Clark, the Supreme Court justice who wrote on behalf of the majority, went on to state that, although confessional instruction and religious indoctrination in publicly funded schools were both unconstitutional, one's "education is not complete without a study of comparative religion or the history of religion and its relationship to the advancement of civilization." The majority of the justices therefore interpreted the First Amendment to state that, although the government cannot force a student to be either religious or nonreligious, the government certainly can— and probably even should—support classes that study the history of particular religions, the comparison of two or more religions, and the role of religion in human history. As some overly eager scholars have gone on to conclude since then, we might say that the academic study of religion is among the few fields of study mandated by a Supreme Court decision.

Fundamental to its decision was the Court's distinction between, as earlier scholars of religion might have phrased it, *religious instruction* and *instruction about religion*. The academic and anthropocentric study of religion, practiced as part of the human sciences, is therefore concerned to study *about* religion and religions.

The History of "Religion"

But it gets a little more complicated. For although you may have never thought about it before, this term "religion" that we've been using all along has a history of its own, and it is not necessarily obvious just how we ought to define the term when going about our work as scholars.

To begin with, "religion" is obviously an English word that is commonly used by people as they go about their daily lives; therefore, we might ask, "Do non-English speakers have religions?" or "Would an ancient Egyptian name something as 'my religion'?" Well, we know that the word "religion" has equivalents in such other modern languages as French and German. For example, when practiced in Germany the study of religion is known as *Religionswissenschaft* (the systematic study, or *Wissenschaft*, of religion) and when practiced in France it is known as *sciences religieuses*. So even just a quick comparison of these and other related languages therefore helps us to see that pretty much all modern languages that can be traced back to Latin possess something equivalent to the English term "religion." This means that, *for language families outside those that are historically related to Latin, there is no equivalent term to "religion"*—unless, of course, Latin-based European cultures have somehow exerted influence on these other cultures and their languages, an influence most evident, as already mentioned, in the history of trade or conquest.

For instance, although "religion" is hardly a traditional concept in India, the long history of British colonialism has ensured that English-speaking Indians have no difficulty conceiving of what some refer to as Hinduism as being their "religion"— although, technically speaking, to a devout person there it might not be seen as a religion at all but, instead, simply understood as *sanatana dharma* (the eternal, cosmic duty, obligation, and order). Even the New Testament is not much help in settling these issues since its language of composition—Greek—lacked the later Latin concept *religio*. So English New Testaments will routinely use "religion" to translate such earlier Greek terms as *eusebia* (see, e.g., 1 Timothy 3:16; 2 Timothy 3:5)—an ancient term that is, in fact, closer to the Sanskrit *dharma* or the Latin *pietas* than it is to our modern term "religion," given that none of these terms meant believing in a god or having faith, as many today would commonly define religion; instead, all of these ancient terms had something to do with maintaining proper social relations (if we include in our idea of the social group everyone from powerful beings who control the universe to our peers and social inferiors).

In fact, even in ancient Latin itself our term "religion" has no equivalent—again, if, by "religion" you mean the sort of things that many of us do when using the term today, for example, worshiping God, believing in an afterlife, or just trying to be a good person. Instead, the closest that we come when looking for Latin precursors to our modern term "religion" are such ancient terms as *religare* or *religere*, which, in their original contexts, simply meant such things as "to bind something tightly together" or "to pay close or careful attention to something." As should be evident, then, words are themselves historical products and they can change considerably over time, even if their users sometimes take them for granted.

Where to from Here?

This leaves us with a lot of questions in need of investigation: Just what do we mean by "religion"? If a group does not have the concept or the word, can we study "their religion"? Is there such as thing as "the Hindu religion" or "ancient Greek religion"?

Why do some people today distinguish between things that they designate as "religions" and those they call "cults"? And, regardless of the history of our vocabulary, is this thing that many of us call religion a universal human phenomenon, exemplified in those things that we commonly refer to as religions or the world religions, or is it simply one among many ways that people name, classify, and authorize their particular social worlds, making religions indistinguishable from ideologies or even cultures or what some call worldviews?

So where does this leave us? Well, it opens the door to a lot of interesting work on how people, both past and present, act, organize, and talk about both themselves and others—whether those others are thought to be powerful, invisible beings or just people who strike "us" as unfamiliar and strange.

Discussion Questions

1. What is the difference between descriptive accuracy and normative judgments? Can you think of a question that concerns descriptive accuracy about a religious tradition? Can you think of a normative judgment that someone might make about a religious tradition?

2. Why are the First Amendment of the Bill of Rights and the Supreme Court case *Abington v. Schempp* (1963) significant to the academic study of religion?

3. The concept of "religion" has a history. Why is it important for those who study religion to understand this history? Or, conversely, why is it problematic for those who study religion to be ignorant of this history?

Reading 2

Name It and Disclaim It: A Tool for Better Discussion in Religious Studies

Joseph P. Laycock and Natasha L. Mikles

This essay was written by two religious studies professors after discussing some of the challenges they have encountered while trying to lead class discussions. They realized the problem was not with the students, but rather with their own inability to explain to students how their analysis could be better. Part of the problem is that it is hard to explain abstract problems for which there are no clear terms. The essay is an experiment in creating new vocabulary to describe some of the unproductive patterns we fall into when we first begin the academic study of religion. Have you noticed these patterns in your own classroom?

Anyone who has led discussion in an introductory undergraduate religious studies class has experienced frustrating comments from students such as, "Jews practice empty ritual," or "Buddhists are more spiritual than other religions." It seems that regardless of efforts to set up "ground rules" at the beginning of the course, comments likes these still crop up. The worst is when they appear in final exam essays, causing one to wonder whether all of their instruction has fallen on deaf ears.

In fairness to our students, doing analysis within a religious studies classroom is a unique beast. It may seem comparable to discussions they have in a philosophy class or a history class, but there are important differences. Religious studies does entail a critical examination of intellectual propositions and establishing frameworks for determining what we can know about the past. But it also involves cultivating an understanding of how other people see the world, learning how to thoughtfully set up comparisons, and—perhaps above all—interrogating one's own assumptions. J. Z. Smith (1982, p. xi) famously wrote that for the student of religion "self-consciousness constitutes his primary expertise, his foremost object of study." Unfortunately, by the time most students have any sense of *how to do religious studies,* the semester is over. While a few will go on to take more courses in religious studies, the majority will not. This problem is even worse in a world religions classroom, where the students must master course content at the same time they are learning to think like a religion scholar.

While everyone must muddle through, certain students demonstrate assumptions and patterns of thinking that are uniquely aggravating to religious studies professors. Usually what makes these patterns so exasperating is that they conceal some form of *intellectual laziness:* the problem is not that the student has some unique perspective the professor disagrees with, but rather that they are deploying a rhetorical maneuver to avoid the hard work of critical analysis.

The challenge for faculty lies in identifying these patterns and explaining to the student what we want them to do differently. In a perfect world, this would occur through a heartfelt conversation during office hours, as it is much harder to explain such problems while grading a mountain of blue books. What follows is an experiment in identifying certain recurring patterns that emerge in religious studies classes and creating *labels* for them. These labels are a heuristic. They provide a vocabulary to discuss these patterns more easily. The list below is inspired in part by a poster created by School of Thought International called "Thou shalt not commit logical fallacies." It lists and names twenty-four fallacies such as "strawman" (now often referred to as "straw-person"), "begging the question," and "tu quoque," and even features a simple "logo" illustrating each fallacy. The purpose is to help people hone their critical thinking skills by providing a reference to identify and articulate fallacies.

In the same way, we have identified seven such problematic patterns that tend to occur again and again. Our purpose is not to perfect a taxonomy of poor or incorrect approaches to religious studies. Rather, we aim to create a tool that both professors and students can use to expedite the process of learning to think like a religious studies scholar. We encourage pedagogues in religious studies to identify the patterns that occur most often in *their* courses, name them appropriately, and then share this vocabulary with the students as needed. These terms can be introduced early in the course and then referred to again, especially during discussion or when giving feedback on student writing. They could also be included on the syllabus or a course website for future reference. Again, their purpose is to help students apprehend larger patterns in what makes a strong or weak argument when doing religious studies.

The Less-Than-Magnificent Seven

1. Square Peg, Round Hole: This label refers to analyzing a religious tradition in terms of another religious tradition—and almost always this tradition is Protestantism. Describing religious beliefs and practices in terms of "empty ritual," "superstition," or "a lack of morality" are all examples of "Square Peg, Round Hole." So too are comparative essays with statements like this: "Instead of a church, Jews have a synagogue. Instead of the Bible, Jews read the Torah. Instead of a pastor, Jews have a rabbi." All of this is technically correct, but it doesn't demonstrate much understanding of Judaism as a tradition.

"Square Peg, Round Hole" should not be misconstrued to say that we never use comparisons in our classroom. Students are always making comparisons, whether we ask them to or not, so it behooves us as educators to embrace the comparative strategy when appropriate. "Square Peg, Round Hole" encompasses comparisons that tacitly and uncritically take one tradition as the norm and everything else as a distortion or aberration of that norm.

To point out the fallacy of "Square Peg, Round Hole" is also not the same as claiming that we must take religious traditions at their word or can never apply the hermeneutics of suspicion. We reject Wilfred Cantwell Smith's (1974, p. 42) proposition that "[n]o statement about a religion is valid unless it can be acknowledged by that religion's believers." But before we can apply critiques we need some understanding of the *internal* logic and worldview of the tradition. It is hard to do this if we are constantly contorting the data so that we can measure it solely in terms of some other religious tradition.

2. No True Scotsman: This well-known fallacy is generally attributed to English philosopher Antony Flew (*The Scotsman*, 2010). It takes its name from an anecdote that usually goes something like this: a Scot claims that Scotsmen never put sugar in their porridge. When shown another Scotsman who *does* put sugar in his porridge, the first Scot specifies that no *true* Scotsman puts sugar in his porridge. In other words, any counterexample to the original claim is dismissed *ipso facto*.

Franklin Graham invoked this fallacy in 2009 when he stated on CNN that "true Islam" is about beating your wife and murdering your children (CNN Wire Staff, 2010). Presumably an infinite number of peaceful Muslim counterexamples would be irrelevant to this claim because they are not practicing "true Islam" as defined by Graham.

Unchallenged, the "No True Scotsman" argument is very effective for belief perseverance. As such, students may be tempted to reach for it when their preconceived notions about a religious tradition are challenged. Just as Graham used this argument to dismiss peaceful Muslims, students may claim that Buddhists who support nationalism or who are more interested in blessed amulets than meditation are not "true Buddhists."

The "No True Scotsman" argument is also frequently applied to the category of religion itself. In his essay "Everyday Miracles: The Study of Lived Religion," Robert Orsi describes how his students felt Catholics in the Bronx using holy water from a replica of the Lourdes grotto was *not* an example of religion. This led Orsi (2001, p. 5) to ask, "So if this is not religion, what is?" Orsi's work demonstrates that numerous labels including "cult" and "superstition" serve the same function as the "No True Scotsman" argument, preserving biases about what religion is and does by screening out counterexamples. But we cannot get into the hard work of doing religious studies until we have stopped making such excuses with the data. As Jeffrey Kripal states, "It is very easy to explain everything on the table if you have just taken off the table everything that you cannot explain" (Strieber and Kripal, 2017, p. 11).

3. Loaded Questions: The classic example of a loaded question is the prosecutor asking, "Do you still beat your wife?" We find these kinds of indictments framed as questions are often coupled with anecdotal evidence. For example, one student asked, "I went to Turkey and everyone glared at me. Why are Muslims so intolerant?" Invoking a completely subjective experience of Muslim intolerance reinforced a rhetorical maneuver in which the class was pressured to accept the claim that Muslims are intolerant instead of challenging this idea.

But the loaded question can also take a more subtle form. Instead of just trying to mask a claim, in a religious studies classroom it can also be used to abdicate the burden of analysis. When a student asks, "Why would *anyone* believe that?" they are actually making the statement, "This tradition is inscrutable and making sense of it is *not* my responsibility." But when students sign up for a religious studies class they forfeit the ability to make these kinds of dismissals. As long as they are in the course, it *is* their job to figure out why anyone would believe that.

4. Medical Materialism: This term, famously coined by William James, refers to the practice of "explaining away" religious experiences in terms of medical diagnoses (James, 1982, p. 13). Common examples include the claim that Paul was epileptic or that Islam arose because "Muhammad suffered a hallucination from too much sun."

As James noted, the problem with medical materialism isn't that these diagnoses are necessarily incorrect (although they are usually made with minimal evidence or medical expertise). Rather, the problem is that they function to dismiss the cultural and historical significance formed around these experiences. James noted that *all* thoughts and mental states can be reduced to the functions of the nervous system, but we only engage in this analysis when examining ideas we don't like.

5. The Dumb Ancestors Assumption: Related to medical materialism is a facile attempt to explain all accounts of the supernatural as a misunderstanding of mental illness or some other natural phenomenon. This maneuver conceals a certain smugness that we have greater powers of reasoning and familiarity with the natural world than our ancestors. The Dumb Ancestors Assumption is particularly an obstacle when interpreting myths or accounts of the supernatural. Our ability to imagine the significance of these stories is limited if our default assumption is that these are just-so stories told by intellectually primitive people to explain the natural world. Biblical scholar John Dominic Crossan alludes to this lack of imagination when he writes, "My point, once again, is *not* that those ancient people told literal stories and we are now smart enough to take them symbolically, but that they told them symbolically and we are now dumb enough to take them literally" (Crossan and Watts, 1999, p. 79).

6. Dan Brown Syndrome: This label refers to an assumption that a historical claim about a religious tradition is more likely to be true if it is not believed by the tradition's practitioners or if the claim would upset them. The most common examples of Dan Brown Syndrome concern early Christianity and include simplistic mythicist claims about the historicity of Jesus or claims that Jesus studied mysticism in India.[1] Less common examples of Dan Brown Syndrome include hyperdiffusionist theories used to explain, for example, why there are five pillars in Islam and five skandhas in Buddhism.[2] Of course, there is good evidence for many historical claims that contradict the official histories of religious institutions. The problem with Dan Brown Syndrome is that it eschews reasoned historical arguments in favor of contrarianism.

---

1 For an overview of these theories see Ehrman (2013).
2 On hyperdiffusionism and its role in pseudoarchaeology, see Fagan (2010, pp. 362–367).

7. Epistemological Nihilism: This label refers to claims that we cannot engage in any sort of analysis or discussion unless we have perfect empirical knowledge. One of our students told us it was unreasonable when she was asked questions during class discussion like, "What would Bertrand Russell say about this?" because only Bertrand Russell could ever answer this. Another student chose to write an essay on Elie Wiesel's exegesis of the Book of Job and wrote that Wiesel did not live in the time of Job and therefore was utterly unqualified to say anything about this story and arrogant for attempting to.

This is one of the most galling maneuvers because, while these arguments are often framed in terms of critical thinking or the scientific method, their function is usually to dodge the hard work of analysis. If we can know nothing, claims the epistemological nihilist, then attempting to learn or understand anything is a waste of time.

Conclusions

These seven terms could be incorporated into a syllabus, made into a handout, or otherwise used as a reference for class discussion. This list is just a preliminary exploration. Readers should consult with colleagues to identify and name the patterns that recur in their classes. This should go without saying, but the purpose of these labels is not to shame students or condemn their ideas. Rather, giving names to these patterns makes it possible to talk about them and therefore to *think* about them. This makes the patterns possible to avoid and challenges students to seek out deeper strategies of analysis. We all were students once and probably at least a little bit intellectually lazy until someone pushed us; we hope to do the same for our students now.

REFERENCES

CNN Wire Staff. 2010. "Graham Disinvited from Prayer Event over Islam Comments." https://www.cnn.com/2010/US/04/23/graham.islam.controversy/index.html. Accessed July 21, 2020.

Crossan, John Dominic, and Richard G. Watts. 1999. *Who Is Jesus? Answers to Your Questions about the Historical Jesus.* Louisville, KY: Westminster John Knox Press.

Ehrman, Bart D. 2013. *Did Jesus Exist? The Historical Argument for Jesus of Nazareth.* New York: HarperOne.

Fagan, Garrett G., editor. 2010. *Archaeological Fantasies: How Pseudoarchaeology Misrepresents the Past and Misleads the Public.* London: Routledge.

James, William. 1982. *The Varieties of Religious Experience: A Study in Human Nature.* New York: Penguin Books. (Original work published 1902.)

Orsi, Robert. 2001. "Everyday Miracles: The Study of Lived Religion." In *Lived Religion in America: Toward a History of Practice*, edited by David D. Hall, pp. 3–21. Princeton, NJ: Princeton University Press.

Smith, Jonathan Z. 1982. *Imagining Religion: From Babylon to Jonestown*. Chicago: University of Chicago Press.

Smith, Wilfred Cantwell. 1974. "Comparative Religion: Whither—and Why?" In *The History of Religions: Essays in Methodology*, edited by Mircea Eliade and Joseph M. Kitagawa, pp. 31–59. Chicago: University of Chicago Press.

Strieber, Whitley, and Jeffrey J. Kripal. 2017. *The Super Natural: Why the Unexplained Is Real*. New York: TarcherPerigee.

The Scotsman. 2010. "Obituary: Professor Antony Flew." April 16, https://www.scotsman.com/news/obituaries/obituary-professor-antony-flew-1-799918. Accessed July 21, 2020.

Discussion Questions

1. What do you think J. Z. Smith meant when he wrote that for the student of religion "self-consciousness constitutes his primary expertise, his foremost object of study"?

2. Have you noticed any of the seven patterns described here in college courses that study religion?

3. Are there other patterns you have noticed that make it difficult to understand and analyze religious traditions? If so, what are they?

Hinduism

Arguably the oldest religious traditions in Asia, Hindu ideas, texts, and practices have provided inspiration for many of the subsequent religious and philosophical traditions to develop on the Indian subcontinent. Hindu understandings of humanity's central problem focus on *samsara*, which they understand to be the unsatisfactory cycle of life, death, and rebirth. The solution is *moksha*, an expansive term that has variously meant eternal life in a heavenly abode, union with a personal God, union with an impersonal God, and one's cosmic realization of wisdom and accompanying transformation. Regardless of how the goal is conceptualized, however, moksha ultimately signifies a release from the cycle of samsara. This problem, and its solution, are reflected in a selection from the Katha Upanishad. Composed sometime between the seventh and third centuries BCE, the Katha Upanishad relates an exchange between the Brahmin boy Nachiketa and King Yama, the Lord of Death. During the conversation, Yama explains the true nature of man, the cycle of reincarnation, and the possibility of freedom from rebirth. Many of the metaphors he uses to describe the transcendent and eternal self (*atman*) remain some of the most frequently used rhetorical devices to explain what, at its foundation, is considered beyond words. As evidenced in the multiplicity of interpretations surrounding the term "moksha," Hinduism offers a diverse range of practices to attain release from samsara. To reflect this, we have selected a chapter from the Bhagavad Gita that outlines these practices as three paths of action (*karma*), wisdom (*jnana*), and devotion (*bhakti*). While the text here offers them as three separate paths, many contemporary Hindu thinkers such as "Amma," a South Indian woman known as the "hugging saint," conceptualize them as three parts of one path, and most Hindus engage in religious practices related to all three.

Among this wide range of Hindu practices, the path of bhakti devotionalism has been perhaps the most popular because of its welcoming of women as well as Dalits and other low-caste individuals. Indeed, one of the primary exemplars within Hinduism has been the fervently devoted poet-saint, an example of which is reflected in this selection of poetry from the sixteenth-century mystic Mirabai. Originally a princess born into a royal family in Rajasthan, Mirabai is known for her tremendous and single-minded devotion to the god Krishna in the face of extreme persecution from her parents, her husband, and her husband's family. Her poetry speaks to the pain of separation from Lord Krishna, often using a terminology rich with romantic longing. In this selection, we see many themes prevalent in bhakti discourse, including the disregarding of caste, craving an emotional connection with Krishna, and loving Krishna above all else. In contrast to Mirabai's passionate yearning for union with Krishna, Swami Vivekananda represents a different type of exemplar—a yogi whose practice is defined by the pursuit of wisdom. A devotee of the Bengali mystic Ramakrishna and Advaita Vedanta Hinduism, Swami Vivekananda is perhaps best known for his appearance at the World's Parliament of Religions held in Chicago in 1893. There, he enthralled the crowd as a handsome and well-spoken representative of Hinduism. In this selection from two of his speeches given at the World's Parliament of Religions, we see reflected both his efforts to explain Advaita Vedanta Hinduism and his defense of Hinduism as the originator of the perennialist philosophy, speaking to the ultimate unity of all religions.

In the aftermath of British colonialism in India, there was widespread debate among Indian intellectuals as to whether India would have a secular or Hindu government. While the defenders of a secular government won and the Indian Constitution defends India as a multireligious nation, the movement to govern India as an explicitly Hindu country has remained strong. Known as Hindutva, which translates as "Hinduness," the Hindu Nationalist movement has identified various "enemies" of India's Hindu majority, including both Christians and communists. In its contemporary manifestations, however, Hindutva proponents have particularly targeted India's Muslim minority as a threat to Hindu safety and an "Indian" way of life, leading to significant violence against the Muslim community. From a political standpoint, advocates of Hindu nationalism have also had substantial success in recent years, including the 2014 and 2019 elections of Narendra Modi as prime minister through the Hindutva-sympathetic Bharatiya Janata Party (BJP). In a selection from the website *The Conversation*, scholar of contemporary India Chandrima Chakraborty analyzes Modi's 2019 victory speech for its unique reliance on imagery of asceticism to portray the politician as both a political and religious figure.

From the Katha Upanishad

While the Vedas are the oldest writings in the Hindu canon, the Upanishads are perhaps the most influential in the development of Hindu thought. Composed in roughly the seventh to third centuries BCE, these texts represent the philosophical foundation of Hinduism, answering questions like the meaning of life, the nature of divinity, and the relationship between the gods and oneself. If the Vedas detail what rituals you must complete in order to obtain a son, the Upanishads ask you to instead reflect on your reasons for wanting a son and whether a son will help you escape the cycle of reincarnation. In the selection from the Katha Upanishad highlighted here, Nachiketa disturbs his father and causes him to exclaim the ancient Indian equivalent of "Go to hell!" As a dutiful son, Nachiketa follows his father's wishes and the presumably surprised Lord of Death, King Yama, grants the child three wishes. Nachiketa rejects gold and worldly glory as trappings of samsara; instead he uses his three wishes to obtain knowledge on how to properly perform the Vedic rituals and what happens to the self after one dies. Yama's answers provide an important description of the atman's transcendent nature.

Valli 1

Usan, the son of Vajasravas, once gave away all his possessions. He had a son named Nachiketa. ² Young as he was, faith took hold of him while the cows presented as sacrificial gifts were being led away, and he reflected:

> ³ "They've drunk all their water, eaten all their fodder,
> They have been milked dry, they are totally barren—
> 'Joyless' are those worlds called,
> to which a man goes
> who gives them as gifts."

⁴ So he asked his father: "Father, to whom will you give me?" He repeated it for a second time, and again for a third time. His father yelled at him: "I'll give you to Death!"

[NACHIKETA *reflects*.] ⁵ I go as the very first of many.
I go as the middlemost of many.
What is it that Yama must do,
That he will do with me today?

[A VOICE]
6 Look ahead! See how they have gone,
      those who have gone before us!
Look back! So will they go,
      those who will come after us.
A mortal man ripens like grain,
And like grain he is born again.

7 A Brahmin guest enters a house
      as the fire in all men.
Bring water, O Vaivasvata,[1]
      that is how they appease him.

8 Hopes and expectations, fellowship and goodwill,
Children and livestock, rites and gifts—
      all these a Brahmin wrests from the foolish man,
      in whose house he resides without any food.

[DEATH]
9 Three nights, O Brahmin [child], you stayed in my house,
      a guest worthy of homage, without any food;
Three wishes, therefore, deign to make in return.
      So homage to you, O Brahmin [child]!
      And may I fare well!

[NACHIKETA]
10 That with his temper cooled, his anger subdued,
      O Death, be to me well-disposed.
That he greet me with joy, when by you I'm dismissed—
      this is the first of my three wishes.

[DEATH]
11 He'll be affable in the future, just as before;
      Great philosopher, I have dismissed you.
He'll have restful nights, his anger subdued,
      seeing you released from the jaws of Death.

[NACHIKETA]
12 In the world of heaven there is no fear;
      there one has no fear of old age or you.
Transcending both these—both hunger and thirst,
      beyond all sorrows, one rejoices in heaven.

---

1 Sanskrit term indicating a divine king.

¹³ You, O Death, are studying,
      the fire-altar that leads to heaven;
Explain that to me, a man who has faith;
People who are in heaven enjoy the immortal state—
      It is this I choose with my second wish.

[DEATH]
    ¹⁴ I shall explain to you—
      and heed this teaching of mine,
      O Nachiketa, you who understand—
the fire-altar that leads to heaven,
to the attainment of an endless world,
and is its very foundation.
      Know that it lies hidden,
      In the cave of the heart.

[NARRATOR]
    ¹⁵ He described to him that fire-altar—
      the beginning of the world—
What type the bricks, how many; and how they are to be laid;
      and he repeated it exactly as described.
Delighted at him, then, Death said to him again;
¹⁶ Well-pleased, the large-hearted one said to him:

[DEATH]
    Here I grant you another wish today.
This fire-altar will bear your very name.
Take also this glittering disk of gold.

    ¹⁷ This is a three-Nachiketa man—
Uniting with the three, performing the triple rite,
      he crosses over birth and death.
Perceiving the *brahman* that is being born,
      as the god who is to be adored,
      recognizing this disk of gold to be that,
      he attains unending peace.

    ¹⁸ This is a three-Nachiketa man—
Knowing these three, and, with that knowledge,
Piling the altar of Nachiketa,
      he shoves aside the fetters of death before him,
      passes beyond sorrow,
      and rejoices in heaven.

¹⁹ This, Nachiketa, is your fire that leads to heaven,
　　　　which you chose with your second wish.
People will proclaim this your very own fire.
　　　　Choose your third wish, O Nachiketa.

[NACHIKETA]　　²⁰ There is this doubt about a man who is dead.
　　　　"He exists," say some, others, "He exists not."
I want to know this, so please teach me.
　　　　This is the third of my three wishes.

[DEATH]　　²¹ As to this even the gods of old had doubts,
　　　　for it's hard to understand, it's a subtle doctrine.
Make, Nachiketa, another wish.
　　　　Do not press me! Release me from this.

[NACHIKETA]　　²² As to this, we're told, even the gods had doubts;
　　　　and you say, O Death, it's hard to understand.
But another like you I can't find to explain it;
　　　　and there's no other wish that is equal to it.

[DEATH]　　²³ Choose sons and grandsons who'd live a hundred years!
Plenty of livestock and elephants, horses and gold!
Choose as your domain a wide expanse of earth!
And you yourself live as many autumns as you wish!

²⁴ And if you would think this is an equal wish—
You may choose wealth together with a long life;
Achieve prominence, Nachiketa, in this wide world;
And I will make you enjoy your desires at will.

²⁵ You may ask freely for all those desires,
　　　　hard to obtain in this mortal world;
Look at these lovely girls, with chariots and lutes,
　　　　girls of this sort are unobtainable by men—
I'll give them to you; you'll have them wait on you;
　　　　but about death don't ask me, Nachiketa.

[NACHIKETA]　　²⁶ Since the passing days of a mortal, O Death,
　　　　sap here the energy of all the senses;

And even a full life is but a trifle;
> so keep your horses, your songs and dances!

27 With wealth you cannot make a man content;
Will we get to keep wealth, when we have seen you?
And we get to live only as long as you will allow!
So, this alone is the wish that I'd like to choose.

> 28 What mortal man with insight,
who has met those that do not die or grow old,
himself growing old in this wretched and lowly place,
looking at its beauties, its pleasures and joys,
> would delight in a long life?

29 The point on which they have great doubts—
> what happens at that great transit—
> tell me that, O Death!
This is my wish, probing the mystery deep.
> Nachiketa wishes for nothing
> other than that.

Valli 2

[DEATH]
The good is one thing, the gratifying is quite another;
> their goals are different, both bind a man.
Good things await him who picks the good;
> by choosing the gratifying, one misses one's goal.

2 Both the good and the gratifying
> present themselves to a man;
The wise assess them, note their difference;
> and choose the good over the gratifying;
But the fool chooses the gratifying
> rather than what is beneficial.

3 You have looked at and rejected, Nachiketa,
> things people desire, lovely and lovely to look at;
This disk of gold, where many a man founders,
> you have not accepted as a thing of wealth.

4 Far apart and widely different are these two:
> ignorance and what's known as knowledge.

I take Nachiketa as one yearning for knowledge;
    the many desires do not confound you.

5 Wallowing in ignorance, but calling themselves wise,
Thinking themselves learned, the fools go around,
    staggering about like a group of blind men,
    led by a man who is himself blind.

6 This transit lies hidden from a careless fool,
    who is deluded by the delusion of wealth.
Thinking "This is the world; there is no other,"
    he falls into my power again and again.

7 Many do not get to hear of that transit;
    and even when they hear,
    many don't comprehend it.
Rare is the man who teaches it,
    lucky is the man who grasps it;
Rare is the man who knows it,
    lucky is the man who's taught it.

8 Though one may think a lot, it is difficult to grasp,
    when it is taught by an inferior man.
Yet one cannot gain access to it,
    unless someone else teaches it.
For it is smaller than the size of an atom,
    a thing beyond the realm of reason.

9 One can't grasp this notion by argumentation;
Yet it's easy to grasp when taught by another.
    You're truly steadfast, dear boy,
    you have grasped it!
    Would that we have, Nachiketa,
    one like you to question us!

[NACHIKETA]   10 What you call a treasure, I know to be transient;
    for by fleeting things one cannot gain the perennial.
Therefore I've built the fire-altar of Nachiketa,
    and by things eternal I have gained the eternal.

[DEATH]   ¹¹ Satisfying desires is the foundation of the world;
Uninterrupted rites bring ultimate security;
Great and widespread praise is the foundation—
these you have seen, wise Nachiketa,
and having seen, firmly rejected.

¹² The primeval one who is hard to perceive,
wrapped in mystery, hidden in the cave,
residing within the impenetrable depth—
Regarding him as god, an insight
gained by inner contemplation,
both sorrow and joy the wise abandon.

¹³ When a mortal has heard it, understood it;
when he has drawn it out,
and grasped this subtle point of doctrine;
He rejoices, for he has found
something in which he could rejoice.
To him I consider my house
to be open, Nachiketa.

[NACHIKETA?]   ¹⁴ Tell me what you see as—
Different from the right doctrine and from the wrong;
Different from what's done here and what's left undone;
Different from what has been and what's yet to be.

[DEATH?]   ¹⁵ The word that all the Vedas disclose;
The word that all austerities proclaim;
Seeking which people live student lives;
That word now I will tell you in brief—
It is OM!

¹⁶ For this alone is the syllable that's *brahman*!
For this alone is the syllable that's supreme!
When, indeed, one knows this syllable,
he obtains his every wish.

¹⁷ This is the support that's best!
This is the support supreme!
And when one knows this support,
he rejoices in *brahman*'s world.

[DEATH]   ¹⁸ The wise one—

> he is not born, he does not die;
> he has not come from anywhere;
> he has not become anyone.
>
> He is unborn and eternal, primeval and everlasting.
> And he is not killed, when the body is killed.

[The dialogue between Nachiketa and Death appears to end here.]

¹⁹ If the killer thinks that he kills;
If the killed thinks that he is killed;
Both of them fail to understand.
> He neither kills, nor is he killed.

²⁰ Finer than the finest, larger than the largest,
> is the self (*atman*) that lies here hidden
> in the heart of a living being.
Without desires and free from sorrow,
> a man perceives by the creator's grace
> the grandeur of the self.

²¹ Sitting down, he roams afar.
Lying down, he goes everywhere.
The god ceaselessly exulting—
> Who, besides me, is able to know?

²² When he perceives this immense, all-pervading self,
as bodiless within bodies,
as stable within unstable beings—
> A wise man ceases to grieve.

²³ This self cannot be grasped,
> by teachings or by intelligence,
> or even by great learning.
Only the man he chooses can grasp him,
> whose body this self chooses as his own.

²⁴ Not a man who has not quit his evil ways;
Nor a man who is not calm or composed;
Nor even a man who is without a tranquil mind;
> Could ever secure it by his mere wit.

²⁵ For whom the Brahmin and the Ksatriya
are both like a dish of boiled rice;
and death is like the sprinkled sauce;
Who truly knows where he is?

Valli 3

Knowers of *brahman*, men with five fires,
and with the three fire-altars of Nachiketa,
They call these two "Shadow" and "Light,"
the two who have entered—
the one into the cave of the heart,
the other into the highest region beyond,
both drinking the truth
in the world of rites rightly performed.

² May we master the fire-altar of Nachiketa,
a dike
for those who have sacrificed;
the imperishable, the highest *brahman*,
the farther shore
for those who wish to cross the danger.

³ Know the self as a rider in a chariot,
and the body, as simply the chariot.
Know the intellect as the charioteer,
and the mind, as simply the reins.

⁴ The senses, they say, are the horses,
and sense objects are the paths around them;
He who is linked to the body (*atman*), senses, and mind,
the wise proclaim as the one who enjoys.

⁵ When a man lacks understanding,
and his mind is never controlled;
His senses do not obey him,
as bad horses, a charioteer.

⁶ But when a man has understanding,
and his mind is ever controlled;
His senses do obey him,
as good horses, a charioteer.

⁷ When a man lacks understanding,
             is unmindful and always impure;
He does not reach that final step,
             but gets on the round of rebirth.

⁸ But when a man has understanding,
             is mindful and always pure;
He does reach that final step,
             from which he is not reborn again.

⁹ When a man's mind is his reins,
             intellect, his charioteer;
He reaches the end of the road,
             that highest step of Vishnu.

¹⁰ Higher than the senses are their objects;
Higher than sense objects is the mind;
Higher than the mind is the intellect;
Higher than the intellect is the immense self;

¹¹ Higher than the immense self is the unmanifest;
Higher than the unmanifest is the person;
Higher than the person there's nothing at all.
That is the goal, that's the highest state.

¹² Hidden in all the beings,
             this self is not visibly displayed.
Yet, people of keen vision see him,
             with eminent and sharp minds.

¹³ A wise man should curb his speech and mind,
             control them within the intelligent self;
He should control intelligence within the immense self,
             and the latter, within the tranquil self.

¹⁴ Arise! Awake! Pay attention,
             when you've obtained your wishes!
A razor's sharp edge is hard to cross—
             that, poets say, is the difficulty of the path.

¹⁵ It has no sound or touch,
             no appearance, taste, or smell;

It is without beginning or end,
> undecaying and eternal;
When a man perceives it,
> fixed and beyond the immense,
He is freed from the jaws of death.

16 The wise man who hears or tells
the tale of Nachiketa,
an ancient tale told by Death,
will rejoice in *brahman*'s world.

17 If a man, pure and devout, proclaims this great secret
in a gathering of Brahmins,
or during a meal for the dead,
it will lead him to eternal life!

Discussion Questions

1. This text uses several metaphors to describe the atman. Do these metaphors appear to be describing the same thing as far as attributes, qualities, and atman's relationship with the body? If there is contradiction or disagreement between the various metaphors, what might be the value of this?

2. Why put this information about the self and the nature of the world in the context of Nachiketa's conversation with Yama? Is it important to believe this story actually happened in order to understand the idea of atman? Why or why not?

3. Early in the text, Yama seems not to want to tell Nachiketa about the nature of the self and what happens after death, trying to convince him instead to wish for a long life, great wealth, or prestige. Why might that be the case? Is this a test? Is this knowledge dangerous somehow?

Technique

From the Bhagavad Gita

Perhaps one of the most influential religious texts in the world, the Bhagavad Gita is a segment of the lengthy Hindu epic the Mahabharata. Composed around 100 BCE, it relates a conversation between the warrior Arjuna and divine Lord Krishna. The conversation occurs on the cusp of a battle where Arjuna must fight his cousins to win back the throne that rightfully belongs to his older brother. Not wanting to fight his own cousins, Arjuna becomes upset and declares to his charioteer Krishna that he refuses to go into battle. What follows is a heart-to-heart between Krishna and Arjuna, where Krishna succinctly explains the nature of reality and practices (yoga) that may be performed to obtain moksha, which has classically been divided into three paths: the path of action (karma), the path of wisdom (jnana), and the path of devotion (bhakti). Krishna, disguised as a neighboring prince, aids Arjuna, and Arjuna is unaware that his conversation is actually with God; however, one can see hints of it throughout the text and by the end of the text, Krishna reveals his true form as reality itself. For its beautiful poetry, mystical reflections, and compelling message of all-consuming devotion to God, the Bhagavad Gita has been a favorite of many important thinkers, including Henry David Thoreau, Mahatma Gandhi, and Ralph Waldo Emerson.

Reading the Third

ARJUNA *SPOKE.*

If knowledge is deemed by you to be better than action, O destroyer of foes! why do you engage me to this dreadful deed, Keśava?[1]

You bewilder my mind by these ambiguous words:

THE HOLY ONE *SPOKE.*

There is in this world a twofold rule of life, as I said before, O pure one!—those who seek salvation through devotion to knowledge and those who seek salvation through devotion to work.

A man who does not undertake works attains not to freedom from work, nor does he obtain the perfect state by mere renunciation.

For no man ever continues to cease from action, even for a short time, since every one is compelled by his property of nature to act, even against his will.

He who, restraining the organs of action, remains inactive, but yet remembers in his heart the objects of sense, he, confused in soul, is called a "false devotee."

But he who, having subdued the senses by the heart, Arjuna, undertakes the devotion of work by the organs of action without attachment and is highly esteemed.

Do every appointed work, for action is better than inaction, and even the means of subsistence for the body cannot be gained by you if inactive.

This world is bound by the bonds of action, except in work done on account of sacrifice. Apply yourself to work for this purpose, O son of Kuntī!

When the Lord of all things had created mankind of old, together with sacrifice, he said, "By this shall offspring be obtained: be this your cow of plenty for (the attainment of) your desires."

---

1 Keśava is a name for Vishnu in the Hindu tradition.

Nourish the gods by this, and let the gods also nourish you. Thus, nourishing with each other, you shall obtain the highest good;

For the gods, nourished by sacrifice, shall give to you the desired foods. He who eats the things which are given by them without offering to them (in return) is a thief.

Good men, who eat the remains of sacrifices, are freed from all their sins, but the evil, who cook only for themselves, eat sin.

All creatures live by food; food is produced by rain; rain is (caused) by sacrifice; sacrifice is wrought by action.

Know that action springs from Brahmā; Brahmā proceeds from the Indivisible One. Therefore Brahma, the all-pervading, is ever present in sacrifice.

He who causes not this appointed cycle to revolve here below, he, living in sin and gratifying the sense, lives in vain, O son of Kuntī!

But the man who can be happy in himself, pleased with himself, and contented with himself alone, for him nothing remains to be done.

For this man has no interest whatever in what is done or left undone here below, nor for him is there any occasion whatever of seeking for succour from any living thing.

Therefore apply your energies to work that ought to be done, but always without attachment, for the man who applies himself to work without attachment attains to the Supreme.

For Janaka[2] and others have attained to perfection even by work. You should work, also, from regard to the masses of mankind.

Whatever is done by one who is high in position, that other men do, whatever it may be. Whatever example he offers, the people follow it.

Nothing whatever, O son of Kuntī, must needs be done by me in the three worlds, nor is anything to be attained that is unattained, yet I am occupied in work.

For if I should not be ever at work, unwearied,

These worlds would sink in ruin. If I should not work, I should be the author of confusion, and I should destroy this race of men.

As ignorant men do works with attachment, O son of Bharata![3] so the wise man should work without attachment, desiring to promote the general good.

Let him not cause distraction of mind in ignorant men who are attached to works: let the wise and devout man promote every kind of work, co-working therein.

Works are done entirely by man's nature. He whose soul is bewildered by vanity thinks, "I am the doer;"

But he who knows the truth of the universe, O mighty-armed one, is free and unbound.

---

2 An ancient Indian king honored for his wisdom and spiritual attainment.
3 Arjuna's kingdom.

[. . .]

Renouncing all works in Me, fixed in thought on the Supreme Spirit, free from hope and selfishness, put away your sorrow and fight!

The men who ever follow this my doctrine, full of faith and unreviling, are set free even by works.

Reading the Fourth

THE HOLY ONE *SPOKE.*

This eternal (doctrine of) yoga I taught of old to the sun itself; the sun taught it to the first man, the first man taught it to his son.

This being handed down from one to another, the royal sages knew. This yoga (doctrine) was lost in this world by length of time, O destroyer of foes!

This same ancient doctrine is now declared to you by me, who have said, "You are my worshipper and friend," for it is a supreme mystery.

ARJUNA *SPOKE.*

The birth of my Lord was later; the birth of the sun was prior (to you). How then may I understand this saying of yours, "I taught it in the beginning?"

THE HOLY ONE *SPOKE.*

Many have been in past time the births of me and of you also, Arjuna! All these I know, but you know them not, O slayer of foes!

Though I am unborn, and my nature is eternal, and I am the Lord also of all creatures, yet taking control of my natural form, I am born by my illusive power.

For whenever piety decays, O son of Bharata, and impiety is in the ascendant, then I produce myself.

For the protection of good men, for the destruction of evil-doers, for the re-establishment of piety, I am born from age to age.

He who truly knows my birth and this divine work of mine, comes nevermore to birth again when he quits the body: he comes to Me, Arjuna!

Freed from passion, fear, and wrath, thinking on Me and finding refuge in Me, many, purified by the ascetic rite of knowledge, enter into my being.

As men devote themselves to Me, even so do I honour them. Men follow my path, O son of Kuntī, from every side.

They who desire success in works offer sacrifice here to the gods, for soon in this world of mortals success is gained by works.

The four castes were created by me, according to the apportionment of qualities and works. Know that I, the uncreating and unchanging, am the creator of them.

Works defile me not; in me there is no desire for the fruit of works. He who comprehends me thus is not bound by works.

Knowing this, works were wrought by men of old, who sought for (final) deliverance. For this reason, do you engage in work as it was done aforetime by the men of old.

Even the wise are troubled if one should ask, "What is action and what is inaction?" I will teach you the kind of action by the knowledge of which you will be free from evil.

For action must be well understood, so must forbidden action, and also inaction: tangled is the path of works.

He who can see inaction in action, and also action in inaction, he among men is wise; he is devout, and has fulfilled every work.

He whose effort is free from the impulse of desire, whose work has been burnt up by the fire of knowledge, is called by the wise a learned man.

Renouncing all attachment to the fruit of works, ever contented, self-reliant, this man, though engaged in work, works not at all.

Void of hope, self-restrained in thought, and rejecting all surroundings, performing merely bodily work, he contracts no guilt.

Contented with whatever he may receive, unaffected by pairs of opposites (pleasure and pain, etc.), free from envy, the same in good and evil fortune, he, though he works, is not bound.

The work of one in whom attachment is dead, who is freed from sense pleasures, whose mind is stayed on knowledge, wholly dissolves away, though he engage in sacrifice.

Brahma is the oblation; Brahma is the sacrificial butter; Brahma is in the fire; the burnt-offering is by Brahma. Into Brahma will he enter who meditates on Brahma in his work.

Some devotees attend sacrifices offered to the gods; other offer sacrifice by sacrificing only in the fire of Brahma:

Others sacrifice hearing and the other senses in the fire of self-restraint; others sacrifice the objects of the senses, sound and the rest, in the fire of the senses.

Others, too, sacrifice all the functions of the senses and of life in the mystic fire of self-restraint, kindled by knowledge.

Others also, subdued in mind and bound by vows austere, offer the sacrifice of wealth or penance or devotion (*yoga*), or the sacrifice of silent reading and knowledge.

So also others sacrifice the inward breath in the outward, and the outward breath in the inward, obstructing the channels of inspiration and expiration, intent on the restraint of breath.

Others, who practise abstinence, sacrifice their life in life. All these are skilled in sacrifice, and by sacrifice their sins are destroyed.

They who feed on the ambrosial remains of sacrifices go to the Eternal Brahma. This world is not for him who offers no sacrifice; how then the other, O best of Kurus.[4]

Thus many kinds of sacrifice are offered in the presence of Brahma. Know that all these proceed from action: knowing this, you will be free.

The sacrifice of knowledge is better than the sacrifice of wealth, O slayer of foes! Every work, in its completeness, is contained in knowledge.

Learn this (knowledge) by doing reverence, by questions, and by service. The wise, who see the truth, will teach you knowledge.

When you will not be reborn to this trouble (of mind), O son of Pandu[5]; for you will see all things, without exception, in both yourself and then in Me.

Even if you are the most sinfull of all sinful men, you will pass over all transgression by the bark of knowledge.

As the kindled fire reduces all fuel to ashes, Arjuna, so the fire of knowledge reduces all works to ashes.

For no purifier is found on earth equal to knowledge. One who is perfect in devotion finds it in course of time in himself.

This knowledge is obtained by the believer, who is devoted to it and has subdued the senses: when he has obtained it, he reaches without delay the supreme repose (*nirvana*).

The ignorant man and the unbeliever, and he whose soul is full of doubt are lost. He whose soul is full of doubt has neither this world, nor the next, nor (final) blessedness.

Works do not bind the man who is master of himself, who has abandoned work in devotion, and in whom doubt is destroyed by knowledge, O subduer of wealth!

Therefore slay this doubt, which is born of ignorance, and is seated in the heart by the sword of knowledge; give yourself to devotion, and arise, O son of Bharata!

Reading the Twelfth

ARJUNA *SPOKE.*

Of those who, ever devoutly worshipping, do your service, and those who serve the Imperishable and the Unmanifested—which of these (classes) is best acquainted with Yoga?

THE HOLY ONE *SPOKE.*

They who have stayed their hearts on Me, and do Me service with a constant devotion, being endowed with perfect faith, these I deem to be the most devout.

---

4 The clan to which Arjuna and his brothers belong.
5 Arjuna's father.

But they who serve the Imperishable, Unseen, Unmanifested One, All-pervading and Incomprehensible, who dwell on high, the Immutable and Eternal;

Who, subduing all the senses, are equal-minded to all around and rejoice in the good of all, these attain to Me.

The trouble of those whose minds are fixed on the Unmanifested is the greater, because the unseen path is hard to be gained by those who are embodied;

But they who renounce all works in Me, for whom I am chief object, who, meditating on Me, serve with an exclusive devotion;

These I raise from the ocean of this mortal world without delay, O son of Kuntī, their minds being stayed on Me.

Fix thy heart on Me alone; let thy mind be stayed on Me; then hereafter you shall dwell in Me on high: of that there is no doubt.

But if you are not able to fix thy thoughts constantly on Me, then by frequent devotion seek to gain Me, O subduer of wealth!

If you are not able to provide this frequency of devotion, be you intent on doing works for Me; if you do works for Me alone, you will attain the perfect state.

If you are also not able to do this, then, having found refuge with Me in devotion, renounce thus the fruit of works;

For knowledge is better than diligence, meditation is better than knowledge, and renouncing of the fruit of works better than meditation; for the renouncer peace is very nigh.

He who hates no single being, is friendly and compassionate, free from self-regard and vanity, the same in good and evil, patient;

Contented, ever devout, subdued in soul, firm in purpose, fixed on Me in heart and mind, and who worships Me, is dear to Me.

He whom the world troubles not, and who troubles not the world, who is free from the emotions of joy, wrath, and fear, is dear to Me.

The man who has no selfish bias, is pure, upright, unconcerned, free from distress of mind, who renounces every enterprise and worships Me, is dear to Me.

He who has neither delight nor aversion, who neither mourns nor desires, who renounces good and evil fortune, and worships Me, is dear to Me.

He who is the same to friend and foe, and also in honour and dishonour, who is the same in cold and heart, pleasure and pain, who is wholly free from attachment;

To whom praise and blame are equal, who is silent, content with every fortune, home-renouncing, steadfast in mind, and worships Me, that man is dear to Me.

But they who sit at (the banquet of) that sacred nectar, which has been described before, endowed with faith, making Me their highest aim and worshipping (Me), these are the most dear to Me.

1. Does Krishna's speech actually solve Arjuna's dilemma of not wanting to fight and kill his own family? Why frame this important declaration of Hindu practice within the epic story of the Mahabharata?

2. Do these three yogas, or paths, to moksha seem incompatible with each other? Does Krishna's speech indicate that a practitioner of the path of action could also do bhakti practices? Or would these three paths contradict each other?

3. Does bhakti practice as described by Krishna seem like something easy to do? Would it be hard to keep someone focused in their mind at all times—when working, eating, and playing?

Exemplar 1

Poetry of Mirabai

A poet famous for her devotion to Krishna, Mirabai—sometimes known affectionately as Mira or Meera—was born a princess in Rajasthan in the sixteenth century. Her family forced her to marry a local prince, but her love for Krishna made her unable to properly fulfill her wifely role. For this, the prince's family persecuted her, in some stories even trying to kill her with poison. Inspired by a vision of Lord Krishna, Mirabai eventually ran away to become a follower of Krishna devotee and low-caste Hindu saint Ravidas. Thousands of poems have been attributed to her, though likely many of these are later imitations. Important themes of bhakti practice are highlighted in the selection of poetry here. Notable among them is the poem about a low-caste woman ("The Bhil Woman Tasted Them") who offers the god Rama a plum; because she tasted the plums first to offer him the best, the plums were polluted, yet still Rama found her offering praiseworthy. Another is Mirabai's own expression of passionate longing for Krishna such that she gratefully embraces death when her husband tries to poison her ("I'm Colored with the Color of Dusk"). While Mirabai represents the North Indian Hindu tradition, it is important to note that South India has had its own rich tradition of bhakti poet-saints, including Nammalvar and Akka Mahadevi.

I'm Colored with the Color of Dusk

The male bhakti saints often speak with the voices of women—the voices of Krishna's mother, his lover, the lover's friend. But Mirabai can speak in her own voice, simultaneously as herself and as one of the cowherd women. The *rana*, the ruler, the man of Mirabai's warrior class, her husband, is poison to her; while the god, Krishna, has so thoroughly pervaded her that he has dyed her with his own dark color. He is called the "Mountain Lifter" in recognition of the time when the god of rain sent a devastating monsoon but Krishna lifted up Mount Govardhana to form an umbrella for the cowherd village. "The Maddening One" refers both to Krishna and to Kama, the god of erotic love; together, they have intoxicated Mira and driven her mad.

> I'm colored with the color of dusk, oh rana,
> 　　colored with the color of my Lord.
> Drumming out the rhythm on the drums, I danced,
> 　　dancing in the presence of the saints,
> 　　　　colored with the color of my Lord.
> They thought me mad for the Maddening One,
> 　　raw for my dear dark love,
> 　　　　colored with the color of my Lord.
> The rana sent me a poison cup:
> 　　I didn't look, I drank it up,
> 　　　　colored with the color of my Lord.
> The clever Mountain Lifter is the lord of Mira.
> 　　Life after life he's true—
> 　　　　colored with the color of my Lord.

Life without Hari

In this poem detailing Mirabai's longing for Krishna, whom she affectionately calls "Hari," we catch a glimpse of her difficulties with her husband's family. Their demands for her to abandon her love for Krishna and devote herself fully to her husband cause great tension.

> Life without Hari is no life, friend,
> And though my mother-in-law fights,
> 　　my sister-in-law teases,
> 　　the rana is angered,
> A guard is stationed on a stool outside,
> 　　and a lock is mounted on the door,
> How can I abandon the love I have loved
> 　　in life after life?
> Mira's Lord is the clever Mountain Lifter:
> 　　Why would I want anyone else?

The Bhil Woman Tasted Them

This poem is based on a story that Indian bhakti writers Valmiki and Kabir told before Mirabai told it and that Tulsidas would tell after her. When Prince Rama was exiled in the forest, a woman from the low-caste Bhil tribe offered him a piece of fruit (a large, slightly sour fruit from the ber tree, something like a plum). He accepted it despite her low caste. Mirabai adds a woman's touch that makes the fruit doubly untouchable: the tribal woman first tastes the fruit herself, to make sure that it is not too sour, not realizing that the fluids from her mouth are polluting. Though Mirabai notes that such a woman could never have learned to recite the Vedas, her love carries her straight to heaven.

The Bhil woman tasted them, plum after plum,
    and finally found one she could offer him.
What kind of genteel breeding was this?
    And hers was no ravishing beauty.
Her family was poor, her caste quite low,
    her clothes a matter of rags,
Yet Ram took that fruit—that touched, spoiled fruit—
    for he knew that it stood for her love.
This was a woman who loved the taste of love,
    and Ram knows no high, no low.
What sort of Veda could she ever have learned?
    But quick as a flash she mounted a chariot
And sped to heaven to swing on a swing,
    tied by love to God.
You are the Lord who cares for the fallen;
    rescue whoever loves as she did:
Let Mira, your servant, safely cross over,
    a cowherding Gokul girl.

Sister, I Had a Dream

Past lives, like unremembered dreams, here reward the dreamer with a vision of union with the Mountain Lifter (Krishna, who held up Mount Govardhana), also called "Lord of Braj" (Krishna's village). And as the Upanishads teach us, in many ways dreams are more real than waking life.

Sister, I had a dream that I wed
    the Lord of those who live in need:
Five hundred sixty thousand people came
    and the Lord of Braj was the groom.
        In dream they set up a wedding arch;
        in dream he grasped my hand;
        in dream he led me around the wedding fire
        and I became unshakably his bride.
Mira's been granted her mountain-lifting Lord:
    from living past lives, a prize.

Oh, the Yogi

Mira sends a message, through a female friend, to a yogi, telling him that now, in the season of rains, when the monsoon makes travel almost impossible and lovers are reunited, it is time to stop wandering and settle down—or else, after the rains, to wander together, yogi with yogini (female yogi). Mira often depicts Krishna as a yogi, perhaps because he is so distant, wandering away from her, and she depicts herself as a yogini, leaving behind conventional marriage in order to take up her idealized marriage, the union of a yogi and a yogini. Such a union contradicts the conventional Hindu categories of marriage and the householder life but not the more esoteric mythology of the god Shiva, the erotic ascetic whose clothing and jewelry are made of snakes. Mira often invokes Shiva, sometimes, as here, together with the god Ram, not the Rama of the Ramayana, Sita's Rama, but Kabir's Rama, a god without qualities (*nirguna*).

Oh, the yogi—
>   my friend, that clever one
>   whose mind is on Shiva and the Snake,
>   that all-knowing yogi—tell him this:

"I'm not staying here, not staying where
>   the land's grown strange without you, my dear,
But coming home, coming to where your place is;
>   take me, guard me with your guardian mercy,
>   please.
I'll take up your yogic garb—
>   your prayer beads,
>   earrings,
>   begging-bowl skull,
>   tattered yogic cloth—
>   I'll take them all
And search through the world as a yogi does
with you—yogi and yogini, side by side.

"My loved one, the rains have come,
>   and you promised that when they did, you'd come too.
And now the days are gone: I've counted them
>   one by one on the folds of my fingers
>   till the lines at the joints have blurred
And my love has left me pale,
>   my youth grown yellow as with age.
Singing of Ram,
>   your servant Mira

has offered you an offering:
        her body and her mind."

Let Us Go to a Realm Beyond Going

In this vision of a land beyond all the heavens, giving form and expression to the formless and indescribable land of moksha (release), the royal geese or swans settle on the lake of the heart (*manasarovar*) at the foot of Mount Kailasa, where Shiva meditates. There the devotees of Krishna dance, as the cowherd women danced in his village on earth; and they are married to him. The sixteen signs of beauty are the traditional cosmetics and ornaments of a married woman, such as the mark on the forehead and along the part of the hair, a pearl in the nostril, the gold bangles on the arm.

Let us go to a realm beyond going,
Where death is afraid to go,
Where the high-flying birds alight and play,
Afloat in the full lake of love.
There they gather—the good, the true—
To strengthen an inner regimen,
To focus on the dark form of the Lord
And refine their minds like fire.
Garbed in goodness—their ankle bells—
They dance the dance of contentment
And deck themselves with the sixteen signs
Of beauty, and a golden crown—
There where the love of the Dark One comes first
And everything else is last.

Discussion Questions

1. In many of her poems, Mirabai discusses how her passionate love for Lord Krishna makes her appear "mad." If developing this kind of extreme emotional connection is what one should do in order to obtain moksha, why do others call Mirabai "mad"?

2. Do Mirabai's reflections on the superiority of low-caste devotion to Krishna in "The Bhil Woman Tasted Them" offer any kind of "this world" change for the Bhil woman's social status? What does this tell us about the caste system in Hindu history and thought?

3. Is bhakti devotional practice as expressed in Mirabai's poetry similar to any other religious practices with which you may be familiar? How is it different?

Speech to the World's Parliament of Religions

Swami Vivekananda

Swami Vivekananda (1863–1902) was the first Hindu missionary to the United States. He was invited to speak at the World's Parliament of Religions in Chicago in 1893, where he presented the following speech explaining Hinduism. At the time, India was ruled by the British, who generally regarded Hinduism as the superstitious religion of a people that would benefit from European colonization. The Reverend John Henry Barrows, the Presbyterian minister who organized the World's Parliament, hoped the event would demonstrate the superiority of Protestant Christianity. But Vivekananda, who had studied Christianity, science, and Western philosophy, surprised his audience with his eloquent speeches. He defended Hinduism as an ancient religion that has always promoted tolerance and is compatible with modern science.

In 1894, he founded the Vedanta Society, the first Hindu organization in the United States designed to attract American converts. By the 1920s, that organization had spread to Boston, San Francisco, and Los Angeles.

Hinduism

Three religions stand now in the world which have come down to us from time prehistoric—Hinduism, Zoroastrianism, and Judaism.

They all have received tremendous shocks and all of them prove by their survival their internal strength; but while Judaism failed to absorb Christianity, and was driven out of its place of birth by its all-conquering daughter, and a handful of Parsees, are all that remains to tell the tale of his grand religion, sect after sect have arisen in India and seemed to shake the religion of the Vedas to its very foundation, but like the waters of the seashore in a tremendous earthquake, it receded only for a while, only to return in an all-absorbing flood, a thousand times more vigorous, and when the tumult of the rush was over, they have been all sucked in, absorbed and assimilated in the immense body of another faith.

From the high spiritual flights of Vedantic philosophy, of which the latest discoveries of science seem like the echoes, the agnosticism of the Buddhas, the atheism of the Jains, and the low ideas of idolatry with the multifarious mythology, each and all have a place in the Hindu's religion.

Where then, the question arises, where is the common center to which all these widely diverging radii converge; where is the common basis upon which all these seemingly hopeless contradictions rest? And this is the question I shall attempt to answer.

The Hindus have received their religion through their revelation, the Vedas. They hold that the Vedas are without beginning and without end. It may sound ludicrous to this audience, how a book can be without beginning or end. But by the Vedas no books are meant. They mean the accumulated treasury of spiritual law discovered by different persons in different times. Just as the law of gravitation existed before its discovery, and would exist if all humanity forgot it, so with the laws that govern the spiritual world. The moral, ethical and spiritual relation between soul and souls and between individual spirits and the Father of all spirits were there before their discovery and would remain even if we forgot them.

The discoverers of these laws are called Rishis, and we honor them as perfected beings, and I am glad to tell this audience that some of the very best of them were women.

Here it may be said that the laws as laws may be without end, but they must have had a beginning. The Vedas teach us that creation is without beginning or end. Science has proved to us that the sum total of the cosmic energy is the same throughout all. Then if there was a time when nothing existed, where was all this manifested energy? Some say it was in a potential form in God. But then God is sometimes potential and sometimes kinetic, which would make him mutable, and everything mutable is a compound, and everything compound must undergo that change which is called destruction. Therefore God would die. Therefore there never was a time when there was no creation. If I may be allowed to apply a simile, creation and creator are two lives, without beginning and without end, running parallel to each other, and God is power, an ever-active providence, under whose power systems after systems are being evolved out of chaos,—made to run for a time and again destroyed. This is what the Hindu boy repeats every day with his *guru*: "The sun and the moon, the Lord created after other suns and moons." And this agrees with science.

Here I stand, and if I shut my eyes and try to conceive my existence, I, I, I—what is the idea before me? The idea of a body. Am I, then, nothing but a combination of matter and material substances? The Vedas declare "No," I am a spirit living in a body. I am not the body. The body will die, but I will not die. Here am I in this body, and when it will fail, still I will go on living, and also I had a past. The soul was not created from nothing, for creation means a combination, and that means a certain future dissolution. If, then, the soul was created, it must die. Therefore it was not created. Some are born happy, enjoying perfect health, beautiful body, mental vigor, and with all wants supplied. Others are born miserable; some are without hands or feet, some idiots, and only drag on a miserable existence. Why, if they are all created, does a just and merciful God create one happy and the other unhappy—why is he so partial? Nor would it mend matters in the least by holding that those that are miserable in this life will be perfect in a future. Why should a man be miserable here in the reign of a just and merciful God? In the second place, it does not give us any cause, but simply a cruel act of an all-powerful being, and therefore unscientific. There must have been causes, then, to make a man miserable or happy before his birth, and those were his past actions. Are not all the tendencies of the mind and those of the body answered for by inherited aptitude from parents? Here are the two parallel lines of existence—one that of the mind, the other that of matter. If matter and its transformation answer for all that we have, there is no necessity of supposing the existence of a soul. But it cannot be proved that thought has been evolved out of matter, and if a philosophical monism is inevitable, a spiritual monism is certainly logical and no less desirable, but neither of these is necessary here.

We cannot deny that bodies inherit certain tendencies from heredity, but these tendencies only mean the secular configuration, through which a peculiar mind alone can act in a peculiar way. The cause of those peculiar tendencies in that soul have been caused by his past actions, and a soul with a certain tendency would go and take birth in a body which is the fittest instrument of the display of that tendency by the laws of affinity. And this is in perfect accord with science, for science wants to explain everything by habit, and habit is got through repetitions. So these repetitions are also necessary to explain the natural habits of a new-born soul—and they were not got in this present life; therefore they must have come down from past lives.

But there is another suggestion; taking all these for granted, how is it that I do not remember anything of my past life? This can be easily explained. I am now speaking English. It is not my mother tongue, in fact no words of my mother tongue are present in my consciousness, but let me try to bring them up, they rush into my consciousness. That shows that consciousness is the name only of the surface of the mental ocean, and within its depths is stored up all our experiences. Try and struggle and they will come up and you would be conscious.

This is the direct and demonstrative evidence. Verification is the perfect proof of a theory and here is the challenge, thrown to the world by the Rishis. We have discovered precepts by which the very depths of the ocean of memory can be stirred up—try it and you would get a complete reminiscence of your past life.

So then the Hindu believes that he is a spirit.

Him the sword cannot pierce—him the fire cannot burn—him the water cannot melt—him the air cannot dry. And that every soul is a circle whose circumference is nowhere, but whose center is located in a body, and death means the change of this center from body to body. Nor is the soul bound by the conditions of matter. In its very essence, it is free, unbounded, holy and pure and perfect. But some how or other it has got itself bound down by matter, and thinks itself as matter? Why should the free, perfect and pure being be under the thraldom of matter, is the next question.

How can the perfect be deluded into the belief that he is imperfect, is the question. We have been told that the Hindus shirk the question and say that no such question can be there, and some thinkers want to answer it by the posing of one or more quasi perfect beings, and big scientific names to fill up the gap. But naming is not explaining. The question remains the same. How the perfect becomes the quasi perfect; how can the pure, the absolute, change even a microscopic particle of its nature? But the Hindu is more sincere. He does not want to take shelter under sophistry. He is brave enough to face the question in a manly fashion. And his answer is, I do not know. I do not know how the perfect being, the soul came to think itself as imperfect, as joined to and conditioned by matter. But the fact is a fact for all that. It is a fact in everybody's consciousness that he thinks himself as the body. We do not attempt to explain why I am in this body. The answer that it is the will of God, is no explanation. It is nothing more than what they say themselves. "We do not know."

Well, then, the human soul is eternal and immortal, perfect and infinite, and death means only a change of center from one body to another. The present is determined by our past actions, and the future will be by the present; that it will go on evolving up or reverting back from birth to birth and death to death. But here is another question; is man a tiny boat in a tempest, raised one moment on the foaming crest of a billow and dashed down into a yawning chasm the next, rolling to and fro at the mercy of good and bad actions—a powerless, helpless wreck in an ever-raging, ever-rushing, uncompromising current of cause and effect—a little moth placed under the wheel of causation, which rolls on crushing everything in its way, and waits not for the widows' tears or the orphans' cry? The heart sinks at the idea, yet this is the law of nature. Is there no hope? Is there no escape? was the cry that went up from the bottom of the heart of despair. It reached the throne of mercy, and words of hope and consolation came down and inspired a Vedic sage, and he stood up before the world and in trumpet voice proclaimed the glad tidings to the world. "Hear ye children of immortal bliss, even ye that reside in higher spheres. I have found the Ancient One, who is beyond all darkness, all delusion, and knowing him alone you shall be saved from death over again. Children of immortal bliss, what a sweet, what a hopeful name." Allow me to call you, brethren, by that sweet name, heirs of immortal bliss—yea, the Hindu refuses to call you sinners. Ye are the children of God, the sharers of immortal bliss, holy and perfect beings, ye are divinities on earth. Sinners? It is a sin to call a man so; it is a standing libel on human nature. Come up, Oh, live and shake off the delusion that you are sheep; you are souls immortal, spirits free and blest and eternal; ye are not matter, ye are not bodies; matter is your servant, not you the servant of matter.

Thus it is that the Vedas proclaim not a dreadful combination of unforgiving laws, not an endless prison of cause and effect, but that at the head of all these laws, in and through every particle of matter and force, stands one through whose command the wind blows, the fire burns, the clouds rain, and death stalks upon the earth. And what is his nature?

He is everywhere the pure and formless one. The Almighty and the All-merciful. "Thou art our father, thou art our mother; thou art our beloved friend; thou art the source of all strength; give us strength. Thou art he that bearest the burdens of the universe: help me bear the little burden of this life." Thus sang the Rishis of the Veda; and how to worship him—through love. "He is to be worshipped as the one beloved," "dearer than everything in this and the next life."

This is the doctrine of love preached in the Vedas, and let us see how it is fully developed and preached by Krishna, whom the Hindus believe to have been God incarnate on earth.

He taught that a man ought to live in this world like a lotus leaf, which grows in water but is never moistened by water—so a man ought to live in this world—his heart to God and his hands to work. It is good to love God for hope of reward in this or the next world, but it is better to love God for love's sake, and the prayer goes: "Lord, I do not want wealth, nor children, nor learning. If it be thy will I will go to a hundred hells, but grant me this, that I may love thee without the hope of reward—unselfishly love for love's sake." One of the disciples of Krishna, the then Emperor of India, was driven from his throne by his enemies, and had to take shelter in a forest in the Himalayas with his queen, and there one day the queen was asking him how it was that he, the most virtuous of men, should suffer so much misery; and Yuohistera answered: "Behold, my queen, the Himalayas, how beautiful they are; I love them. They do not give me anything, but my nature is to love the grand, the beautiful, therefore I love them. Similarly, I love the Lord. He is the source of all beauty, of all sublimity. He is the only object to be loved; my nature is to love him, and therefore I love. I do not pray for anything; I do not ask for anything. Let him place me wherever he likes. I must love him for love's sake. I cannot trade in love."

The Vedas teach that the soul is divine, only held under bondage of matter, and perfection will be reached when the bond shall burst, and the word they use is therefore Mukto—freedom, freedom from the bonds of imperfection, freedom from death and misery.

And this bondage can only fall off through the mercy of God, and this mercy comes on the pure, so purity is the condition of his mercy. How that mercy acts. He reveals himself to the pure heart, and the pure and stainless man sees God, yea even in this life, and then, and then only, all the crookedness of the heart is made straight. Then all doubt ceases. He is no more the freak of a terrible law of causation. So this is the very center, the very vital conception of Hinduism. The Hindu does not want to live upon words and theories—if there are existences beyond the ordinary sensual existence, he wants to come face to face with them. If there is a soul in him which is not matter, if there is an all-merciful universal soul, he will go to him direct. He must see him, and that alone can destroy all doubts. So the best proof a Hindu sage gives about the soul, about God, is "I have seen the soul; I have seen God." And that is the only condition of perfection. The Hindu religion does not consist in struggles and attempts to believe a certain doctrine or dogma, but in realizing; not in believing, but in being and becoming.

So the whole struggle in their system is a constant struggle to become perfect, to become divine, to reach God and see God, and this reaching God, seeing God, becoming perfect, even as the Father in Heaven is perfect, constitutes the religion of the Hindus.

And what becomes of man when he becomes perfect? He lives a life of bliss, infinite. He enjoys infinite and perfect bliss, having obtained the only thing in which man ought to have pleasure, God, and enjoys the bliss with God. So far all the Hindus are agreed. This is the common religion of all the sects of India; but then the question comes, perfection is absolute, and the absolute cannot be two or three. It cannot have any qualities. It cannot be an individual. And so when a soul becomes perfect and absolute, it must become one with Brahma, and he would only realize the Lord as the perfection, the reality, of his own nature and existence, the existence absolute, knowledge absolute, and life absolute. We have often and often read about this being called the losing of individuality as becoming a stock or a stone. "He jests at scars that never felt a wound."

I tell you it is nothing of the kind. If it is happiness to enjoy the consciousness of this small body, it must be more happiness to enjoy the consciousness of two bodies, so three, four, five; and the aim, the ultimate of happiness would be reached when it would become a universal consciousness. Therefore, to gain this infinite universal individuality, this miserable little prison individuality must go. Then alone can death cease when I am one with life, then alone can misery cease when I am one with happiness itself; then alone can all errors cease when I am one with knowledge itself; and it is the necessary scientific conclusion, science has proved to me that physical individuality is a delusion, that really my body is one little continuously changing body, in an unbroken ocean of matter, and the Adwaitam is the necessary conclusion with my other counterpart, mind.

Science is nothing but the finding of unity, and as any science can reach the perfect unity, it would stop from further progress, because it would reach the goal, thus chemistry cannot progress farther, when it would discover one element out of which all others could be made. Physics would stop when it would be able to fulfill its services in discovering one energy of which all the others are but the manifestations, and the science of religion become perfect when it discovered Him who is the one life in a universe of death; Him who is the constant basis of an ever-changing world; One who is the only soul of which all souls are but delusive manifestations. Thus was it, through multiplicity and duality, the ultimate unity was reached, and religion can go no farther, and this is the goal of all, again and again, science after science, again and again.

And all science is bound to come to this conclusion in the long run. Manifestation, and not creation, is the word of science of to-day, and he is only glad that what he had cherished in his bosom for ages is going to be taught in some forcible language, and with further light by the latest conclusions of science.

Descend we now from the aspirations of philosophy to the religion of the ignorant? On the very outset, I may tell you that there is no polytheism in India. In every temple, if one stands by and listens, he will find the worshipers applying all the attributes of God, including omnipresence, to these images. It is not polytheism, neither would the name henotheism answer our question. "The rose called by any other name would smell as sweet." Names are not explanations.

I remember, when a boy, a Christian man was preaching to a crowd in India. Among other sweet things he was telling the people that if he gave a blow to their idol with his stick, what could it do? One of his hearers sharply answered, "If I abuse your God what can he do?" "You would be punished," said the preacher, "when you die." "So my idol will punish you when you die," said the villager.

The tree is known by its fruits; and when I have seen amongst them that are called idolatrous men, the like of whom in morality and spirituality and love, I have never seen anywhere, I stop and ask myself, Can sin beget holiness?

Superstition is the enemy of man, bigotry worse. Why does a Christian go to church, why is the cross holy, why is the face turned toward the sky in prayer? Why are there so many images in the Catholic Church, why are there so many images in the minds of Protestants, when they pray? My brethren, we can no more think about anything without a material image than it is profitable for us to live without breathing. And by the law of association the material image calls the mental idea up and *vice versa*. Omnipotent to almost the whole world means nothing. Has God superficial area? if not, when we repeat the word we think of the extended earth; that is all.

As we find that somehow or other, by the laws of our constitution, we have got to associate our ideas of infinity with the ideal of a blue sky, or a sea; the omnipresence covering the idea of holiness with an idol of a church or a mosque, or a cross; so the Hindus have associated the ideas of holiness, purity, truth, omnipresence, and all other ideas with different images and forms. But with this difference: upon certain actions some are drawn their whole lives to their idol of a church and never rise higher, because with them religion means an intellectual assent to certain doctrines and doing good to their fellows. The whole religion of the Hindu is centered in realization. Man is to become divine, realizing the divine, and, therefore, idol or temple or church or books, are only the supports, the helps of his spiritual childhood, but on and on he must progress.

He must not stop anywhere; "external worship, material worship," says the Vedas "is the lowest stage; struggling to rise high, mental prayer is the next stage, but the highest stage is when the Lord has been realized." Mark the same earnest man who was kneeling before the idol tell you here-after of struggles, "Him the sun cannot express, nor the moon nor the stars, the lightning cannot express him, nor what we speak of fire; through him they all shine." But with this difference, he does not abuse the images or call it sin. He recognizes in it a necessary stage of his life. "The child is father of the man." Would it be right for the old man to say that childhood is a sin or youth a sin? Nor is it compulsory in Hinduism.

But if a man can realize his divine nature with the help of an image, would it be right to call it a sin? Nor even when he has passed that stage that he should call it an error. To the Hindu man is not traveling from error to truth, but from truth to truth, from lower to higher truth. To him all the religions from the lowest fetichism to the highest absolutism mean so many attempts of the human soul to grasp and realize the Infinite, determined by the conditions of its birth and association, and each of these mark a stage of progress, and every soul is a child eagle soaring higher and higher; gathering more and more strength till it reaches the glorious sun.

Unity in variety is the plan of nature, and the Hindu has recognized it. Every other religion lays down a certain amount of fixed dogma, and tries to force the whole society through it. They lay down before society one coat which must fit Jack and Job, and Henry, all alike. If it does not fit John or Henry, they must go without coat to cover body. They have discovered that the absolute can only be realized or thought of or stated through the relative, and the image, cross or crescent are simply so many centers,—so many pegs to help the spiritual idea on. It is not that this help is necessary for every one, but for many, and those that do not need it, have no right to say that it is wrong.

One thing I must tell you. Idolatry in India does not mean a horror. It is not the mother of harlots. On the other hand, it is the attempt of undeveloped minds to grasp high spiritual truths. The Hindus have their own faults, they sometimes have their exceptions; but mark this, it is always towards punishing their own bodies, and never to cut the throats of their neighbors. If the Hindu fanatic burns himself on the pyre, he never lights the fire of inquisition; and even this cannot be laid at the door of religion any more than the burning of witches can be laid at the door of Christianity.

To the Hindu, then, the whole world of religions is only a traveling, a coming up, of different men and women, through various conditions and circumstances, to the same goal. Every religion is only an evolving a God out of the material man; and the same God is the inspirer of all of them. Why, then, are there so many contradictions? They are only apparent, says the Hindu. The contradictions come from the same truth adapting itself to the different circumstances of different natures.

It is the same light coming through different colors. And these little variations are necessary for that adaptation. But in the heart of everything the same truth reigns; the Lord has declared to the Hindu in his incarnation as Krishna, "I am in every religion as the thread through a string of pearls. And wherever thou seest extraordinary holiness and extraordinary power raising and purifying humanity, know ye that I am there." And what was the result! Through the whole order of Sanscrit philosophy, I challenge anybody to find any such expression as that the Hindu only would be saved and not others. Says Vyas, "We find perfect men even beyond the pale of our caste and creed." One thing more. How can, then, the Hindu whose whole idea centers in God believe in the Buddhist who is agnostic, or the Jain who is atheist?

The Buddhists do not depend upon God; but the whole force of their religion is directed to the great central truth in every religion, to evolve a God out of man. They have not seen the Father, but they have seen the Son. And he that hath seen the Son hath seen the Father. This, brethren, is a short sketch of the ideas of the Hindus. The Hindu might have failed to carry out all his plans, but if there is to be ever a universal religion, it must be one which would hold no location in place or time, which would be infinite like the God it would preach, whose sun shines upon the followers of Krishna or Christ; saints or sinners alike; which would not be the Brahman or Buddhist, Christian or Mohammedan, but the sum total of all these, and still have infinite space for development; which in its catholicity would embrace in its infinite arms and formulate a place for every human being, from the lowest groveling man who is scarcely removed in intellectuality from the brute, to the highest mind, towering almost above humanity, and who makes society stand in awe and doubt his human nature.

It would be a religion which would have no place for persecution or intolerance in its polity, and would recognize a divinity in every man or woman, and whose whole scope, whose whole force would be centered in aiding humanity to realize its divine nature. Offer religions in your hand, and all the nations must follow thee. Asoka's council was a council of the Buddhist faith. Akbar's, though more to the purpose, was only a parlor-meeting. It was reserved for America to call, to proclaim to all quarters of the globe that the Lord is in every religion.

May He who is the Brahma of the Hindus, the Ahura Mazda of the Zoroastrians, the Buddha of the Buddhists, the Jehovah of the Jews, the Father in Heaven of the Christians, give strength to you to carry out your noble idea. The star arose in the East; it traveled steadily toward the West, sometimes dimmed and sometimes effulgent, till it made a circuit of the world, and now it is again rising on the very horizon of the East, the borders of the Tasifu, a thousand-fold more effulgent than it ever was before. Hail Columbia, mother-land of liberty! It has been given to thee, who never dipped her hand in her neighbor's blood, who never found out that shortest way of becoming rich by robbing one's neighbors, it has been given to thee to march on at the vanguard of civilization with the flag of harmony.

Controversy

Narendra Modi's Victory Speech Delivers Visions of a Hindu Nationalist Ascetic

Chandrima Chakraborty

Narendra Modi was first elected prime minister of India in 2014 amid a sweeping victory of the Bharatiya Janata Party (BJP), a conservative political party with Hindu nationalist leanings. Originally a member of a Hindu nationalist paramilitary organization, Modi served as chief minister of Gujarat from 2002 to 2014. It was during his tenure that Gujarat suffered the 2002 Gujarat riots, in which perhaps as many as two thousand Muslims were killed by Hindu mobs as retaliation for a deadly train fire that killed sixty Hindu pilgrims—though it is unclear if the fire was set intentionally. As prime minister, he has continued to use Hindu nationalist rhetoric to unite adherents of various Indian religions—all of which he considers to fall under the "Hindu" umbrella—against Muslims, whom he considers to be "foreign" invaders despite the fact that many Muslim families have lived in India for generations. These efforts have included the military lockdown of Kashmir, the only Muslim-majority state in India, and a controversial bill that disenfranchised potentially millions of Muslims as noncitizens and denied citizenship to Muslim refugees fleeing to India from surrounding countries. This analysis of Modi's victory speech for his second term as prime minister focuses on his use of Hindu nationalist rhetoric to paint himself as a selfless "ascetic" fighting to preserve the purity of India.

In the recently concluded Indian parliamentary elections, the electorate gave a thumping majority to current Prime Minister Narendra Modi of the Hindu right-wing Bharatiya

Janata Party (BJP) to lead the nation for another five years. In his victory speech at the BJP headquarters, Modi addressed the nation.

Throughout his speech, Modi crafted an image of himself as a Hindu ascetic who renounces worldly possessions, not for personal liberation but to serve the nation's needy—a *karmayogi*. This image of the selfless Hindu ascetic devoted to the nation has been carefully cultivated over decades by the Hindu right.

The creation of this figure is partly a response to the British colonial denigration of Hindu ascetics as willfully idle, otherworldly, apathetic and apolitical. It is also a response to the secular middle class derision of monks in saffron robes entering politics.

India has seen a remarkable public resurgence of Hindu ascetics in politics since the 1980s, with the ascendance of the Hindu right. Notable political figures include the Chief Minister of Uttar Pradesh, Yogi Adityanath, MP Sakshi Maharaj and MP Uma Bharati, among others.

Although not dressed in saffron robes like his compatriots, Modi's biography speaks to nationalist ascetic virtues: celibacy, renunciation of family and service for the nation. He left his home in his teenage years and wandered the Himalayas for two years, joined the militant Rashtriya Swayamsevak Sangh (RSS), the parent organization of the BJP, and abandoned his wife for the nation.

Symbolically, Modi chose Varanasi, one of Hinduism's holiest cities and the spiritual home for Hindu ascetics, as the constituency to represent at the close of his election.

Nationalist asceticism is valorized by the Hindu right, but it also holds appeal for a broad section of Hindus. Modi's victory speech impresses the audience with the popular image of the Hindu ascetic devoted to the nation's cause.

Performance of Ascetic Humility

Amit Shah, national president of the BJP, set the stage for the prime minister's address with a heart-pumping, chest-thumping victory speech offering data on states, towns and personalities that had suffered unprecedented losses for the Congress party. Rejoicing over the BJP's continued supremacy in the Hindi heartland in the 2019 elections, Shah was exuberant about the party's electoral successes in eastern India.

Following these high-pitched, triumphalist accounts of electoral victories, which the audience greeted with thunderous applause, Modi took the podium to address his supporters as the crowd chanted "Modi-Modi."

What ensued was a spectacular public performance of humility. Reminding the masses of his humble origins, Modi repeatedly applauded the generosity of the voters for filling his *fakir's jholi* (ascetic's bag). In sharp contrast to Shah, he instructed his supporters to move ahead with humility.

Modi made three promises and asked the people to hold him accountable on these promises for the tenure of his public office. First, he said he would not do anything with ill intent. Second, he vowed not to do anything for himself. That is, he would not make any personal gains from his public office. Third, he promised he would dedicate every moment of his time and every cell in his body to serving the country.

Modi's self-deprecating speech—replete with references to Hindu mythology (god of clouds), Hindu practices (cleansing oneself with a bath in the river Ganga) and the Hindu epic Mahabharata—speaks to a receptive Hindu majority.

Using Hindu Religious Texts in Politics

Modi's three promises consolidate the image of the *karmayogi*—articulated in one of Hinduism's primary texts, the Bhagavad Gita—without having to name it.

The Bhagavad Gita is the Hindu right's religious text of choice. The book starts at the beginning of an epic war and reveals a battlefield discussion between Prince Arjun and his charioteer Lord Krishna. Arjun feels squeamish going to war against his own family. Lord Krishna encourages him to think of himself as a *karmayogi*: someone who works with detachment without anticipating the fruits of his labor.

In his speech, Modi informed his listeners that he had a busy day. Therefore he did not have the opportunity to look through the poll results and would look later that night. Thus, he put forth himself as a detached and selfless worker for the nation.

As Modi publicly rededicates himself to serve the nation at the beginning of his second five-year political mandate, this coded messaging will appeal to his Hindu sympathizers. Many of them are fed up with corrupt politicians and feel marginalized by privileged liberal elites. A humble, Hindi-speaking prime minister elicits their trust. Others feel encouraged to uphold their religious identity.

Many of these same people believe that secularism is an unmanly appeasement of religious minorities, especially Muslims.

Crafting Images of Devotion

A few days before the election results were declared, images of Modi draped in a saffron shawl meditating in a cave emerged. His election victory speech fleshed out this self-representation as an ascetic. Modi presents himself as a Hindu ascetic walking from door to door seeking alms (votes), thankful for the generosity of the masses.

In an ironic twist, the voter becomes the kind benefactor, rather than the prime minister, who can improve the lives of the poor. Such skillful use of imagery also tells the Indian public that while Modi may be the prime minister of India, he continues to be one of them.

This alms-seeking ascetic narrative invokes Modi's humble origins. It emphasizes his strong personal virtues of dedication and hard work. This is what allowed him to climb through the ranks of the Rashtriya Swayamsevak Sangh to become the leader of the largest democracy in the world.

It's a reminder to those frustrated with the Congress Party's dynastic politics that this humble son of the soil, with limited English fluency, has proven his ascendancy over the privileged, English-speaking Gandhis.

More so, it offers assurances to his supporters, many of whom speak a variety of vernacular tongues—but especially to his Hindi speakers—that the days of the liberal, English-educated elite are over.

Modi's carefully crafted, religiously coded public enactment of unabashed patriotic loyalty is a dog whistle that those who support his vision of a Hindu majoritarian "new India" can hear loud and clear.

Discussion Questions

1. As highlighted by the author, Hindu nationalists often laud the Bhagavad Gita for its poetic imagery and its valorization of battle to defend a nation. How is Modi using the imagery of a practitioner of karma yoga?

2. Politicians around the world often use religious imagery in speeches to make their point. Based on Chandrima Chakraborty's analysis, do you think Modi is using religious imagery differently than his global peers? Why might that be the case?

3. Can we frame Hindu nationalism as largely a reaction to British colonial rule of India, which ended only in 1947? What other forces might be in play?

Buddhism

Sometimes misunderstood as a nihilistic tradition, Buddhists understand humanity's fundamental problem to be suffering, which they believe to be inherent to the human condition. The solution Buddhists offer is nirvana, a rich and complex term that means in Sanskrit "blowing out" and allows for a multiplicity of interpretations—the blowing out of attachments, the blowing out of one's own idea of the self, and the blowing out of suffering itself. To illustrate this problem and solution, we have selected several poems from *Verses of the Elder Nuns* (Therigatha) and *Verses of the Elder Monks* (Theragatha). These two collections of poetry written by early Buddhist monks and nuns may be contemporaneous with the life of Buddha Siddhartha Gautama himself and beautifully reflect the very human nature of suffering. They speak to universal fears of death, old age, and loss, while also exhorting the reader to follow the teachings of the Buddha and not waste a precious human life on frivolous pursuits. To combat suffering and eventually obtain nirvana, Buddhism offers a wide-ranging variety of techniques, including both contemplative practices like meditation and more devotional practices like offerings. All of them, however, take as their foundation the development of attentive awareness to the world around oneself and the true nature of the mind. To reflect this technique, therefore, we have selected two chapters from the *Verses of the Dharma* (Dhammapada), an early anthology of Buddhist aphorisms preserved in the Pali canon. Organized thematically, the chapters selected here detail how systematically developing one's awareness and mental focus breeds wisdom and insight into the true origins of suffering. While it is tempting to read these selections as evidence that the earliest forms of Buddhist practice were devoid of devotional practices, such an assumption would be a mistake. We know that early Buddhist practitioners cherished relics of the Buddha and that soon after his death, devotional offerings were being made at stupas and other sites holding his ashes.

As Buddhism developed in India and eventually spread throughout Asia, a variety of exemplars emerged to guide Buddhist practice. Chief among these in the Mahayana tradition were the compassionate bodhisattvas who had perfected their generosity and worked tirelessly to lead more people on the path to enlightenment. In China, where Mahayana Buddhism has historically been predominant, one of the most important bodhisattvas is Guanyin. Originally known as Avalokiteshvara in India, she is believed to constantly take human form in order to provide salvific aid to devotees and promote Buddhist practice. In this legend detailing her reincarnation as the princess Miao-shan, we see an important statement about the potential for women to act as Buddhist teachers, as well as insight into the social pressure to marry and bear children faced by Chinese women. A contemporary example of an individual identified as a bodhisattva by many Buddhists is antiwar activist Thich Nhat Hanh. Born in Vietnam in 1926, he has engaged in significant peace activism in America, France, and Vietnam, while also establishing Buddhist communities around the globe. So respected is Thich Nhat Hanh that Dr. Martin Luther King, Jr. nominated him for a Nobel Peace Prize in 1967. In this selection, he speaks on the application of Buddhist principles to contemporary social situations like poverty and hatred through a recognition of the interconnection of all phenomena—a term he has inventively labeled "interbeing."

Despite the widespread belief in America that Buddhists are free from the violent struggles that have been recorded in so many other religious traditions, violence has been present in both historical and contemporary Buddhism. The final reading of this chapter explores this controversy through a detailed examination of contemporary Buddhist violence in the country of Myanmar, once known as Burma. In recent years, the Burmese Buddhist majority has disenfranchised and targeted the Rohingya Muslim minority as a threat to a Buddhist way of life, comparing them to a "mad dog" that must be put down. These attacks have been spurred in large part by the activist monk Wirathu, whom *Time Magazine* profiled in 2013. The article, printed in full here, provides insight into the nationalist and religious rhetoric employed by Wirathu to inspire physical assaults against and ostracization of Burmese Muslims. While it is tempting to disavow Wirathu as a "bad" Buddhist or to claim he is twisting the Buddhist religion to fit his nationalist purposes, such a move is a form of essentialism that reduces Buddhism to a limited, Western-defined form of the religion while ignoring the real, lived experiences and actions of Buddhists around the world.

Poems of the Elders

The earliest Buddhist texts were transmitted orally until they were written down sometime before the first century BCE and formed into what is today called the Pali canon. While scholars note that some texts were likely added at a later time or modified over the centuries, many of these texts show evidence of going back directly to the fifth-century BCE community that surrounded Siddhartha Gautama himself. Among these are the *Verses of the Elder Nuns* and the *Verses of the Elder Monks*. These two collections of poetry are the compositions of elderly monastics said to be close to the historical Buddha and are remarkable for not only their age but also their eloquence in describing the fundamentally human problem of suffering. Indeed, the *Verses of the Elder Nuns* is one of the earliest known collections of writing by women discussing their own religious experiences. In these selections identified by the poets' names, the speakers reflect on the impermanence of the body and social prominence, while also encouraging the reader's dedication toward Buddhist teachings.

Selections from *Verses of the Elder Monks*
2:16—Mahākāla

This swarthy woman
[preparing a corpse for cremation]
    —crow-like, enormous—
breaking a thigh and then the other
    thigh,
breaking an arm and then the other
       arm,
cracking open the head,
    like a pot of curds,
she sits with them heaped up beside her.

Whoever, unknowing,
makes acquisitions
    —the fool—
returns over and over
to suffering and stress.
So, discerning,

don't make acquisitions.
May I never lie
with my head cracked open
again.

3:13—Abhibhūta

Listen, kinsmen, all of you,
as many as are assembled here.
I will teach you the Dhamma:
Painful is birth,
again and again.

Rouse yourselves.
Go forth.
Apply yourselves
to the Awakened One's bidding.
Scatter the army of Death
as an elephant would
a shed made of reeds.

He who,
in this Dhamma and Vinaya,
stays heedful,
abandoning birth,
the wandering-on,
will put an end
to suffering and stress.

6:5—Māluṅkyaputta

When a person lives heedlessly,
his craving grows like a creeping vine.
He runs now here
and now there,
as if looking for fruit:
a monkey in the forest.

If this sticky, uncouth craving
overcomes you in the world,
your sorrows grow like wild grass
after rain.

If, in the world, you overcome
this uncouth craving, hard to escape,
sorrows roll off you,
      like water beads off
      a lotus.

To all of you gathered here
I say:
      Good fortune.
      Dig up craving
—as when seeking medicinal roots, wild grass—
      by the root.
Don't let Mara cut you down
—as a raging river, a reed—
over and over again.

Do what the Buddha says.
Don't let the moment pass by.
Those for whom the moment is past
grieve, consigned to hell.
Heedlessness is dust.
Dust follows on heedlessness.
Through heedfulness, knowledge,
pull out
      your own arrow
      on your own.

Selections from *Verses of the Elder Nuns*
13:1—AMBAPĀLĪ

Black was my hair
—the color of bees—
and curled at the tips;
      with age, it looked like coarse hemp.
The Truth-speaker's word
         doesn't change.

Fragrant, like a perfumed basket
filled with flowers: my coiffure.
      With age it smelled musty,
      like animal fur.

The Truth-speaker's word
        doesn't change.

Thick and lush, like a well-tended grove,
made splendid, the tips elaborate
with comb and pin.
        With age, it grew thin
        and bald here and there.
The Truth-speaker's word
        doesn't change.

Adorned with gold and delicate pins,
it was splendid, ornamented with braids.
        Now, with age,
        that head has gone bald.
The Truth-speaker's word
        doesn't change.

Curved, as if well-drawn by an artist,
my brows were once splendid.
        With age, they droop down in folds.
The Truth-speaker's word
        doesn't change.

Radiant, brilliant like jewels,
my eyes: elongated, black—deep black.
        With age, they're no longer splendid.
The Truth-speaker's word
        doesn't change.

Like a delicate peak, my nose
was splendid in the prime of my youth.
        With age, it's like a long pepper.
The Truth-speaker's word
        doesn't change.

Like bracelets—well-fashioned, well-finished—
my ears were once splendid.
        With age, they droop down in folds.
The Truth-speaker's word
        doesn't change.

Like plantain buds in their color,
my teeth were once splendid.
		With age, they're broken and yellowed.
The Truth-speaker's word
			doesn't change.

Like that of a cuckoo in the dense jungle,
flitting through deep forest thickets:
sweet was the tone of my voice.
		With age, it cracks here and there.
The Truth-speaker's word
			doesn't change.

Smooth—like a conch shell well-polished—
my neck was once splendid.
		With age, it's broken down, bent.
The Truth-speaker's word
			doesn't change.

Like rounded door-bars—both of them—
my arms were once splendid.
		With age, they're like dried up pāṭalī trees.
The Truth-speaker's word
			doesn't change.

Adorned with gold and delicate rings,
my hands were once splendid.
		With age, they're like onions and tubers.
The Truth-speaker's word
			doesn't change.

Swelling, round, firm, and high,
both my breasts were once splendid.
		In the drought of old age, they dangle
		like empty old water bags.
The Truth-speaker's word
			doesn't change.

Like a sheet of gold, well-burnished,
my body was splendid.
		Now it's covered with very fine wrinkles.

The Truth-speaker's word
        doesn't change.

Smooth in their lines, like an elephant's trunk,
both my thighs were once splendid.
        With age, they're like knotted bamboo.
The Truth-speaker's word
        doesn't change.

Adorned with gold and delicate anklets,
my calves were once splendid.
        With age, they're like sesame sticks.
The Truth-speaker's word
        doesn't change.

As if they were stuffed with soft cotton,
both my feet were once splendid.
        With age, they're shriveled and cracked.
The Truth-speaker's word
        doesn't change.

Such was this physical heap,
now: decrepit, the home of pains, many pains.
        A house with its plaster all fallen off.
The Truth-speaker's word
        doesn't change.

14—SUBHĀ AND THE LIBERTINE

As Subhā the nun was going through Jīvaka's delightful mango grove, a libertine (a goldsmith's son) blocked her path, so she said to him:

"What wrong have I done you
that you stand in my way?
It's not proper, my friend,
that a man should touch
a woman gone forth.
I respect the Master's message,
the training pointed out by the One Well-Gone.
I am pure, without blemish:
        Why do you stand in my way?

You—your mind agitated, impassioned;
I—unagitated, unimpassioned,
with a mind entirely freed:
　　　　Why do you stand in my way?"

"You are young and not bad-looking,
what need do you have for going forth?
Throw off your ochre robe—
　　　　Come, let's delight in the flowering grove.
A sweetness they exude everywhere,
the trees risen-up with their pollen.
The beginning of spring is a pleasant season—
　　　　Come, let's delight in the flowering grove.
The trees with their blossoming tips
moan, as it were, in the breeze:
What delight will you have
if you plunge into the grove alone?
Frequented by herds of wild beasts,
disturbed by elephants rutting and aroused:
You want to go
　　　　unaccompanied
into the great, lonely, frightening grove?
Like a doll made of gold, you will go about,
like a goddess in the gardens of heaven.
With delicate, smooth Kāsī fabrics,
you will shine, O beauty without compare.
I would gladly do your every bidding
if we were to dwell in the glade.
For there is no creature dearer to me
　　　　than you, O nymph with the languid regard.
If you do as I ask, happy, come live in my house.
Dwelling in the calm of a palace,
　　　　have women wait on you,
　　　　wear delicate Kāsī fabrics,
　　　　adorn yourself with garlands and creams.
I will make you many and varied ornaments
　　　　of gold, jewels, and pearls.
Climb onto a costly bed,
scented with sandalwood carvings,
with a well-washed coverlet, beautiful,
spread with a woolen quilt, brand new.

Like a blue lotus rising from the water
where no human beings dwell,
you will go to old age with your limbs unseen,
if you stay as you are in the holy life."

"What do you assume of any essence,
here in this cemetery grower, filled with corpses,
this body destined to break up?
What do you see when you look at me,
        you who are out of your mind?"

"Your eyes are like those of a fawn,
like those of a sprite in the mountains.
Seeing your eyes, my sensual delight
        grows all the more.
Like tips they are, of blue lotuses,
in your golden face
        —spotless:
Seeing your eyes, my sensual delight
        grows all the more.
Even if you should go far away,
I will think only of your pure,
        long-lashed gaze,
for there is nothing dearer to me
        than your eyes, O nymph with the languid regard."

"You want to stray from the road,
you want the moon as a plaything,
you want to jump over Mount Sineru,
you who have designs on one born of the Buddha.
For there is nothing anywhere at all
in the cosmos with its devas,
that would be an object of passion for me.
        I don't even know what that passion would be,
        for it's been killed, root and all, by the path.
Like embers from a pit—scattered,
like a bowl of poison—evaporated,
        I don't even see what that passion would be,
        for it's been killed, root and all, by the path.
Try to seduce one who hasn't reflected on this,
or who has not followed the Master's teaching.

But try it with this one who knows
        and you suffer.
For in the midst of praise and blame,
        pleasure and pain,
my mindfulness stands firm.
Knowing the unattractiveness
        of things compounded,
my mind cleaves to nothing at all.
I am a follower of the One Well-Gone,
riding the vehicle of the eightfold way:
My arrow removed, effluent-free,
I delight, having gone to an empty dwelling.
For I have seen well-painted puppets,
hitched up with sticks and strings,
made to dance in various ways.
When the sticks and strings are removed,
thrown away, scattered, shredded,
smashed into pieces, not to be found,
        in what will the mind there make its home?
This body of mine, which is just like that,
when devoid of dhammas doesn't function.
When, devoid of dhammas, it doesn't function,
        in what will the mind there make its home?

Like a mural you've seen, painted on a wall,
smeared with yellow orpiment,
there your vision has been distorted,
your perception of a human being—pointless.
Like an evaporated mirage,
like a tree of gold in a dream,
like a magic show in the midst of a crowd—
        you run blind after what is unreal.
Resembling a ball of sealing wax,
set in a hollow,
with a bubble in the middle
and bathed with tears,
eye secretions are born there too:
The parts of the eye
are rolled all together
in various ways."

Plucking out her lovely eye,
with mind unattached
she felt no regret.

"Here, take this eye. It's yours."

Straightaway she gave it to him.
Straightaway his passion faded right there,
and he begged her forgiveness:

"Be well, follower of the holy life.
        This sort of thing
        won't happen again.
Harming a person like you
is like embracing a blazing fire.
It's as if I have seized a poisonous snake.
So may you be well. Forgive me."

And released from there, the nun
went to the excellent Buddha's presence.
When she saw the mark of his excellent merit,
        her eye became
        as it was before.

Discussion Questions

1. How do the authors of these poems suggest that one challenge the craving and attachment that Buddhists claim keep one trapped in the cycle of reincarnation?

2. How do the selections from the *Verses of the Elder Monks* and the selections from the *Verses of the Elder Nuns* differ? How do they express similar concerns?

3. What is the value of religious scriptures like these, which are not explicit moments of instruction or explanation? How do they deepen one's understanding of Buddhist doctrine?

From the Dhammapada

Attributed to Siddhartha Gautama himself, *Verses of the Dharma* is one of the most well-known Buddhist texts and among the first to be examined by Western scholars in the nineteenth century. Consisting of 423 verses organized thematically into twenty-six chapters, the *Verses of the Dharma* represents for many contemporary Buddhists an essential and concise summary of Buddhist teachings and practices, so much so that a choral arrangement of the text was produced in 2010. While this selection comes from the Pali version of the text, there are similar, but not identical, collections in a variety of other South Asian languages, including Gandhari and Sanskrit. These selections from Chapters 2 and 3 highlight the importance of developing a careful awareness of the mind to prevent attachment and move toward enlightenment. Buddhism is noteworthy for its breadth of potential techniques to attain enlightenment; selecting just one text in this reader, therefore, will necessarily exclude other practices that are as important for contemporary Buddhist practice. We encourage readers to understand the technique presented here as one among many and to take these selections as a jumping-off point to explore other important Buddhist practices like offerings, chanting, and visualizations.

Chapter II. Awareness

The path to the Deathless is awareness;
Unawareness, the path of death.
They who are aware do not die;
They who are unaware are as dead.

Having known this distinctly,
Those who are wise in awareness,
Rejoice in awareness,
Delighted in the pasture of the noble ones.

Those meditators, persevering,
Forever firm of enterprise,
Those steadfast ones touch nirvana
Incomparable release from bonds.

By standing alert, by awareness,
By restraint and control too,
The intelligent one could make an island
That a flood does not overwhelm.

Fame increases for the one who stands alert,
Mindful, and of pure deeds;
Who with due consideration acts, restrained,
Who lives dharma being aware.

People deficient in wisdom, childish ones,
Engage in unawareness.
But the wise one guards awareness
Like the greatest treasure.

Engage not in unawareness,
Nor in intimacy with sensual delight.
Meditating, the one who is aware
Attains extensive ease.

When the wise one by awareness expels unawareness,
Having ascended the palace of wisdom,
He, free from sorrow, steadfast,
The sorrowing folk observes, the childish,
As one standing on a mountain
[Observes] those standing on the ground below.

Among those unaware, the one aware,
Among the sleepers, the wide-awake,
The one with great wisdom moves on,
As a race horse who leaves behind a nag.

By awareness, Maghavan[1]
To supremacy among the gods arose.
Awareness they praise;
Always censured is unawareness.

The monk who delights in awareness,
Who sees in unawareness the fearful,
Goes, burning, like a fire,
The fetters subtle and gross.

The monk who delights in awareness,
Who sees in unawareness the fearful—

---

1 A title for Indra, king of the gods, whom early Buddhists believed to be an early disciple of the Buddha.

He is not liable to suffer a fall;
In nirvana's presence is such a one.

Chapter III. The Mind

The quivering, wavering mind,
Hard to guard, hard to check,
The sagacious one makes straight,
Like a fletcher, an arrow shaft.

Like a water creature
Plucked from its watery home and thrown on land,
This mind flaps;
[Fit] to discard [is] Mara's sway.

Commendable is the taming
Of mind, which is hard to hold down,
Nimble, alighting wherever it wants.
Mind subdued brings ease.

The sagacious one may tend the mind,
Hard to be seen, extremely subtle,
Alighting wherever it wants.
The tended mind brings ease.

They who will restrain the mind,
Far-ranging, roaming alone,
Incorporeal, lying abiding—
They are released from Mara's bonds.

For one of unsteady mind,
Who knows not dhamma true,
Whose serenity is adrifting,
Wisdom becomes not full.

No fear is there for the wide-awake
Who has mind undamped
And thought unsmitten—
The wholesome and the detrimental left behind.

Knowing this body as a pot of clay,
Securing this mind as a citadel,

One may fight Mara with wisdom's weapon,
Guard what has been gained—and be unattached.

Soon indeed
This body on the earth will lie,
Pitched aside, without consciousness,
Like a useless chip of wood.

What a foe may do to a foe,
Or a hater to a hater—
Far worse than that
The mind ill held may do to him.

Not mother, father, nor even other kinsmen,
May do that [good to him—]
Far better than that
The mind well held may do to him.

Discussion Questions

1. Several times, the text discusses Mara, the demon of illusion that keeps one trapped in the cycle of samsara. Based on your reading of the text, is Mara considered a real, physical entity that might harm a practitioner? Or is he a symbol representing those things that might distract one from attaining nirvana?

2. While meditation is perhaps the most well-known Buddhist method to develop one's awareness and mental acuity, what other methods might Buddhists use? How might performing devotional practices like giving alms or chanting the *nembutsu* develop the skill of mental awareness?

3. Does developing awareness as described in the text seem like an easy or difficult thing to do? Is this something every Buddhist will have the opportunity to do?

Exemplar 1

The Legend of Miao-shan

As Buddhism developed in China, Indian Buddhist figures often changed to fit local contexts, as we see with the male bodhisattva Avalokiteshvara's transformation into Guanyin, whom Jesuit interpreters called the Goddess of Mercy. Meaning literally "[the one who] perceives all sounds [of suffering]," Guanyin is considered a bodhisattva endeavoring to provide personal salvation and religious guidance for those in pain; for this, she is worshipped throughout East Asia in a variety of forms. Perhaps most popular among these is Miao-shan, whose legend is detailed below. Although the narrative has several variants—including versions in which she tours hell on the back of a supernatural tiger—this particular telling represents one of the oldest; it was found inscribed on two eleventh-century stone pillars at a Buddhist monastery in Hangzhou. Beyond this particular story, Miao-shan has been especially celebrated as the "Calmer of Waves" who saves stranded sailors and fishermen.

Once in the past, the Lü Master [Dao]xuan dwelt in the Zhongnan Mountains. His pure conduct drew in response a divine spirit to attend upon him.

The Master asked the divine spirit: "I have heard that the Mahāsattva [bodhisattva] Guanyin has an affinity with this land, but I do not know in which place the divine traces are most abundantly manifest."

The divine spirit replied: "The appearances of Guanyin have no fixed place, yet for the physical incarnation it is Fragrant Mountain which has the strongest affinity."

The Master enquired: "Fragrant Mountain—where is it located now?"

The divine spirit then narrated the story of Miao-shan: Over two hundred li to the south of Mount Song there are three hills in a row. The middle one is Fragrant Mountain, and that is the place where the Bodhisattva attained enlightenment. North-east of the hill there was in the past a king whose name was King Zhuang. He had a consort named Baode. The king's mind believed in error, and he paid no respect to the Three Treasures. He had no crown prince, only three daughters—the eldest Miao-yen, the second Miao-yin, the youngest Miao-shan. Of these three daughters, two were already married. At the time of Miao-shan's conception the consort had dreamed that she swallowed the moon. When the night of the birth came round the whole earth quaked, strange fragrance filled the chamber, light shone within and without. The people of the land were shocked and amazed, thinking there was a fire in the palace. That night she became incarnate, clean without being washed, her holy marks noble and majestic, canopied over with many colored auspicious clouds. The people of the land said that perhaps a sage had appeared in their country. The king her father thought this singular and gave her the name Miao-shan.

When she grew up her actions and demeanor far transcended the common run. She always wore soiled clothes and used no adornment, she ate only once a day and never ate strongly flavored food. She talked much of cause and effect, impermanence, illusion, and falsity. In the palace she was known as "buddha-hearted." Those who followed her instruction were all able to convert to goodness. They pursued the life of abstinence and religious discipline without faltering in resolve.

One day, the king said to his daughter: "You are now grown up. You must follow my instructions. . . . I and your mother will bring in a husband for you. From now on you must follow orthodox ways, not study false doctrines which corrupt the customs of my land."

Miao-shan heard her father's command and replied with a smile: "The river of desire has mighty waves, the sea of suffering has fathomless depths. I would never, for the sake of one lifetime of pleasure, plunge into eons of misery. When I reflect on this matter it causes me strong revulsion. I am resolved to seek to become a nun, to pursue religious discipline and study the true way, to achieve the Buddha's perfect wisdom, to repay my parents' love and deliver all living beings from their suffering."

The king's consort sent for her and tried to coax her, but Miao-shan said: "Why do you try so hard to make your daughter marry? I will obey my mother's command if it will prevent three misfortunes. The first is this: when the men of this world are young their face is as fair as the jade-like moon, but when old age comes their hair turns white, their face is wrinkled, in motion or repose they are in every way worse off than in their youth. The second is this: a man's limbs may be lusty and vigorous, he may step as if flying through the air, but once an illness befalls him he lies in bed without a single pleasure in life. The third is this: a man may have a great assembly of relatives, may have all his nearest and dearest before him, but when one day impermanence (*anitya*) comes, even such close kin as father or son cannot take his place. If a husband can prevent these three misfortunes, I will marry him. If he cannot, then I vow not to marry. I pity the people of this world, plunged into such suffering. If we are to prevent this, it can only be through Buddhism. My purpose is to become a nun in the hope of gaining, through religious discipline, the fulfilment of preventing these great misfortunes on behalf of all mankind."

The king was even more angry. He cast his daughter into the rear garden where her food and drink were cut off and none of the palace staff were allowed to go near her. One day, her mother and sisters came to clasp her, loudly weeping, and said: "Since you left the palace my two eyes have nearly withered away, my insides have been torn apart. How can you be at ease when you have brought your mother to this state? Your father in the palace has been so worried that for days he has not held court, and the nation's affairs are not attended to. He has told me and your sisters to come together and urge you: if you have any thought for your father, then return to good practices."

Miao-shan said, "Your child suffers no hardship here—why should my parents go this far? In all the emotional entanglements of this world there is no term of release. If close kin are gathered together, they must inevitably be sundered and scattered. Even should my parents remain together until the age of a hundred, impermanence (*anitya*) would be on its way, and they must needs be parted. Rest at ease, Mother. Fortunately you have my two elder sisters to care for you. To what purpose do you need this child? Take yourself home to the palace, for your daughter has no intention of turning back."

Miao-yan and Miao-yin then said: "When you look at the people nowadays who leave their family for religious practice, which of them manages to radiate light and make the earth tremble, or to become a buddha or patriarch, repaying their parents' love and delivering all beings? Better surely to follow human ways according to the rites and make a family. You have caused your parents such vexation and concern!"

Hearing their words, Miao-shan said to her two sisters: "You are coveting honor and glory, married love has you entangled, and you pursue present joys without realizing that joy is the cause of suffering. At such a time, even if you have a husband, is he able to take your place? Sisters, each of you has a single life and death: examine yourselves now, and do not lay such strong persuasions on me. With the signs of karma so visible in front of you, there is nothing to be gained from vain remorse. Urge our lady mother to return to the palace and announce to the king our father that empty things come to an end, while my vow has no end. Let the king decide if I should live or die!"

Furious at hearing this, the king summoned Huizhen, a nun of the White Sparrow monastery, [and charged her] to take [Miao-shan] off to the monastery to grow vegetables, and to devise ways to induce her to return to the palace [by treating her harshly].

The community of five hundred nuns welcomed Miao-shan inside, where she burned incense before the images. The next day the community addressed Miao-shan: "You were born and grew up in a royal palace, Miao-shan, why ever should you seek solitude for yourself? Far better to return to the palace than dwell silently in a convent."

Miao-shan smiled when she heard their words and said: "Now I see your level of knowledge is such that it leads me to despise you. If even you, as disciples of the Buddhist order, are capable of uttering those words, then how much more would layfolk put blame on me? Perhaps there is reason for my father the king to loathe you all and refuse to let me become a nun. Surely you know what the round scalp and square robe basically mean? To become a nun is to shy away from honor and glory, to gain release from feelings and affections. Our Buddha, the World-honored One, clearly left the precept that those who leave the family should lay the hand on their own head and abandon adornment, they should wear discolored robes and seek their living by holding up the begging bowl. Why is it that you all pursue splendor and extravagance, that your comportment is seductive, your clothing fine and showy? You have irresponsibly entered the Buddhist order, openly broken the pure precepts, undeservedly received alms from believers, vainly consumed your time. When you all became nuns your minds did not conform to where the truth lay."

Huizhen, the nun, answered: "I am under the king's orders. This is nothing to do with me." She then gave an account of the king's royal injunction, and appealed to Miao-shan, quickly to change her mind and save this community of nuns or else she feared the king would destroy them.

Miao-shan said: "Surely, you remember how the prince Mahāsattva threw himself from a cliff to feed the tiger, achieving the fulfilment of no-birth. King Sivi cut off his flesh to save the dove, gaining transcendence on the yonder shore. Since you all have sought to leave the family, you should view the illusory body as impermanent and detestable, the four empirical elements as fundamentally non-existent. Your every thought should be to depart from the cycle of transmigration, all your minds should seek for release. Why should you fear death and love life, or still long for that stinking mess in the bag of skin? My one wish is that the king's heart should aspire to release from death."

When the nuns heard these words they debated together, saying: "Miao-shan was born in the palace and knows nothing of the hardships outside. She thinks that becoming a nun is a pleasurable thing. We ought to burden her with hard and demeaning duties, so that she will know remorse and fear." They then told Miao-shan: "Since you desire to become a nun, there are no vegetables in the kitchen garden, and you must provide some. There must be enough by the appointed time, whatever the state of supply."

Miao-shan went into the garden and saw that the vegetables were few indeed. She then reflected on how she could supply enough for everyone the following day. As the thought arose in her mind, the dragon spirit of the convent came to her aid with divine power, and when morning came the vegetables in the garden were lush and sufficient for needs. Huizhen then knew that this was no ordinary mortal, for she could attract the aid of the dragon spirit. So now she announced the matter to the king, who in a great rage ordered troops to surround the monastery, behead the nuns, and burn down their quarters.

Although Miao-shan came out to meet her death, at the moment she was about to receive the blade, the mountain god of Dragon Mountain snatched away Miao-shan and set her down at the mountain foot. When the envoy reported this to the king, his consort and the royal family all wept bitterly, saying that her daughter was already dead and beyond hope of rescue. The king said to his consort: "Do not grieve. This young girl was no kin of mine. She must have been some demon who was born into my family. We have managed to get rid of the demon: that is cause for great delight!"

Now that Miao-shan had been snatched away by divine power she went up into Fragrant Mountain, climbed to the summit, and looked around. It was peaceful, without any trace of man, and she said to herself: "This place is for my destined work of transformation." So she went to the summit and built a shelter for her religious cultivation. She dressed in grasses, ate from trees, and no one knew of it for three whole years.

Meanwhile her father the king sickened with jaundice in return for his crimes of destroying a monastery and killing the religious, and could not find rest.

The best doctors throughout the land were unable to heal him. His consort and the royal family were morning and night in anxiety about him. One day a strange monk stood in front of the inner palace, saying: "I have a divine remedy which can heal the king's sickness."

The king asked, "What medicine do you have that can cure my sickness?"

The monk said, "The medicine can be made by using the hands and eyes of one without anger."

The king said: "Do not speak so frivolously. If I take someone's hands and eyes, must they not be angry?"

The monk said: "Such a one does exist in your land. In the southwest of your dominion is a mountain named Fragrant Mountain. On its summit is a hermit practicing religious cultivation with signal merit, though none knows of it. This person has no anger. If you put your request to her she will certainly make the gift."

The king ordered an envoy to take incense into the hills and bow to the holy one, saying: "The king of the land has suffered jaundice for three years now. The great physicians, the wonder drugs of all the land are alike unable to cure him. A monk has presented a cure: by using the hands and eyes of one without anger, a medicine can be made. We venture to beg you for your hands and eyes to cure the king's sickness."

Miao-shan reflected: "My father the king showed disrespect to the Three Treasures, he persecuted and suppressed Buddhism, he burned monastic buildings, he executed a community of nuns. He invited the retribution of this sickness. With my hands and eyes I shall save the king in his distress." She said to the envoy: "It must be your king's refusal to believe in the Three Treasures that has caused him to suffer this evil malady. I shall give my hands and eyes to provide medicine for him. My one desire is that the remedy may match the ailment and will drive out the king's disease. The king must direct his mind towards enlightenment and commit himself to the Three Treasures: then he will achieve recovery."

With these words, the holy one gouged out both her eyes with a knife and then told the envoy to sever her two hands. At that moment the whole mountain shook, and from the sky came a voice commending her: "Rare, how rare! She is able to save all living beings, to do things impossible in this world!"

The envoy returned to the king, who made the monk blend the medicine. Before ten days were out he recovered completely from his sickness. He brought his palms together and said, "Tomorrow I shall go to visit Fragrant Mountain and make thanks-offerings to the hermit." The next day, the king with his consort, two daughters, and palace retinue set out from the walled city and came up Fragrant Mountain. Reaching the hermitage, they lavishly laid out the finest offerings. When the royal family saw the holy one with no arms or eyes, the king and his lady were deeply moved to a painful thought: "The holy one looks very like our daughter."

The hermit suddenly spoke: "I am indeed Miao-shan. When my father the king suffered the foul disease, your child offered up her hands and eyes to repay the king's love."

Hearing these words, the king and his consort embraced her with loud weeping, stirring heaven and earth with their grief. He said: "Our evil ways have caused my daughter to lose her hands and eyes and endure this suffering. I am going to lick my child's two eyes with my tongue and join on her two hands, and desire the gods and spirits of heaven and earth to make my child's withered eyes grow again, her severed arms once more to be whole!"

When the king had expressed this resolve, but before his mouth had touched her eyes, Miao-shan was suddenly not to be found. At that moment heaven and earth shook, radiance blazed forth, auspicious clouds enclosed all about, heavenly drums resounded. And then was seen the All-Compassionate Guanyin of the Thousand Hands and Thousand Eyes, solemn and majestic in form, radiant with dazzling light, lofty and magnificent like the moon amid the stars.

When the king with his consort and palace maidens beheld the form of the Bodhisattva, they rose and struck themselves, beat their breasts with loud lament, and raised their voices in repentance: "We your disciples with our mortal sight failed to recognize the Holy One. Evil karma has obstructed our minds. We pray you to extend your saving protection to absolve our earlier misdeeds. From this time on we shall turn towards the Three Treasures, we shall rebuild Buddhist monasteries. We pray you, Bodhisattva, in your compassion, to return to your original body and permit us to make offerings." In a moment the hermit returned to her original person, with her hands and eyes quite intact. She sat cross-legged, brought her palms together, and with great solemnity passed away, as though entering into meditation.

The king and his consort burned incense and made a vow: "We your disciples will provide an offering of fragrant wood, will commit your holy body to the funeral pyre, and when we return to the palace will build a stupa and make offerings to it in all perpetuity." Having made his vow, the king surrounded the numinous body with all kinds of pure incense, cast flames upon it, and burned it. The king then reverently established a precious shrine into which he placed the Bodhisattva's true body, and outside he built a precious stupa. In all solemnity he buried her on the summit of the mountain, beneath the site of her hermitage. And there on the mountain, with court and kin, he watched and protected her day and night, without sleeping.

Back with Master Daoxuan, the divine spirit spoke: "Master, you have asked your disciple about the numinous traces of the Bodhisattva, and I have given a summary account of the broad essentials."

The Lü Master again asked: "What is the present state of the precious stupa on Fragrant Mountain?"

The divine spirit said: "The stupa has long been abandoned. Now there is only the earthen pagoda, and no one knows of it. The traces left on earth by a holy one prosper and decay in their due time. After three hundred years there will be a revival."

On hearing this through the Lü Master brought his palms together and uttered these words of praise: "Such is the spiritual power of the Mahāsattva Guanyin! Were it not for the amplitude of the Bodhisattva's vow, these signs could not have been revealed. If the living beings of that land had not brought their karmic conditions to maturity, they could not have attracted this response. How mighty, this merit without measure! It cannot be conceived!"

Discussion Questions

1. The Buddhist idea of "no self" challenges the idea of a single unified self with one inherent essence; however, here we see Guanyin taking rebirth as Miao-shan to help spread Buddhism. Guanyin/Miao-shan appears to have a self despite being enlightened. How do we make sense of this contradiction?

2. What do the difficulties faced by Miao-shan as she attempts to devote her life to Buddhist practice tell us about the historic realities of doing Buddhist practice as a woman in China?

3. Many Westerners perceive Buddhism as a "rational" and "scientific" religion that lacks miracle stories or other features of the supernatural. This narrative, however, challenges that perception and features many things that seem miraculous or otherwise a challenge to scientific understandings of the world. What does this tell us about Buddhism? Are Western perceptions accurate? If not, why do they persist?

Exemplar 2

Interbeing

Thich Nhat Hanh

Thich Nhat Hanh is one of the best-known contemporary Buddhist teachers, writers, and antiwar activists who has been active since the 1950s in Europe, Vietnam, and abroad. Through this work, he also represents an important Buddhist innovator; after beginning his Buddhist training in the Vietnamese Thien order, Thich Nhat Hanh founded the Order of Interbeing in 1966—a group of lay and monastic Buddhist practitioners who seek to bring traditional bodhisattva precepts into dialogue with the modern world through Thich Nhat Hanh's Fourteen Mindfulness Trainings. This work reflects Thich Nhat Hanh's larger commitment to using Buddhist ideas and practices to engage with pressing social problems, a feature that has become a defining trait of his Plum Village Tradition. In this selection from his commentary on the *Heart Sutra* (*Prajnaparamita*), he elaborates on what he calls "interbeing"—a term created by himself to describe the fundamental interpenetration and collective arising of all things.

Interbeing

If you are a poet, you will see clearly that there is a cloud floating in this sheet of paper. Without a cloud, there will be no rain; without rain, the trees cannot grow; and without trees, we cannot make paper. The cloud is essential for the paper to exist. If the cloud is not here, the sheet of paper cannot be here either. So we can say that the cloud and the paper *inter-are*. "Interbeing" is a word that is not in the dictionary yet, but if we combine the prefix "inter-" with the verb "to be," we have a new verb, *inter-be*. Without a cloud, we cannot have paper, so we can say that the cloud and the sheet of paper *inter-are*.

If we look into this sheet of paper even more deeply, we can see the sunshine in it. If the sunshine is not there, the forest cannot grow. In fact, nothing can grow. Even we cannot grow without sunshine. And so, we know that the sunshine is also in this sheet of paper. The paper and the sunshine inter-are. And if we continue to look, we can see the logger who cut the tree and brought it to the mill to be transformed into paper. And we see the wheat. We know that the logger cannot exist without his daily bread, and therefore the wheat that became his bread is also in this sheet of paper. And the logger's father and mother are in it too. When we look in this way, we see that without all of these things, this sheet of paper cannot exist.

Looking even more deeply, we can see we are in it too. This is not difficult to see, because when we look at a sheet of paper, the sheet of paper is part of our perception. Your mind is in here and mine is also. So we can say that everything is in here with this sheet of paper. You cannot point out one thing that is not here—time, space, the earth, the rain, the minerals in the soil, the sunshine, the cloud, the river, the heat. Everything co-exists with this sheet of paper. That is why I think the word inter-be should be in the dictionary. "To be" is to inter-be. You cannot just *be* by yourself alone. You have to inter-be with every other thing. This sheet of paper is, because everything else is.

Suppose we try to return one of the elements to its source. Suppose we return the sunshine to the sun. Do you think that this sheet of paper would be possible? No, without sunshine nothing can be. And if we return the logger to his mother, then we have no sheet of paper either. The fact is that this sheet of paper is made up only of "non-paper elements." And if we return these non-paper elements to their sources, then there can be no paper at all. Without non-paper elements, like mind, logger, sunshine, and so on, there will be no paper. As thin as this sheet of paper is, it contains everything in the universe in it.

But the *Heart Sutra* seems to say the opposite. Avalokiteśvara tells us that things are empty. Let us look more closely.

Roses and Garbage

Neither defiled nor immaculate.

Defiled or immaculate. Dirty or pure. These are concepts we form in our mind. A beautiful rose we have just cut and placed in our vase is immaculate. It smells so good, so pure, so fresh. It supports the idea of immaculateness. The opposite is a garbage can. It smells horrible, and it is filled with rotten things.

But that is only when you look on the surface. If you look more deeply you will see that in just five or six days, the rose will become part of the garbage. You do not need to wait five days to see it. If you just look at the rose, and you look deeply, you can see it now. And if you look into the garbage can, you see that in a few months its contents can be transformed into lovely vegetables, and even a rose. If you are a good organic gardener and you have the eyes of a bodhisattva, looking at a rose you can see the garbage, and looking at the garbage you can see a rose. Roses and garbage inter-are. Without a rose, we cannot have garbage; and without garbage, we cannot have a rose. They need each other very much. The rose and garbage are equal. The garbage is just as precious as the rose. If we look deeply at the concepts of defilement and immaculateness, we return to the notion of interbeing.

In the *Majjhima Nikaya* there is a very short passage on how the world has come to be. It is very simple, very easy to understand, and yet very deep. "This is, because that is. This is not, because that is not. This is like this, because that is like that." This is the Buddhist teaching of Genesis.

In the city of Manila there are many young prostitutes, some of them only fourteen or fifteen years old. They are very unhappy young ladies. They did not want to be prostitutes. Their families are poor and these young girls went to the city to look for some kind of job, like a street vendor, to make money to send back to their families. Of course this is not true only in Manila, but in Ho Chi Minh City in Vietnam, in New York City, and in Paris also. It is true that in the city you can make money more easily than in the countryside, so we can imagine how a young girl may have been tempted to go there to help her family. But after only a few weeks there, she was persuaded by a clever person to work for her and to earn perhaps one hundred times more money. Because she was so young and did not know much about life, she accepted, and became a prostitute. Since that time, she has carried the feeling of being impure, defiled, and this causes her great suffering. When she looks at other young girls, dressed beautifully, belonging to good families, a wretched feeling wells up in her, and this feeling of defilement has become her hell.

But if she had an opportunity to meet with Avalokitśvara, he would tell her to look deeply at herself and at the whole situation, and see that she is like this because other people are like that. "This is like this, because that is like that." So how can a so-called good girl, belonging to a good family, be proud? Because their way of life is like this, the other girl has to be like that. No one among us has clean hands. No one of us can claim it is not our responsibility. The girl in Manila is that way because of the way we are. Looking into the life of that young prostitute, we see the non-prostitute people. And looking at the non-prostitute people, and at the way we live our lives, we see the prostitute. This helps to create that, and that helps to create this.

Let us look at wealth and poverty. The affluent society and the society deprived of everything inter-are. The wealth of one society is made of the poverty of the other. "This is like this, because that is like that." Wealth is made of non-wealth elements. It is exactly the same as with the sheet of paper. So we must be careful. We should not imprison ourselves in concepts. The truth is that everything is everything else. We can only inter-be, we cannot just be. And we are responsible for everything that happens around us. Avalokiteshvara will tell the young prostitute, "My child, look at yourself and you will see everything. Because other people are like that, you are like this. You are not the only person responsible, so please do not suffer." Only by seeing with the eyes of interbeing can that young girl be freed from her suffering. What else can you offer her to help her be free?

We are imprisoned by our ideas of good and evil. We want to be only good, and we want to remove all evil. But that is because we forget that good is made of non-good elements. Suppose I am holding a lovely branch. When we look at it with a nondiscriminative mind, we see this wonderful branch. But as soon as we distinguish that one end is the left and the other end is the right, we get into trouble. We may say we want only the left, and we do not want the right (as you hear very often), and there is trouble right away. If the rightist is not there, how can you be a leftist? Let us say that I do not want the right end of this branch, I only want the left. So, I break off half of this reality and throw it away. But as soon as I throw the unwanted half away, the end that remains become right (the new right). Because as soon as the left is there, the right must be there also. I may become frustrated and do it again. I break what remains of my branch in half, and still, I have the right end here.

The same may be applied to good and evil. You cannot be good alone. You cannot hope to remove evil, because thanks to evil, good exists, and vice versa. When you stage a play concerning a hero, you have to provide an antagonist in order for the hero to be a hero. So, Buddha needs Mara to take the evil role so Buddha can be a Buddha. Buddha is as empty as the sheet of paper; Buddha is made of non-Buddha elements. If non-Buddhas like us are not here, how can a Buddha be? If the rightist is not there, how can we call someone a leftist?

In my tradition, every time I join my palms together to make a deep bow to the Buddha, I chant this short verse:

The one who bows and pays respect,
And the one who receives the bow
And the respect,

Both of us are empty.
That is why the communion is perfect.

It is not arrogant to say so. If I am not empty, how can I bow down to the Buddha? And if the Buddha is not empty, how can he receive my bow? The Buddha and I inter-are. Buddha is made of non-Buddha elements, like me. And I am made of non-me elements, like the Buddha. So the subject and object of reverence are both empty. Without an object, how can a subject exist?

Discussion Questions

1. What do you think of Thich Nhat Hanh's claim that if one is not empty, one cannot bow down to a Buddha, because oneself and the Buddha "inter-are"? Does this sound nihilistic or pessimistic, as some Western commentators have claimed about Buddhism?

2. Some might say that "interbeing" has the same meaning as the traditional Buddhist concept of interdependence and, therefore, a new word is not needed. What is gained in Thich Nhat Hanh coining the term "interbeing"? Does it confuse the tradition or enrich it?

3. If one takes seriously Buddhist ideas of interbeing as expressed here, what sorts of ethical positions does it lead to?

Controversy

The Face of Buddhist Terror

Hannah Beech

Monk-activist Wirathu, profiled here in a July 2013 *Time Magazine* article, has become the public face of Buddhist violence and terroristic activities in contemporary Myanmar, formerly known as Burma. He is de facto leader of the nationalistic "969" movement, which is largely made up of Burmese Buddhist monks and draws its name from the number of special attributes possessed, respectively, by Siddhartha Gautama, the Buddhist teachings (*dharma*), and the Buddhist monastic community (*sangha*). Since 2012, Buddhist monks associated with the 969 movement have expressed concern over what they perceive as a spread of Muslim culture that threatens Myanmar's traditionally Buddhist way of life. This rhetoric has led to both the forcible displacement of the Rohingya Muslims, who make up 5 percent of Myanmar's population, and anti-Muslim riots in which rioters have burned Muslim homes, businesses, and mosques. In their actions, Burmese Buddhist monks are largely shielded from public prosecution by both their religious status and their close connections with the military, whom they supported in the 2007 "Saffron Revolution." Although Wirathu states that he publicly disavows violence, some Burmese Buddhist organizations have banned him from preaching in response to his vehement political rhetoric.

His face as still and serene as a statue's, the Buddhist monk who has taken the title "the Burmese bin Laden" begins his sermon. Hundreds of worshippers sit before him, palms pressed together, sweat trickling down their sticky backs. On cue, the crowd chants with the man in burgundy robes, the mantras drifting through the sultry air of a temple in Mandalay, Burma's second biggest city after Rangoon. It seems a peaceful scene, but Wirathu's message crackles with hate. "Now is not the time for calm," the monk intones, as he spends 90 minutes describing the many ways in which he detests the minority Muslims in this Buddhist majority land. "Now is the time to rise up, to make your blood boil."

Buddhist blood is boiling in Burma, also known as Myanmar—and plenty of Muslim blood is being spilled. Over the past year, Buddhist mobs have targeted members of the minority faith, and incendiary rhetoric from Wirathu—he goes by one name—and other hard-line monks is fanning the flames of religious chauvinism. Scores of Muslims have been killed, according to government statistics, although international human-rights workers put the number in the hundreds. Much of the violence is directed at the Rohingya, a largely stateless Muslim group in Burma's far west that the U.N. calls one of the world's most persecuted people. The communal bloodshed has spread to central Burma, where Wirathu, 46, lives and preaches his virulent sermons. The radical monk sees Muslims, who make up at least 5% of Burma's estimated 60 million people, as a threat to the country and its culture. "[Muslims] are breeding so fast, and they are stealing our women, raping them," he tells me. "They would like to occupy our country, but I won't let them. We must keep Myanmar Buddhist."

Such hate speech threatens the delicate political ecosystem in a country peopled by at least 135 ethnic groups that have only recently been unshackled from nearly half a century of military rule. Already some government officials are calling for implementation of a ban, rarely enforced during the military era, on Rohingya women's bearing more than two children. And many Christians in the country's north say recent fighting between the Burmese military and Kachin insurgents, who are mostly Christian, was exacerbated by the widening religious divide.

Radical Buddhism is thriving in other parts of Asia too. This year in Sri Lanka, Buddhist nationalist groups with links to high-ranking officialdom have gained prominence, with monks helping orchestrate the destruction of Muslim and Christian property. And in Thailand's deep south, where a Muslim insurgency has claimed some 5,000 lives since 2004, the Thai army trains civilian militias and often accompanies Buddhist monks when they leave their temples. The commingling of soldiers and monks—some of whom have armed themselves—only heightens the alienation felt by Thailand's minority Muslims. Although each nation's history dictates the course radical Buddhism has taken within its borders, growing access to the Internet means that prejudice and rumors are instantly inflamed with each Facebook post or tweet. Violence can easily spill across borders. In Malaysia, where hundreds of thousands of Burmese migrants work, several Buddhist Burmese were killed in June—likely in retribution, Malaysian authorities say, for the deaths of Muslims back in Burma.

In the reckoning of religious extremism—Hindu nationalists, Muslim militants, fundamentalist Christians, ultra-Orthodox Jews—Buddhism has largely escaped trial. To much of the world, it is synonymous with nonviolence and loving kindness, concepts propagated by Siddhartha Gautama, the Buddha, 2,500 years ago. But like adherents of any other religion, Buddhists and their holy men are not immune to politics and, on occasion, the lure of sectarian chauvinism. When Asia rose up against empire and oppression, Buddhist monks, with their moral command and plentiful numbers, led anticolonial movements. Some starved themselves for their cause, their sunken flesh and protruding ribs underlining their sacrifice for the laity. Perhaps most iconic is the image of Thich Quang Duc, a Vietnamese monk sitting in the lotus position, wrapped in flames, as he burned to death in Saigon while protesting the repressive South Vietnamese regime 50 years ago. In 2007, Buddhist monks led a foiled democratic uprising in Burma: images of columns of clerics bearing upturned alms bowls, marching peacefully in protest against the junta, earned sympathy around the world, if not from the soldiers who slaughtered them. But where does political activism end and political militancy begin? Every religion can be twisted into a destructive force poisoned by ideas that are antithetical to its foundations. Now it's Buddhism's turn.

Mantra of Hate

Sitting cross-legged on a raised platform at the New Masoeyein monastery in Mandalay, next to a wall covered by life-size portraits of himself, the Burmese bin Laden expounds on his worldview. U.S. President Barack Obama has "been tainted by black Muslim blood." Arabs have hijacked the U.N., he believes, although he sees no irony in linking his name to that of an Arab terrorist. About 90% of Muslims in Burma are "radical, bad people," says Wirathu, who was jailed for seven years for his role in inciting anti-Muslim pogroms in 2003. He now leads a movement called 969—the figure represents various attributes of the Buddha—which calls on Buddhists to fraternize only among themselves and shun people of other faiths. "Taking care of our own religion and race is more important than democracy," says Wirathu.

It would be easy to dismiss Wirathu as an outlier with little doctrinal basis for his bigotry. But he is charismatic and powerful, and his message resonates. Among the country's majority Bamar ethnic group, as well as across Buddhist parts of Asia, there's a vague sense that their religion is under siege—that Islam, having centuries ago conquered the Buddhist lands of Indonesia, Malaysia, Pakistan and Afghanistan, now seeks new territory. Even without proof, Buddhist nationalists stoke fears that local Muslim populations are increasing faster than their own, and they worry about Middle Eastern money pouring in to build new mosques.

In Burma, the democratization process that began in 2011 with the junta's giving way to a quasi-civilian government has also allowed extremist voices to proliferate. The trouble began last year in the far west, where machete-wielding Buddhist hordes attacked Rohingya villages; 70 Muslims were slaughtered in a daylong massacre in one hamlet, according to Human Rights Watch. The government has done little to check the violence, which has since migrated to other parts of the country. In late March, the central town of Meiktila burned for days, with entire Muslim quarters razed by Buddhist mobs after a monk was killed by Muslims. (The official death toll: two Buddhists and at least 40 Muslims.) Thousands of Muslims are still crammed into refugee camps that journalists are forbidden to enter. In the shadow of a burned-down mosque, I was able to meet the family of Abdul Razak Shahban, one of at least 20 students at a local Islamic school who were killed. "My son was killed because he was Muslim, nothing else," Razak's mother Rahamabi told me.

Temple and State

In the deep south of Burma's neighbor Thailand, it is the Buddhists who complain of being targeted for their faith. This part of the country used to be part of a Malay sultanate before staunchly Buddhist Thailand annexed it early last century, and Muslims make up at least 80% of the population. Since a separatist insurgency intensified in 2004, many Buddhists have been targeted because their positions—such as teachers, soldiers and government workers—are linked with the Thai state. Dozens of monks have been attacked too. Now the Buddhists have overwhelming superiority in arms: the Thai military and other security forces have moved into the wat, as Thai Buddhist temples are known. If Buddhists feel more protected by the presence of soldiers in their temples, it sends quite another signal to the Muslim population. "[The] state is wedding religion to the military," says Michael Jerryson, an assistant professor of religious studies at Youngstown State University in Ohio and author of a book about Buddhism's role in the southern-Thailand conflict. Muslims too are scared: more of them have perished in the violence than Buddhists. (By proportion of population, more Buddhists have died, however.) Yet Buddhists are the ones who receive the greater state protection, and I listen to monk after monk heighten tensions by telling me that Muslims are using mosques to store weapons or that every imam carries a gun. "Islam is a religion of violence," says Phratong Jirat-amo, a former marine turned monk in the town of Pattani. "Everyone knows this."

It's a sentiment the Burmese bin Laden would endorse. I ask Wirathu how he reconciles the peaceful sutras of his faith with the anti-Muslim violence spreading across his Bamar-majority homeland. "In Buddhism, we are not allowed to go on the offensive," he tells me, as if he is lecturing a child. "But we have every right to protect and defend our community." Later, as he preaches to an evening crowd, I listen to him compel smiling housewives, students, teachers, grandmothers and others to repeat after him, "I will sacrifice myself for the Bamar race." It's hard to imagine that the Buddha would have approved.

Discussion Questions

1. Where does the perception of Buddhism as a religion free from violence come from? What makes the idea so persistent?

2. How are global concerns about Islamic terrorism and public violence being used to oppress peaceful Muslim minorities in Myanmar? Are other countries you've studied or read about outside of this class engaged in similar practices?

3. Some people might say Wirathu and other Buddhist monks who promote violence are not "real" Buddhists. Why might it be problematic for college students in North America to make judgments about whether people in Myanmar are practicing Buddhism "correctly" or not?

Sikhism

In the Sikh tradition the fundamental problem is the ego (*haumai*), a prideful self-centeredness that constantly focuses on "me" and "mine." The solution to this problem of ego is union with God through service and meditation on the divine name (*nam simran*). To reflect this problem/solution and technique, we have two hymns found in the Guru Granth—Sikhism's primary scripture, which is revered as a living guru by Sikhs around the world. One of only a few religious texts to contain scriptures from other religious traditions, in this case Hinduism and Islam, the Guru Granth is a collection of 5,871 devotional hymns compiled in the sixteenth century by Sikhism's fifth leader, Guru Arjan. Intended to be sung via a collection of sixty different classical Indian musical melodies called ragas, these hymns work to evoke a memory of God's majesty, while also reflecting certain emotional states one might experience in the quest to join God. The raga used in the first reading is Bihagra, which is meant to evoke extreme sadness and pain at one's distance from God. This "Prayer for Forgiveness," therefore, speaks to humanity's distance from God caused by its own focus on the worldly ego, covetousness, and prioritizing of money over spiritual concerns. The hymn ends by describing how remembering and uniting with God can help the reader overcome this painful separation and return to divine bliss. The technique to bring about this transformation is highlighted in the second reading, a selection from the Guru Granth sung in the raga of Gauri, a raga intended to reflect one's dedicated labor to achieve a specific objective. This particular hymn is generally considered the masterpiece of Guru Arjan's composition, and it reflects the profound personal and social transformations that arise from the constant contemplation of God.

As the ideal exemplars of religious practice, Sikhs celebrate gurus, a Sanskrit title meaning "teacher" or "guide." After the death of Sikhism's founder Guru Nanak, a series of ten Gurus were selected to lead the community and continue developing the Sikh tradition in line with Nanak's vision. The tenth (and, for most Sikhs, final) Guru, Guru Gobind Singh, tells his story of sacrifice and service in this selection from the Dasam Granth, or the "Book of the Tenth Guru." Considered by many Sikhs to be a scripture second only to the Guru Granth, the Dasam Granth contains a variety of hymns, poetry, letters, and narratives. In the excerpt here, Guru Gobind Singh relates his own story of sacrifice and service to God, as well as the sacred duty of protecting the distinctiveness of the Sikh people with which he has been tasked. While the second exemplar selected is not a guru, Jagmeet Singh represents a contemporary realization of Sikh values in daily life. During the British occupation of India, Sikhs spread from the Punjab throughout the English-speaking world, with the largest diaspora population developing in Canada. Trained as a lawyer, Singh was elected leader of Canada's New Democratic Party in 2017 and member of Parliament in 2019. In this selection from his autobiography *Love and Courage*, Singh discusses how his mother's efforts to model the importance of the Sikh practice of service (*seva*) have guided his political aspirations.

Despite Sikhism's commitment to racial and class equality, Sikhism continues to struggle with issues related to the status of women. The final reading of the section explores this controversy through the eyes of a contemporary Sikh woman, Harbani Ahuja. Ahuja describes her childhood realization that her options as a Sikh woman were limited to marriage and patriarchal regulation and the resulting dedication she feels to reinvigorating the egalitarian principles prescribed by Guru Nanak—a process identified by scholar Nikky-Guninder Kaur Singh as the "refeminization" of Sikhism.

Problem/Solution

Prayer for Forgiveness
FROM THE GURU GRANTH

In this prayer from the Guru Granth we see reflected the Sikh experience of being separated from God because of the development of ego (*haumai*). Composed by Guru Arjan, the prayer is written in a musical melody intended to invoke extreme pain, loss, and agitation, which, the text makes clear, can only be solved by uniting once more with God. The text itself seems to move between perspectives—praising God as the absolute creator and sustainer of all things and then bemoaning the errors of the singer who neglected God in favor of other pursuits. As reflected in the final stanza, the solution is to refocus one's attention on God's praises through song, which will return the devotee to their former state of joy and peace.

Hear my supplication, O my Lord God,
Though I am full of millions of sins, nevertheless I am Your slave.
O You Dispeller of grief, merciful, fascinating, Destroyer of trouble and anxiety,
I seek Your protection, protect mine honour; You are in all things, O spotless One,
You hear and behold us; You are with us all, O God; You are the nearest of all to us.
O Lord, hear Nanak's prayer, save the slave of Your household.
You are ever omnipotent; we are poor and beggars.
O God, save us who are involved in the love of mammon.
Bound by covetousness and worldly love, we have committed various sins.
The Creator is distinct and free from entanglements; man obtains the fruit of his acts.
Show us kindness, You purifier of sinners; we are weary of wandering through many a womb.
Nanak represents—I am the slave of God who is the Support of the soul and life.
You are great and omnipotent; my understanding is feeble.
You cherish even the ungrateful; You look equally on all.
Unfathomable is Your knowledge, O infinite Creator; I am lowly and know nothing.
Having rejected the gem of Your name, I have amassed money; I am a degraded and silly being.
By the commission of sin I have amassed what is very unstable and forsakes man.
Nanak has sought Your protection, O omnipotent Lord; preserve his honour.
When I sang God's praises in the association of the saints,
He united me, who had been separated from Him, with Himself.
By ever thoroughly singing God's praises, He who is happiness itself becomes manifest.
My couch, when God accepts me as His own, is adorned by Him.
Having dismissed anxiety I am no longer anxious, and suffer no further pain.
Nanak lives beholding God and singing the praises of the Ocean of excellences.

1. You are reading this text in a book, but it is intended to be sung—either individually or together as a community. How do you think hearing it as a song would change its reception and interpretation?

2. Based on this reading, who is the one capable of rebuilding the connection between the devotee and God that was lost due to haumai: God or the devotee?

3. What does the text frame as the opposition to God that causes haumai to develop?

Technique

Remembering God
FROM THE GURU GRANTH

The following selection from a hymn in the Guru Granth is considered so important by the tradition as to be given its own title: the Sukhmani Sahib, or the Great Jewel of Peace. Composed in 1602 by Sikhism's fifth leader, Guru Arjan (1563–1606), it covers all facets of Sikh life, including the importance of meditation on the divine name (*nam simran*), the centrality of service (*seva*), the primacy of gurus, and the evils of materialism and serving one's own ego. The text is thirty-five pages long, and devout Sikhs will often gather to recite the full Sukhmani Sahib as contemplative practice, with some doing the hour-long recitation as frequently as twice a day. The selection below highlights the extensive personal, spiritual, and societal effects that arise from the remembrance of God, including combating an individual's selfishness and material desires.

Sukhmani

I bow to the primal Guru;
I bow to the Guru of the primal age;
I bow to the true Guru;
I bow to the holy divine Guru.
Remember, remember God; by remembering Him you shall obtain happiness,
And erase from your hearts trouble and affliction.
Remember the praises of the one all-supporting God.
Numberless persons utter God's various names.
Investigating the Vedas, the Puranas, and the Smritis,

Men have made out the one word which is God's name.
His praises cannot be recounted,
Who treasures God's name in his heart even for a moment.
Says Nanak, save me, O Lord, with those who are desirous of one glance of You.
The name of God is like ambrosia, bestowing happiness.
And giving peace to the hearts of the saints.
By remembering God man does not again enter the womb;
By remembering God the tortures of Death disappear;
By remembering God death is removed;
By remembering God enemies retreat;
By remembering God no obstacles are met;
By remembering God we are watchful night and day;
By remembering God fear is not felt;
By remembering God sorrow troubles not:
Men remember God in the company of the saints—
Nanak, by the love of God all wealth is obtained.
By remembering God we obtain wealth, supernatural power, and the nine
    treasures;
By remembering God we obtain divine knowledge, meditation, and the essence
    of wisdom;
Remembrance of God is the real devotion, penance, and worship;
By remembering God the conception of duality is dispelled;
By remembering God we obtain the advantages of bathing at places of
    pilgrimage;
By remembering God we are honoured at His court;
By remembering God we become reconciled to His will;
By remembering God men's lives are very profitable:
They whom He has caused to do so remember Him—
Nanak, touch the feet of such persons.
To remember God is the most exalted of all duties.
By remembering God many are saved;
By remembering God thirst is quenched;
By remembering God man knows all things;
By remembering God there is no fear of death;
By remembering God our desires are fulfilled;
By remembering God mental impurity is removed,
And the ambrosial Name fills the heart.
God abides on the tongue of the saint
Whose most humble slave Nanak is.
They who remember God are wealthy;
They who remember God are honoured;

They who remember God are acceptable;
They who remember God are distinguished;
They who remember God feel not want;
They who remember God rule the world;
They who remember God dwell in happiness;
They who remember God live forever;
They to whom God shows mercy ever remember Him—
Nanak prays for the dust of such men's feet.
They who remember God are philanthropic;
I am ever devoted to those who remember God.
The faces of those who remember God look bright;
They who remember God pass their lives in bliss;
They who remember God chasten their hearts;
The ways of those who remember God are holy;
They who remember God feel extreme joy;
They who remember God dwell near Him,
And by the favour of the saints are watchful night and day—
Nanak, meditation on God is obtained by complete good fortune.
By remembering God everything is accomplished;
By remembering God man never grieves;
By remembering God man utters His praises;
By remembering God man is easily absorbed in Him;
By remembering God man finds an immovable seat;
By remembering God the lotus of man's heart blooms;
By remembering God man hears the unbeaten melody;
The happiness which is obtained by remembering God has no end or limit:
They to whom God is merciful remember Him;
Nanak seeks the protection of such men.

Discussion Questions

1. In the Sikh perspective, how does the technique of "remembering God" combat the problem of "ego"? Wouldn't "forgetting the ego" be a more straightforward solution than "remembering God"?

2. Based on this text, who does the act of remembering God benefit? Is it oneself, one's family, or one's whole society?

3. How does this text perceive the relationship between Sikhism and Hinduism? Does it state that the Vedas, Puranas, and other Hindu texts are incorrect?

Guru Gobind Singh's Story
FROM THE DASAM GRANTH

Sometimes called Sikhism's "second founder," Guru Gobind Singh (1666–1708) had a significant impact on Sikh identity through the founding of the Khalsa in 1699 and the installation of the Guru Granth as the living, everlasting guru on his death. His father, the ninth Guru Tegh Bahadur, was executed on the orders of the Mughal Emperor Aurangzeb when Gobind Singh was only ten, thrusting him into a leadership role in a difficult and potentially hostile environment. As seen in its explicit use of martial imagery, the Khalsa reflects this challenging environment and had an important role in forming a cohesive Sikh identity in the face of oppression. In this selection from the Dasam Granth, Guru Gobind Singh relates his own spiritual journey through a mystic vision of conversations with God before his birth, as well as his investiture as leader of the Sikh community. While some Sikhs dispute the authority of the entirety of the Dasam Granth because of the inclusion of Hindu narratives and deities, it remains perhaps the most important collection of Guru Gobind Singh's writings.

I shall now tell my own history,
How God brought me into the world as I was performing penance
On the mountain of Hem Kunt,[1]
Where the seven peaks are conspicuous—
There I performed very great austerities
And worshipped the Unseen One.
I performed such penance
That I became blended with God.
My father and mother had also worshipped the Unseen One,
And strove in many ways to unite themselves with Him.
The Supreme Guru was pleased
With their devotion to Him.

When God gave me the order
I assumed birth in this degraded age.
I did not desire to come,
As my attention was fixed on God's feet.
God remonstrated earnestly with me,

---

1 A mountain in India that today represents an important place of pilgrimage for Sikhs.

And sent me into this world with the following orders:
"When I created this world
I first made the demons, who became enemies and oppressors.
They became intoxicated with the strength of their arms,
And ceased to worship Me, the Supreme Being.
I became angry and at once destroyed them.
In their places I established the gods:
They also busied themselves with receiving sacrifices and worship,
And called themselves supreme beings.
Mahadev called himself the imperishable God.
Vishnu too declared himself to be God;
Brahma called himself the supreme Brahma,
And nobody thought Me to be God.

. . .

Brahma made the four Vedas
And caused all to act according to them;
But they whose love was attached to My feet
Renounced the Vedas.
They who abandoned the tenets of the Vedas and of other religious books,
Became devoted to Me, the supreme God.
They who follow true religion
Shall have their sins of various kinds blotted out.
They who endure bodily suffering
And cease not to love Me,
Shall all go to paradise,
And there shall be no difference between Me and them.
They who shrink from suffering,
And, forsaking Me, adopt the way of the Vedas and Smritis
Shall fall into the pit of hell,
And continually suffer transmigration.

. . .

I then created Muhammad,
And made him king of Arabia.
He too established a religion of his own,
Cut off the foreskins of all his followers,
And made every one repeat his name;
But no one fixed the true Name in man's heart.
All these were wrapped up in themselves,
And none of them recognized Me, the Supreme Being.
I have cherished thee as My son,
And created thee to extend My religion.

Go and spread My religion there,
And restrain the world from senseless acts."

I stood up, clasped my hands, bowed my head, and replied:
"Your religion shall prevail in the world when You vouch Your assistance."

On this account God sent me.
Then I took birth and came into the world.
As He spoke to me so I speak unto men:
I bear no enmity to anyone.
All who call me the Supreme Being
Shall fall into the pit of hell.
Recognize me as God's servant only:
Have no doubt whatever of this.
I am the slave of the Supreme Being,
And have come to behold the wonders of the world.
I tell the world what God told me,
And will not remain silent through fear of mortals.

As God spoke to me I speak,
I pay no regard to any one besides.
I am satisfied with no religious garb;
I sow the seed of the Invisible.

I am not a worshipper of stones,
Nor am I satisfied with any religious garb.
I will sing the Name of the Infinite,
And obtain the Supreme Being.
I will not wear matted hair on my head,
Nor will I put on earrings;
I will pay no regard to anyone but God.
What God told me I will do.
I will repeat the one Name
Which will be everywhere profitable.
I will not repeat any other name,
Nor establish any other god in my heart.
I will meditate on the name of the Endless One,
And obtain the supreme light.
I am imbued with Your name, O God;
I am not intoxicated with any other honour.
I will meditate on the Supreme,

And thus remove endless sins.
I am enamoured of Your form;
No other gift hath charms for me.
I will repeat Your name,
And avoid endless sorrow.

Sorrow and sin have not approached those
Who have meditated on Your name.
They who meditate on any one else
Shall die of arguments and contentions.
The divine Guru sent me for religion's sake:
On this account I have come into the world—
"Extend the faith everywhere;
Seize and destroy the evil and the sinful."
Understand this, you holy men, in your souls.
I assumed birth for the purpose
Of spreading the faith, saving the saints,
And extirpating all tyrants.

Discussion Questions

1. As the tenth Guru, Guru Gobind Singh already had authority as the leader of the Sikh community. What purpose, therefore, might this account of a prebirth conversation with God serve? How might devout Sikh readers at the time have understood this conversation?

2. How does this selection demonstrate Sikhism's distinctiveness as a religious community, separate from both Hinduism and Islam?

3. How do Guru Gobind Singh's writings reflect the practices and philosophies of Guru Nanak, who founded Sikhism? How does he transform them?

Exemplar 2

From *Love and Courage*
Jagmeet Singh

Jagmeet Singh is a prominent Canadian Sikh, who has served as the leader of the New Democratic Party since 2017 and as a member of Parliament since 2019. As the first person of color to head a major political party in Canada, Singh represents both the achievement of the Sikh diaspora and many of the public struggles faced by turban-wearing Sikhs who may be ostracized or mistaken for Muslims. He openly credits Sikh principles for his commitment to social justice and egalitarianism. In this selection from his autobiography *Love and Courage*, Singh describes his mother's commitment to the central Sikh value of *seva*, or service. As portrayed in this selection, many Sikhs perform seva as a part of preparing and serving the *langar* meal—a free, vegetarian meal that is open to all, and one *gurdwara* may serve tens of thousands of people in one day. During the coronavirus pandemic and the protests surrounding the murder of George Floyd, many Sikh gurdwaras became unexpected community centers, providing meals, supplies, and services for those who needed them during a critical time.

My mom and dad had different approaches to supporting their kids. My dad would make sure we had access to any and every opportunity and he was interested in how we carried ourselves. He wanted us to be confident. His philosophy could be summed up by his favourite phrase: "If my kids want blood, I'll give them the marrow." My mom tried to focus less on how the world saw us and more on how we saw ourselves. She would often say, "Happiness comes from the inside."

My mom often tried to pass along her wisdom through stories. One of my favourites of hers was a story of Guru Nanak, the founder of Sikhi.[1] In the story, Guru Nanak joined a group of people gathered in a river. They were busily cupping their hands with water and throwing it toward the sun. Guru Nanak did the same, only he threw the water in the opposite direction. The group laughed at Guru Nanak and said he was doing it wrong. Guru Nanak explained he was watering his fields.

"Your fields are hundreds of kilometres away," they said. "That's impossible."
"Where are you throwing the water?" he asked.
"We're sending water to our ancestors."
"How far away are the ancestors?" he asked them.
"Our ancestors are in the next world."
"If you can send water into the next world, then my fields aren't too far away," he said.

I enjoyed the spirit of rebelliousness and the willingness to challenge the status quo that these stories conveyed. Maybe in a small way, they inspired me to try to do the same. My mom also introduced me to something a lot of Sikh kids learn, *seva*. *Seva*, or "selfless service," is a fundamental part of Sikhi. A spiritual journey is incomplete if it doesn't also focus on what we give back to society and the world

---

1 Acknowledging that "Sikhism" is a term created by Western scholars, many Sikhs prefer to call their tradition "Sikhi," which means to continuously dedicate oneself to the tenets of Guru Nanak, the Gurus who followed him, and the everlasting Guru, the Guru Granth.

around us. At its core, *seva* is a lesson in love. The idea of serving others puts unconditional love into practice.

Mom started me young on *seva*. Every Sunday at Windsor's humble gurdwara—a small, slipshod, cinder-block building on the outskirts of town—I'd work in the free community kitchen that all gurdwaras must have, handing out napkins to the eighty or so attendees before food was served. Gurdwaras are supposed to be open 24/7, with four doors welcoming all people from the north, south, east, and west, without a specifically designated spiritual day. But Windsor's Sikh population was too small to sustain an around-the-clock gurdwara, so we got together mainly on Sundays.

"You are serving people you do not know with the same love you would serve your family," my mom explained to me as I handed out napkins and she filled people's plates with food. "As a Sikh, you have a personal spiritual journey. And that journey includes ensuring justice for all. It doesn't matter if that person is a Sikh, Christian, Muslim, Hindu, or atheist—the goal is to see everyone around us as one. To feel love for a stranger equal in strength to the love you have for your brother and sister."

My mom had a great fascination with other religions and languages, and would often remark on how beautiful the world was because we all looked different.

"Everyone has their own uniqueness," she said. "There is a place for everybody in the world."

Just as she did with our summer lessons in science and math, my mom left me room to explore Sikhi for myself. She encouraged me and my siblings to walk the path, but she allowed us space to discover a lot of it on our own.

Inspired by the stories my mom told, I began reading books on Sikh spirituality, and each discovery reinforced why I enjoyed it so much. I read about the Ninth Guru, who sacrificed his life for freedom of thought, defending a religion he didn't actually agree with. The story clearly showed the Sikh principle of pluralism, or respecting people no matter what they believed in. It made sense to me and was even a bit of a relief, as I thought about the fact that Walid and his family were Muslim, and how it had never seemed wrong that they believed something different from me.

Through my mom's teachings, the spiritual poetry I read, and *seva*, I gradually understood that the spiritual goal in Sikhi was to love unconditionally. But that's not something that happens overnight. It takes work to realize that we're all connected, to feel our connection to everything around us, to realize we are all one, and to love unconditionally. Just like working out in the gym builds the strength to eventually deadlift four hundred pounds, meditating, reading spiritual poetry, and *seva* all help to develop unconditional love.

"How can I be more connected to the world?" I asked my mom one night.

"You should try meditating," she suggested. "Meditation helps us connect with the infinite energy inside us."

She sat down on the floor beside my bed and patted a space on the rug beside her for me to sit.

"We're going to repeat the *gur mantr*," she said. *Gur* means "enlightened" and *mantr* is a word that one reflects on. In Sikhi, the *gur mantr* is *Waheguru*. It is contemplated and repeated out loud as a way to realize and experience the oneness of the universal energy.

I repeated the word "*Waheguru*" out loud. "*Wahe*" means "wonderful" and "*guru*" means "light in darkness" or "enlightener."

"Good, now say it with me," my mom said.

She began repeating the *gur mantr* rhythmically, in a sing-song manner. I copied her, trying my best to focus. I thought about the connection between this *gur mantr* and the one energy that I had learned connects, binds, surrounds, and constitutes everything—the energy that is everything and everywhere, the reason we are all one. Then, after a while, I stopped and simply got lost in the repetition. I felt something new. It's hard to describe a sense of contentment and peace, but that's what it was. I felt grounded and motivated. I was hooked. I wanted to walk down the path of love and to connect with the world. I also wanted to live up to the meaning of my name.

But I would learn that being a "friend to the world" would be a lot harder than I expected.

Discussion Questions

1. How does Jagmeet Singh situate himself within the larger pattern of Sikh history in this selection? What prior Sikh exemplars inspire him?

2. In 2013, Singh was the first Western legislator to be denied a visa to India for his description of the 1984 anti-Sikh riots in India as a "genocide." What kind of relationship do members of the Sikh diaspora have with the Punjab and the contemporary country of India? Does rising Hindu nationalism harm Sikhs as well as Muslims?

3. In this selection, we see Jagmeet Singh reciting the word *Waheguru*, a name for God, as a form of meditation. Before taking this course, is this how you envisioned meditation? What other things in your life might be considered a form of mediation?

Controversy

A Revolution Called Love
Harbani Ahuja

Compared with other thinkers of his time, Guru Nanak was incredibly forward-thinking, repeatedly stating that women and men were equal in the eyes of God. While all the Sikh gurus were men, their wives played important roles in the community, including organizing the *langar* meal, assisting with the first Khalsa initiation, and even leading men into battle. Despite this noble history, however, Sikh women have historically faced oppression both in India and abroad. These include taboos on menstruating women handling the Guru Granth, an expectation of staying home with children, and the highest rate of sex-selective abortions in India. In this selection from a volume written by Sikh women about their faith, essayist Harbani Ahuja describes her realization that the egalitarian ideals of Sikhism do not always translate into reality both within her Sikh community in America and in the Sikh homeland of Punjab. While heartbreaking, Ahuja's essay also describes how her Sikh identity and Sikh exemplars throughout history fuel her fight for justice and equality.

Aavahu bhainae gal mileh ank sehaelarreeaah//
Mil kai kareh kehaaneeaa samrathh kanth keeaah//

Come, my dear sisters and spiritual companions;
Hug me close in your embrace.
Let's join together and tell stories of our All-powerful Husband Lord.
(Guru Granth Sahib, page 17)

As a little girl, I crawled into my mumma's lap at night; she sang *shabads*[1] and whispered *saakhis*[2] of Mai Bhago. I listened, in awe of the strength and unwavering loyalty of Mai Bhago as she rallied the soldiers to reignite their commitment to the Guru. A courageous warrior, she fought valiantly, unafraid of death to defend Sikhism during the sixteenth century in India. I'd drift into sleep dreaming of a fearless Kaur[3] riding a horse onto a battlefield, a warm light radiating from her silhouette.

At that young, impressionable age, Sikhi was not much more than my birthright, a safe place to retreat to where there would be warm *langar*, a meal served at the Staten Island gurdwara, and Gurmukhi books filled with *Oora, Aara, Eeree*, the Punjabi alphabet. Sikhi was my long braid that Mumma weaved in the morning, and the soothing *kirtan*, spiritual hymns, that echoed through the rooms in her home. It was the *Japji Sahib* prayer I read from a small red *gutka*[4] every morning before school, my head bobbing with sleep every so often. Sikhi was attending our local gurdwara every Sunday and learning how to recite shabads on the harmonium. It was the answer I gave my friends when asked about my religion. But as I got older, Sikhi became so much more to me than my birthright. As I began to fall deeply in love with Sikhi, I found my life's calling.

I realized early in life that being a Sikh woman and being an Indian woman is a contradiction. The countless martyrs in our rich history and the revolutionary words

---

1 Punjabi word for "hymn."
2 Punjabi word for "story," generally used to indicate a story from the time of the Gurus.
3 Last name given to Sikh women who undergo the Khalsa initiation.
4 Book with selections from the Guru Granth used in devotional prayers.

of Guru Nanak inspired my passion to fight for justice and equality. To me, equality was an ocean of *amrit* (holy water). Refreshing, awakening, transformative—it washed away all barriers and biases. Mata Jeeto, Guru Gobind Singh Ji's wife, added sweet *pataase* (wafers), to the amrit that Guru Gobind Singh prepared for the *Khalsa*, a community of purity in consciousness and actions. By adding sweetness and love, qualities personified by women, she made the Khalsa genderless. The Khalsa was to me the very essence of equality, but I found myself infuriated by the discrimination in our Sikh communities across the globe.

When I was fourteen years old, I attended the wedding of my eighteen-year-old girl-friend from our gurdwara. She was fresh out of high school, and her parents had arranged her marriage. She was the first of a series of girlfriends at our gurdwara who were married off at early ages. They were never asked if they wanted to attend college or have a career. Each time it happened, it was as if their futures had been snatched away from them. It was as if their opinions about their own futures were not necessary.

At home, I found myself listening to cousins say that they'd marry a housewife over a woman with a good career, and elders who wouldn't be happy with the birth of a girl in the family. I realized that I was surrounded by Sikhs who chose to view Sikh women through the Indian cultural lens, with its patriarchal dominance. Their bias against women wasn't always open or spoken. Sometimes it was a hushed whisper that floated over conversations. I desperately wanted to expose it, to call people out on the veiled prejudice that surfaced from time to time. As I became frustrated with the world around me, I retreated back to Sikhi, falling in love with its message of equality. My Gurus empowered me as a woman, and I clung to Sikhi because it inspired me to demand that Sikh women, all women, have a voice in the twenty-first century around the world. I used Sikhi as my shield against the world silencing me.

I didn't know the meaning of the shabads Mumma would sing at night; I just remember how beautifully the words rolled off her tongue.

Kahu naanak ho nirabho hoee so prabh maeraa oulhaa//
Says Nanak, I am fearless; God has become my Shelter and Shield.
(Guru Granth Sahib, page 870)

I soon found that the bias I was experiencing in my life was nothing compared to what was happening in India. It pained me to read about and understand how female infanticide, domestic violence, and rape were spreading like plagues in Punjab. I knew that being a Kaur meant that my Gurus had placed responsibility on my shoulders to fight for women, Sikhism, and equality throughout the world. And I knew I had to carry out that responsibility with the grace and fire of the Kaurs before me. All my life, I was drowning, suffocating in a sea of silence, discrimination, and female expectations. When I decided to pursue law and dedicate my life to advocating for human rights, I finally came up for air.

My passion for human rights led me to Chandigarh, India, where I accepted an offer to intern with a human rights attorney. I had begun what I thought was the most exciting experience of my life, and I was unbelievably terrified. I cried before getting on the plane, waving good-bye to my parents, leaving the sanctuary of my home for the first time in twenty-one years to go out on my own into the world.

I'm not sure exactly what I went looking for in India, but once I was there I was overcome with emotion. The bias I had experienced back home was nothing compared to the horrors of what I read in case files at the legal office. Never had I felt more blessed to be a Sikh, to be a Kaur, than I did in that moment. Looking out at the injustices India is facing now, I can only imagine how incredibly revolutionary Guru Nanak was to claim that women were equal to men in the sixteenth century.

The case files I read outlined details of horrific acts of violence against women. I heard a firsthand testimony from a newly married young woman about how her husband had abandoned her, returned to beat her, and let his parents abuse her and kick her out of her home. I read about girls who were hunted down and killed by their own parents because they'd made the mistake of falling in love and marrying a man of their own free will. I read reports about the biased judiciary that set rapists free. While I was in India, a woman was gang-raped and brutally killed on a bus in Delhi. Learning of all of this made me sick. My disgust with the state of the world, with the brutality of what was happening to my own people, with my utter powerlessness—all of this merged into a burning knot that lodged itself in my chest. I'd come to India with the hope of finding something that would empower me to make a difference, but instead what I'd found made me feel small. I didn't know why I was there.

On my last day as an intern, as I left the office, I passed the walls covered with shelves on which rested volumes of legal books such as *Judgements Today* and *Indian Law Reports* placed in chronological order. Next to the shelves of books, I noticed some images framed on the walls. When I realized who the paintings were of, my heart jumped and I froze in my tracks. There she was in my life again, just as beautiful and courageous as I remembered her. As I gazed upon the image of Mai Bhago—a *dastaar*[5] on her head, fearlessly raising a sword, majestically riding her horse into battle, light radiating from her silhouette—the knot in my chest melted away. I remembered why I was there. There was also a battle ahead of me, and like this valiant Kaur, there was only love for my Guru in my heart. In that moment, I knew my Guru was asking me to fight this war against injustice for as long as I lived.

Jaa ko har rang laago eis jug mehi so keheeath hai sooraa//
He alone is called a warrior, who is attached to the Lord's Love in this age.
(Guru Granth Sahib, page 94)

---

5 Turban.

Discussion Questions

1. Harbani Ahuja makes some effort to present the oppression of Sikh women as a feature of Indian culture, not something inherent to Sikhism itself. Is this a fair interpretation? How can one distinguish whether a social problem is due to a religious tradition, local culture, government policies, or other factors? And how does this issue relate to the problem of essentialism in analyzing religious cultures?

2. Sikhism is practiced differently in North America than in the Punjab. What factors might shape whether Sikh immigrants choose to preserve a part of their culture as essential or leave it behind and adapt to a new culture?

3. While Ahuja points to important examples of Sikh women acting prominently in their communities, one could also argue that the history of Sikhism continues to reflect a pattern of patriarchal dominance—none of the gurus were women, many gurus took multiple wives, and so forth. How do we as contemporary readers and cultural interpreters make sense of this seeming contradiction?

Judaism

Judaism is a religion that is particularly difficult to generalize about, especially because Jews have always welcomed debate and dissent. While the religion of Judaism has been understood and expressed in many ways, there are certain themes that saturate Jewish tradition. The problem for Judaism can be described as exile, both in the sense of being distant from God and from one's true home. For most of their history Israelites lived in exile from their promised homeland. They also live in exile from God. And in some mystical traditions part of the Godhead is also in exile from the world. The solution to exile is return, both to God and one's true home. The theme of exile is conveyed here through the poem "Lament on the Devastation of the Land of Israel" by the medieval poet Abraham ben Meir ibn Ezra. Here, the fall of Zion is not so much a historical event but a condition of the world unmoored from time and space; it is always happening everywhere. Ibn Ezra calls on Jews (whom he calls "his brothers") both to weep and to be mindful of ongoing oppression. Born in Spain, Ibn Ezra lived a life of exile himself, traveling the world as a wandering and impoverished scholar.

The techniques of Judaism include stories and the laws. These two techniques are intimately connected, as stories explain the origin of the laws and the laws ensure Jews remember their stories. Outsiders, especially Christians, often misunderstand the significance of law in Judaism. Jews do not follow the laws in order to avoid damnation or attain a reward in heaven. Instead, many practicing Jews have explained that obeying God's laws is a privilege and a source of joy. Solomon Schechter, a leading thinker in Conservative Judaism, helped to dispel this misunderstanding in his essay "The Law Is Not a Burden."

In ancient times the exemplars of Judaism included prophets and priests, but in the modern era rabbis are the living exemplars for Judaism. The two rabbis presented here—each beloved by their community—are meant to demonstrate the diversity of Jewish traditions. Rabbi Israel ben Eliezer, also known as the Baal Shem Tov (Master of the Good Name), was a founding figure of Hasidic Judaism, which formed in the Ukraine in the eighteenth century. The Baal Shem Tov was not only a scholar but a mystic, and Hasidic folklore is replete with legends about miracles he performed. Rabbi Alysa Stanton was born in the twentieth century to a black Pentecostal household in Cleveland, Ohio. She converted to Judaism and became the first African American female rabbi, serving a congregation of Conservative and Reform Jews in Greenville, North Carolina.

Like most ancient religions, Judaism has inherited texts and practices that may strike modern people as patriarchal or even misogynistic. Responding to this problem can be difficult for a religion where tradition is so precious: what one Jew celebrates as progress, another may regard as mocking the Torah. An editorial by Yochi Rappeport, executive director of the group Women of the Wall, offers a look at this controversy. Women of the Wall seek the right for Jewish women to read from the Torah aloud, wear prayer shawls, and engage in other religious activities traditionally prohibited for women, all while being present at the Kotel (also known as the Western Wall)—the most sacred site of Judaism. Some Jewish women regard their efforts as heroic, while others see them as insensitive or sacrilegious.

Problem/Solution

Lament on the Devastation of the Land of Israel
Abraham ben Meir ibn Ezra

Abraham ben Meir ibn Ezra (c. 1093–1167) was a Jewish poet as well as a biblical commentator, philosopher, and physician. He was born in Spain but traveled widely throughout Europe and the Middle East. These journeys may have been precipitated when his son converted to Islam and Ibn Ezra traveled to the Middle East in an unsuccessful attempt to retrieve him. Many found it surprising that he managed to be such a prolific writer while living as an impoverished roving scholar. In legends about Ibn Ezra he arrives to help when Jewish communities are in trouble, only to disappear afterward, returning to his wandering existence.

> Weep, my brothers, weep and mourn
> Over Zion with great moan,
> Like the lament of Hadadrimmon,
> Or of Josiah, son of Amon.

Weep for the tender and delicate ones
Who barefoot now tread upon thorns,
Drawing water for barbarians,
Felling trees at their commands.

Weep for the man who is oppressed,
In bondage inexperienced.
They say to him: "Carry! Make haste!"
And he, among burdens, finds no rest.

Weep for the fathers when they see
Their sons, none more praiseworthy,
Whose price gold cannot buy,
At the hands of Cushites condemned to die.

Weep for the blind who wander on,
Defiled, through the land of Zion,
With the blood of pregnant women,
The blood of the aged and young children.

Weep for the pious, whom the unclean goad,
Force them to eat forbidden food,
To make them forget their bond with God,
And the land, where their joys reside.

Weep for the women pure and chaste,
Whose fidelity had never ceased,
Subject to Hamitic lust,
Conceiving, with terror in their breast.

Weep for the daughters, noble
And upright as sculptured marble,
Forced to be slaves to the ignoble,
Who are themselves a servile rabble.

Weep. Weep and mourn
The synagogues forlorn,
That wild beasts have torn down,
And desert birds have made their own.

Weep for those in the enemies' grip,
Gathered together for a day without hope,
For those poor souls who have drained the cup,
Who are suffering now murder and rape.

Weep, weep for our living.
Do not weep for our dying;
For, as long as we have being,
To be like the dead is our desiring.

Therefore, my friend, do not recall
Consolation for my soul,
For those torn in pieces, all
In Zion, with no burial.

Discussion Questions

1. This poem alludes to terrible things that happened centuries ago or are happening in places far from Europe. Arguably, Ibn Ezra's audience would be happier if they forgot about these events. Why then, are they called to remember?

2. Ibn Ezra was writing for Jews living in diaspora, especially Spain. How might his travels have inspired and influenced this poem?

3. God is never mentioned in this poem. This is unusual for a poem about the plight of God's chosen people. Why might this be?

Technique

The Law Is Not a Burden
Solomon Schechter

Solomon Schechter (1847–1915) was a rabbinic scholar whose ideas led to the development of Conservative Judaism. He was born in Romania but arrived in New York where he became head of the Jewish Theological Seminary in 1902. He was known for his skill as an interpreter of Judaism, explaining Jewish concepts in ways that outsiders could understand. He believed it was possible for Jewish tradition to change, but he resisted the assimilationist tendencies of Reform Judaism and felt that there were "essentials" that could not be abandoned.

It is also an illusion to speak of the burden which a scrupulous care to observe 613 commandments must have laid upon the Jew. Even a superficial analysis will discover that in the time of Christ many of these commandments were already obsolete (as for instance those relating to the tabernacle and to the conquest of Palestine), while others concerned only certain classes, as the priests, the judges, the soldiers, the Nazirites, or the representatives of the community, or even only one or two individuals among the whole population, as the King and the High-Priest. Others again, provided for contingencies which could occur only to a few, as for instance the laws concerning divorce or levirate marriages, whilst many—such as those concerning idolatry, and incest, and the sacrifice of children to Moloch—could scarcely have been considered as a practical prohibition by the pre-Christian Jew; just as little as we can speak of Englishmen under the burden of a law preventing them from burning widows or marrying their grandmothers, though such acts would certainly be considered as crimes.

Thus it will be found by a careful enumeration that barely a hundred laws remain which really concerned the life of the bulk of the people. If we remember that even these include such laws as belief in the unity of God, the necessity of loving and hearing Him, and of sanctifying His name, of loving one's neighbor and the stranger, of providing for the poor, exhorting the sinner, honouring one's parents and many more of a similar character, it will hardly be said that the ceremonial side of the people's religion was not well balanced by a fair amount of spiritual and social elements. Besides, it would seem that the line between the ceremonial and the spiritual is too often only arbitrarily drawn. With many commandments it is rather a matter of opinion whether they should be relegated to the one category or the other.

Thus, the wearing of Tephilin[1] or phylacteries has, on the one hand, been continually condemned as a meaningless superstition, and a pretext for formalism and hypocrisy. But, on the other hand, Maimonides, who can in no way be suspected of superstition or mysticism, described importance in the following words: "Great is the holiness of the Tephilin; for as long as they are on the arm and head of man he is humble and God-fearing, and feels no attraction for frivolity or idle things, nor has he any evil thoughts, but will turn his heart to the words of truth and righteousness." The view which R. Jochanan, a Palestinian teacher of the third century, took of the fulfilment of the Law, will probably be found more rational than that of many a rationalist of today. Upon the basis of the last verse in Hosea, "The ways of the Lord are right, and the just shall walk in them, but the transgressors shall stumble therein," he explains that while one man, for instance, eats his paschal lamb for the sake of the *Mizvah* (that is, to do God's will who commanded it), and thereby commits an act of righteousness, another thinks only of satisfying his appetite by the lamb, so that his eating it (by the very fact that he professes at the same time to

---

1 Worn during prayer, the tefillin (or tephilin) consists of leather straps that attach black boxes to the arm and forehead. Inside the boxes are tiny scrolls of biblical passages.

perform a religious rite) becomes a stumbling-block for him. Thus all the laws by virtue of their divine authority—and in this there was in the first century no difference of opinion between Jews and Christians—have their spiritual side, and to neglect them implies, at least from the individual's own point of view, a moral offence.

The legalistic attitude may be summarily described as an attempt to live in accordance with the will of God. But, nevertheless, on the whole this life never degenerated into religious formalism. Apart from the fact that during the second temple there grew up laws and even beliefs, which show a decided tendency towards progress and development, there were also ceremonies which were popular with the people, and others which were neglected. Men were not, therefore, the mere soulless slaves of the Law; personal sympathies and dislikes also played a due part in their religion. Nor were all the laws actually put upon the same level. With a happy inconsistency men always spoke of heavier and slighter sins, and by the latter—excepting, perhaps, the profanation of the Sabbath—they mostly understood ceremonial transgressions. The statement made by Professor Toy, on the authority of James, that "the principle was established that he who offended in one point was guilty of all," is hardly correct; for the passage seems rather to be laying down a principle, or arguing that logically the law ought to be looked upon as a whole, than stating a fact. The fact was that people did not consider the whole law as of equal importance, but made a difference between laws and laws, and even spoke of certain commandments, such as those of charity and kindness, as outweighing all the rest of the Torah. It was in conformity with this spirit that in times of great persecution the leaders of the people had no compunction in reducing the whole Law to the three prohibitions of idolatry, of incest, and of bloodshed. Only these three were considered of sufficient importance that men should rather become martyrs than transgress them.

These, then, are some of the illusions and misrepresentations which exist with regard to the Law. There are many others, of which the complete exposure would require a book by itself. Meanwhile, in the absence of such a book to balance and correct the innumerable volumes upon the other side, Professor Toy has done the best he could with existing materials, and produced a meritorious work deserving of wide recognition and approval.

Discussion Questions

1. Why might outsiders claim that Jews are "soulless slaves of the Law?" What arguments does Solomon Schechter put forward to debunk this claim?

2. What does it mean to obey a law "for the sake of the *Mitzvah* [*Mizvah*]"? How is this different from other reasons for which people obey religious laws?

3. Where in this essay does Schechter seem open to the idea that Jews can be flexible with how the law is practiced? Where does he identify specific laws, or attitudes toward the law, as essential?

Exemplar 1

In Praise of the Baal Shem Tov

Dan Ben-Amos and Jerome R. Mintz

Rabbi Israel ben Eliezer (c. 1700–1760), better known as the Baal Shem Tov (Master of the Good Name), is regarded as the founder of modern Hasidism, a Jewish revivalist movement that began in the Ukraine in the eighteenth century. "Baal Shem Tov" is frequently shortened to the acronym BeShT or simply "the Besht." Rabbi Dov Ber (also known as Dov Baer ben Samuel) collected over two hundred tales and anecdotes about the Besht into a book called Shivḥei ha-Besht (In Praise of the Besht). Dov Ber was the son-in-law of Rabbi Alexander the Shoḥet, who had been the Baal Shem Tov's scribe for eight years. Manuscripts of this collection circulated in Jewish communities and were first printed in Hebrew in 1814. In 1970 Dan Ben-Amos and Jerome R. Mintz produced the first English translation of this volume, from which the following selections have been excerpted.

The Besht Reveals Himself

. . . [O]ur master and rabbi, Rabbi Gershon, rented a place for the Besht in a certain village where he would be able to earn a living. And there he achieved perfection. He built a house of seclusion in the forest. He prayed and studied there all day and all night every day of the week, and he returned home only on the Sabbath. He also kept there white garments for the Sabbath. He also had a bath house and a mikveh. His wife was occupied with earning a living, and God blessed the deeds of her hand and she was successful. They were hospitable to guests: they gave them food and drink with great respect. When a guest came she sent for the Besht and he returned and served him. The guest never knew about the Besht.

It was the Besht's custom when he came to the city for Rosh Hashanah to remain there for the entire month. Once during the intermediate days of Sukkoth, our master and rabbi, Rabbi Gershon, noticed that he was not putting on tefillin. It was his custom to pray by the eastern wall of the synagogue. And he asked him: "Why don't you put on tefillin today?" He answered: "I saw in the Taich books that he who puts on tefillin during the intermediate days is sentenced to death."

The rabbi became very angry that the Besht followed the customs that are written in the books from Germany. There was no telling what the result would be. He went with him to the rabbi of the community so that the rabbi would admonish him. They considered the Besht to be a pious man, but as the saying goes, "an uncultured person is not sin-fearing."

The rabbi was a very righteous man. When they came to the rabbi's house, Rabbi Gershon kissed the mezuzah, but the Besht put his hand on the mezuzah without kissing it, and our master and rabbi, Rabbi Gershon, became angry with him over this as well.

When they entered the rabbi's house the Besht put aside his mask and the rabbi saw a great light. He rose up before the Besht. Then the Besht resumed the mask and the rabbi sat down. And this happened several times. The rabbi was very frightened since he did not know who he was. Sometimes he seemed to be a holy person and at other times he seemed to be a common man. But when our master and rabbi, Rabbi Gershon, complained to him about the tefillin and the mezuzah, the rabbi took the Besht aside privately and said to him: "I command you to reveal the truth to me." And the Besht was forced to reveal himself to him. But the Besht commanded him in turn not to reveal anything that had transpired.

When they came out the rabbi said to our master and rabbi, Rabbi Gershon: "I taught him a lesson, but I think he would not knowingly commit a fault against our customs. He has acted in innocence." Then the rabbi examined the mezuzah and they discovered that it had a defect.

Rabbi Gershon, the Besht, and the Zohar

I heard this from the Great Light, the Hasid of our community, our master and teacher, Rabbi Gedaliah. Once the Besht borrowed a copy of the Zohar from the rabbi of the holy community of Kuty. On his way back home he encountered his brother-in-law, Rabbi Gershon, who asked him: "What do you have under your arm?"

He did not want to tell him. Rabbi Gershon climbed down from the wagon, took the Zohar from under his arm, and said in wonder: "You need the Zohar?"

After that Rabbi Gedaliah said that the Besht came to the city to pray in the beth-hamidrash. In his prayer he sighed deeply. After the prayer, Rabbi Moses, the head of the court of that holy community, asked him: "Why did I hear a deep sigh from you during the prayer?" And he persuaded him to explain.

The Besht told him: "The truth is that it was a sigh from the heart." He said: "The mezuzah is defective."

The rabbi found that indeed it was as he said. He gave the Besht the copy of the Zohar and blessed him so that he would not encounter Rabbi Gershon.

The Dance of the Hasidim

I heard this upon the arrival of the rabbi of the community of Nemirov. Once on Simhath Torah the followers of the Besht were happy, dancing and drinking a lot of wine from the Besht's cellar.

The Besht's pious wife said: "They will not leave any wine for the blessing of the kiddush and Havdalah," and she entered the Besht's room and said to him: "Tell them to stop drinking and dancing since you will not have any wine left over for the kiddush and Havdalah."

The Besht said to her jokingly: "Well said. Go and tell them to stop and go home."

When she opened the door and saw that they were dancing in a circle and that flames of fire were burning around them like a canopy, she herself took the pots, went to the cellar, and brought them as much wine as they wanted.

After a while the Besht asked her: "Did you tell them to go?"

She said to him: "You should have told them yourself."

The Besht and Shabbetai Tsevi

Rabbi Joel told me [. . .] that Shabbetai Tsevi came to the Besht to ask for redemption. Rabbi Joel said in these words: "The tikkun is done through the connection of soul with soul, spirit with spirit, and breath with breath." The Besht began to establish the connection moderately. He was afraid as Shabbetai Tsevi was a terribly wicked man. Once the Besht was asleep, and Shabbetai Tsevi, may his name be blotted out, came and attempted to tempt him again, God forbid. With a mighty thrust the Besht hurled him to the bottom of hell. The Besht peered down and saw that he landed on the same pallet with Jesus.

Rabbi Joel said that the Besht said that Shabbetai Tsevi had a spark of holiness in him, but that Satan caught him in his snare, God forbid. The Besht heard that his fall came through pride and anger. I was reluctant to write it down, but nevertheless I did so to show to what extent pride can be dangerous.

The Lithuanian Jew and the Besht

I heard this from my brother-in-law, our teacher Mordecai, who heard it from Rabbi Jehiel of Kovel.

Once the Lithuanians sent someone to sound out the nature of the Besht. He stayed as a guest with Rabbi Jehiel and ate with the Besht. When he heard the Besht's prayer on the eve of the holy Sabbath, it appealed to him very much. After the prayer he went with the Besht to his home. When the Besht came home he became angry with his servant and began shouting at him. He told him to go to the stable immediately because a horse was strangling.

The servant pleaded with him and said: "My lord, I will go right away."

The Besht shouted at him again and wanted to hit him. The servant went and saved the horse.

The guest was surprised by the anger of the Besht, and he said to himself: "After such prayer how could he care for one horse so much as to shout at his servant, especially on the Sabbath."

In the morning he heard the Besht's prayer and it pleased him; nevertheless, this reservation haunted him. After the Sabbath when he wanted to return home he revealed it to Rabbi Jehiel, and then he went on his way. Rabbi Jehiel told the Besht about it.

The Besht became angry and said: "Who are they to examine me? I'll tell you what happened. A Jew was traveling on the road on the eve of the holy Sabbath, and evening fell upon him. He could not reach a settlement in time for the Sabbath. It occurred to him to turn off the road into the field and observe the Sabbath there. A thief came and began to hit him and wanted to kill him. This Jew was very coarse and I had no contact with him except through an animal. I frightened my servant, and the more I frightened him the more the thieves were frightened, until they refrained from killing the man. You will see that they will soon bring him to the town." And so it was.

Discussion Questions

1. In one story the Besht's normal persona is described as a "mask" that can be removed to show a "great light." Why does the Besht sometimes show his true nature and other times not? What is the purpose of stories like this?

2. From these stories, what can you tell about how Jews in Poland and the Ukraine celebrated the Sabbath in the Besht's time? What were some of the traditions and social expectations?

3. What is the point of the story "The Dance of the Hasidim?" What does the miracle of flames appearing say about the significance of drinking and dancing on the Sabbath?

Exemplar 2

Pulpit of Color

Stewart Ain

Because Judaism is an ethnicity as well as a religion and a culture, Jews are often imagined as universally sharing a common set of ethnic features and physical characteristics. But both globally and in North America, Jews are much more diverse than many people realize. Judaism is also becoming more diverse as newcomers convert to this tradition. Rabbi Alysa Stanton is a case in point. She converted to Judaism at age 24 and went on to become the first African American female rabbi.

As a student rabbi, Alysa Stanton—who next month becomes the first ever African-American woman rabbi—was assigned to intern in a congregation in Dothan, Ala.

But no sooner did she arrive than the president of the congregation called the Hebrew Union College-Jewish Institute of Religion in Cincinnati to complain.

"He said, 'Are you kidding?'" recalled Rabbi Ken Kanter, director of HUC's rabbinical program.

Stanton said she was told that a "black person ministering to a white congregation in the Deep South was unheard of."

However, Rabbi Kanter said, the congregation "very quickly recognized they had a rabbi who happened to be a woman and who happened to be African-American. She quickly became their rabbi . . . and at the end of the year they wanted her to stay because she was so well loved."

Stanton said the challenge had been to "put aside mutual stereotypes and prejudices and get to know each other on our own merits. We did it and [developed] phenomenal relationships. I will always hold a special place for them in my heart."

That experience gave her the confidence to consider another congregation in the South when it came time to apply for her first full-time position, which she will assume after her ordination June 6. The synagogue is Congregation Bayt Shalom in Greenville, N.C., about 70 miles east of Raleigh in the eastern part of the state.

Stanton and a half-dozen other candidates from both the Reform and Conservative movements were interviewed by phone by the congregation's 10-member search committee, according to Michael Barondes, the congregation's president. Stanton and a Conservative rabbi were then invited for a visit.

"She led an adult education class and met with the youth group and made a tremendous impression on the congregation," Barondes said of Stanton. "She has musical skills and a singing talent that was impressive. And she has interpersonal skills and the ability to engage people—adults and children. She was also able to articulate the desire to help us come up with a plan to unite the diverse Jewish community in a one-synagogue town."

About 70 percent of the 56-family congregation is Reform and the rest Conservative. The congregation is affiliated with both movements.

"The fact that she is a convert was not a factor [in her selection]," Barondes said. "She was not the only Jew-by-choice who applied for the position. . . . And the fact she is African-American played no part. During her three-day visit, she was able to impress so many people that the congregation overwhelmingly supported her candidacy."

Stanton, 45, grew up in a Pentecostal Christian home in Cleveland, Ohio. At the age of 6, her family moved to a Jewish neighborhood in Cleveland Heights, Ohio.

It was there that her Uncle Ed, a devout Catholic who also occasionally attended the local synagogue, explained to her what the mezuzahs meant on the neighbors' doorposts. When she was 10 and already on her own spiritual quest, he gave her a Hebrew grammar book.

"My mother is a woman of faith," Stanton said. "She taught us that we need to have a spiritual base and she gave us the freedom to choose what that is. For me, Judaism was where I found a home."

At the age of 11, Stanton moved with her family to Lakewood, Colo., and by the time she was in her early 20s, she said she had decided to convert to Judaism.

"I sought out a rabbi and each week I traveled 144 miles to meet with him in Denver for intensive, one-to-one study," she said, adding that after a year she converted, appearing before a bet din [Jewish court] and going to the mikveh.

"Initially when I converted my family was shocked," Stanton said, adding that her mother (her father is deceased) and sister and two brothers have been "very supportive—my rock during this long journey."

For about the last 15 years, her rabbi in Denver has been Steven Foster of Temple Emanuel, a Reform congregation. He said he found Stanton to be "a very spiritual person who brings the best of two different cultures together. She is a terrific person and we will be lucky in the Jewish community to have her as a rabbi."

Rabbi Foster said that although Stanton was converted by a "right-wing Conservative rabbi," she later "connected with us because of our history with social justice issues. . . . She used to teach for us and sing for us and when she decided to become a rabbi we all supported her."

One of her professors at HUC, David Weisberg said the fact that Stanton landed a job already in this tight job market—only about half of the graduates have jobs—is evidence of her special qualities.

"She has a love of Judaism and a pull for the study of the Torah," he said. "She is very sensitive about the issues of piety and love of Torah."

Steve Sunderland, a friend at the neighboring University of Cincinnati, called Stanton a "remarkable young lady who has a spiritual commitment to Judaism that is rare. . . . She has it clear in her mind that she is a Jew who happens to be African-American. She sees being an African-American one additional gift she brings to Judaism."

Those thoughts were echoed by Rabbi Samuel Joseph, an HUC professor of Jewish education and leadership development, who said he has "never met anyone more determined."

"She loves being Jewish and wants to serve the Jewish people," he said. "It's always tough being the first, but she wasn't going to let anything stop her. I don't believe she ever thought about becoming a pioneer."

Stanton said, in fact, that she did not know she was the first until after she started rabbinical school.

Rabbi Kanter said Stanton's prior career, as a licensed psychotherapist specializing in grief and loss—she was called upon to counsel people after the Columbine High School massacre in 1999—"is an important talent to bring to the rabbinate."

Stanton is a single mother of a 14-year-old, Shana, who she adopted at the age of 14 months. Stanton later married and divorced. Because of complications from gastric bypass surgery, she was forced to complete her rabbinical studies in seven rather than five years.

Steven M. Cohen, an HUC research professor of Jewish social policy, said it is "no coincidence" that Stanton is being ordained the same year Barack Obama was sworn in as president.

"He is a man who represented the aspiration to cross ancient boundaries, rivalries and conflicts," he said. "She crosses both religious and ethnic boundaries in her own life, representing a pioneering model of Jewish continuity. . . . She is not alone in that the number of converts and others coming to Judaism from non-conventional backgrounds is probably at its peak in American life."

The Institute for Jewish and Community Research in San Francisco estimates that 20 percent of the six million American Jews are racially and ethnically diverse by birth, conversion and adoption. And there have been an estimated 20,000 to 30,000 marriages between Jews and African-Americans since the civil rights movement.

Diane Tobin, the institute's associate director and director of its Be-Chol Lashon program, said her organization has worked with Stanton as part of its mission to "advocate for the growth and diversity of the Jewish people."

Although Stanton is the first female African-American rabbi, there are many black male rabbis worldwide, Tobin said.

"With the election of President Obama, the Jewish community is very interested in its diverse roots," she said. "We have always been a diverse people and young people in particular want to see themselves as part of a global people. . . . Mainstream Jewish communities want to partner with us and introduce diversity as part of their programming."

Although Stanton and her daughter will be the only black members in her Greenville congregation, Tobin said she would be interested to see if they attract blacks to the congregation.

Ernest Adams, 62, an African-American in Manhattan who converted to Judaism in 1997, said he is "meeting more and more black folks in synagogues."

"In the South the Jewish community couldn't be as liberal as the Jews up North, where you could find Jews marching with Martin Luther King," he said. "In the South, the rabbis had to be cautious. But now that a white Southern congregation can hire a black rabbi, there is a significant change. The fact that it has been greeted with equanimity means there's a big shift. The culture is changing."

Stanton said graduation day will be something special, not just because she is the first African-American woman to be ordained a rabbi but because of the medical problems she had to overcome to get there.

"I went back to school in a wheelchair [at one point]," she recalled. "So to be finishing now is so poignant on so many levels. God has sustained me."

Discussion Questions

1. In this article Stanton refers to the need to put aside "mutual stereotypes and prejudices." What stereotypes might the black community have about Jews and vice versa? Or what stereotypes might people who were born into Judaism have about converts? From where do these stereotypes arise?

2. Steven Cohen reports that the number of people converting to Judaism from "non-conventional backgrounds is probably at its peak in American life." Why might people like Rabbi Alysa Stanton convert to Judaism? Why are these conversions happening now?

3. How has the experience of Jews living in the American South been different from those in the north?

Controversy

Well-Behaved Women Seldom Make History

Yochi Rappeport

Women of the Wall was founded in 1988 with the goal of gaining the right for Jewish women to wear prayer shawls, pray, and read from the Torah, collectively and aloud, at the Western Wall, also known as the Kotel. This goal is offensive to many Orthodox Jews (including some Orthodox women who identify as feminists) because they regard the Kotel as a synagogue and believe that women's participation in these activities in a synagogue violates Jewish law. There are, however, Orthodox women who support Women of the Wall. There have been years of legal battles over what exactly women may do at the Kotel, which is overseen by the Ministry of Religious Affairs. Protests by Haredi (ultra-Orthodox) Jews over the group's activities have occasionally escalated into violence. Yochi Rappeport is the executive director of Women of the Wall.

A few years ago, I was interviewed for a leadership course. I was asked if there is a historical figure or event with which I wish I could interact. I replied that my dream would be to meet Susan B. Anthony or Lady Rhondda, significant figures in the history of women's suffrage, and to have them watch as a young woman casts her vote.

Seeing them smile and understand that their struggles and efforts paid off would be an amazing experience.

If you were to ask me the most exciting moment I've experienced with Women of the Wall—the moment that made me feel it was all worth it—I would say it was when a group of religious seminary girls took up two-thirds of the women's section at the Western Wall to sing the Slihot penitential prayers. It was the first time I had witnessed a large gathering like this, young girls praying out loud at the Kotel.

When the seminary girls finished their service, I approached them and expressed my excitement regarding their enthusiastic singing. I then introduced myself and shared that I am from Women of the Wall, the same organization that has been struggling for just this moment for 31 years, to see girls raising their voices in prayer and singing at the holy site.

"Yes, but you do it for the sake of provocation," one of the girls snapped at me. The rest tried to silence her and to thank me for the warm words, but she continued, "Why do you have to be so confrontational? Why not act like we do, in a pleasant way?"

I would love to witness a conversation between a late 19th-century suffragette and a 19-year-old girl in the State of Israel who is learning for the first time that her right to vote today did not come from anyone's good gesture, but was the result of the stubborn struggle of women of the last century.

Change takes courage. Any woman running a marathon today should know that this was made possible only by one cheeky woman, Katherine Switzer, who signed up for the 1967 Boston Marathon on behalf of a man—because women were not allowed to sign up for such an event. Relatedly, every woman who enrolls today for academic studies does so thanks to women who relentlessly demanded women's right to higher education.

Our presence as women in the public sphere is something that was not always taken for granted. It is the result of the determination of "provocative" women. In other words, these bold women of years ago had courage, heroism, boldness and something else: caring. They struggled then because they cared about the future generations of girls and women.

The word provocation has been used to portray the dark side of feminism; it turns people away from hearing what we are trying to express. Like the young woman implied at Slihot, our presence is seen as a demonstration.

The answer is that we have no choice. Provocation is in the eyes of the beholder and it depends on context and time. Just as women's suffrage achieved its goals, Women of the Wall will fight to attain women's freedom of religious expression and women's access to Torah at the Western Wall.

In 1976, Laurel Thatcher Ulrich coined the phrase, "Well-behaved women seldom make history." With those truthful words in mind, we have started acting and stopped apologizing. The future will be better because of strong and resolute women.

Discussion Questions

1. Rappeport describes a Jewish seminary girl "snapping" at her for being too confrontational. Why might some Jewish women disapprove of the goals or methods of Women of the Wall?

2. Rappeport says she is fighting for "women's freedom of religious expression." But many Orthodox Jews, including Orthodox women, counter that the Kotel is a synagogue and that it is deeply offensive for Jewish women to choose *this place* to flaunt their freedom from Jewish law. Do Orthodox Jews have a right to enjoy their sacred site as they see fit? And if so, how should this right be weighed against another group's right to freely express its religion?

3. One reason the Western Wall is so important is that it symbolizes continuity between generations of Jews. Rappeport's essay does not discuss tradition but rather the need for change. Is this a paradox? Why do Jewish women seeking change desire access to an ancient wall?

Christianity

In the Christian tradition, the human problem is sin. While different Christians have different understandings of sin, it generally refers to doing things that are wrong—both in thought and deed. But in addition to the actions we take, human beings are also marked by "original sin": our very nature has been corrupted by the sin of Adam and Eve, and because of this human beings cannot solve the problem of sin without divine help bestowed by God through Jesus. Historians of Christianity often claim that the theology of original sin did not obtain its full formulation and its own terminology until Augustine of Hippo in the early fifth century CE. A selection from *The City of God* illuminates Augustine's ideas about the corrupted nature of humanity and "the ways of the flesh."

While Christians generally agree that salvation from sin comes from Jesus and not human effort, they disagree as to which techniques are necessary to obtain the salvation promised by Jesus. All Christians agree that salvation requires faith. For Roman Catholic and Orthodox Christians faith should be accompanied by good works such as partaking in the sacraments. Protestants disagree, arguing that faith alone is necessary for salvation. In his treatise "The Freedom of a Christian," Martin Luther draws on themes present in the writings of Paul to make his case for why faith is the only technique needed by Christians. Notably, though, Luther rejects "antinomianism" or the idea that because Christians are saved by faith alone, they do not need to follow moral laws. Luther argues that Christians must follow moral laws but rejects the idea that obedience to moral laws *causes* salvation.

Christianity has innumerable exemplars, and only two could be presented here. Desmond Tutu was the Anglican Archbishop of Cape Town, South Africa, now retired. Tutu was the first black head of the Anglican Church in South Africa. He famously invoked Christian ideas of justice and human dignity to combat apartheid and bring racial reconciliation to South Africa, receiving a Nobel Peace Prize in 1984. Dorothy Day was born in New York City and cofounded the Catholic Worker Movement in 1933, a group that cared for the poor and promoted pacifism. There is a movement among American Catholics to canonize Day as a saint, and in 2000 Pope John Paul II allowed Day to be declared "a servant of God," the first step toward sainthood.

Who speaks for Christianity? Although Christianity began in the Middle East and northern Africa, for centuries Europe and North America sent missionaries to colonies in Asia, South America, and Africa. For some, this history contributed to an attitude that Christianity was the West's gift to the world and therefore the West's to define. But today, Christianity is in decline in North America and Europe, while it is exploding in the Global South. This shift in gravity is sometimes referred to as "the browning of Christianity." An accompanying trend has been the rise of Pentecostalism and charismatic Christianity, along with such practices as speaking in tongues, divine healing, and exorcism. These are practices that have always been part of Christian tradition but were largely discarded in the West as superstition or ignorance, particularly in the wake of the Enlightenment. The Azusa Street Revival in Los Angeles in 1906 was a watershed moment for these two trends. The Azusa Street church defied the racial segregation of the day and shocked some by practicing speaking in tongues. A racist newspaper article from the *Los Angeles Times* that suggests the congregation is mentally ill and practicing an ersatz form of Christianity demonstrates some of the anxieties about the role of people of color in shaping the future of Christianity.

Problem/Solution

From *The City of God*
Augustine of Hippo

Augustine (354–430 CE) was the bishop of Hippo in northern Africa. In 410 CE the city of Rome fell to barbarians, and some fleeing Romans claimed this happened because the empire had abandoned the gods for Christianity. These claims inspired Augustine to spend fourteen years writing his massive work, *The City of God*. Because Augustine was debating learned pagans, his work integrates his study of the Bible with Greco-Roman thinkers such as Epicurus, Plato, and Virgil. By doing so, he created a cornerstone of Western thought, expounding important theological ideas including the doctrine of original sin.

Book XIV

1. That All Men Would Have Been Plunged into an Everlasting Second Death by the Sin of the First Man, Had Not God's Grace Redeemed Many

As I have already said in the preceding books, God chose to create the human race from one single man. His purpose in doing this was not only that the human race should be united in fellowship by a natural likeness, but also that men should be bound together by kinship in the unity of concord, linked by the bond of peace. And the individual members of this race would not have been subject to death, had not the first two—one of whom was created from no one, and the other from him—merited it by their disobedience. So great was the sin of those two that human nature was changed by it for the worse; and so bondage to sin and the necessity of death were transmitted to their posterity.

Now the sway of the kingdom of death over men was so complete that all would have been driven headlong, as their due punishment, into that second death to which there is no end, had not some of them been redeemed by the unmerited grace of God. Thus it is that, though there are a great many nations throughout the world, living according to different rites and customs, and distinguished by many different forms of language, arms and dress, there nonetheless exist only two orders, as we may call them, of human society; and, following our Scriptures, we may rightly speak of these as two cities. The one is made up of men who live according to the flesh, and the other of those who live according to the spirit. Each desires its own kind of peace, and, when they have found what they sought, each lives in its own kind of peace.

2. That Life according to the Flesh Is to Be Understood as Arising Not Only from the Faults of the Body, but Also from Those of the Mind

First, therefore, we must see what it is to live according to the flesh and according to the spirit. For anyone who takes what we have just said at face value may err, either because he does not remember how Holy Scripture uses this manner of speaking, or because he pays too little heed to it. On the one hand, he may certainly suppose that the Epicurean philosophers live according to the flesh; for they place man's highest good in the pleasure of the body. And he may suppose that the same is true of the other philosophers who hold in some way that the good of the body is man's highest good. And he may also suppose that it is true of the common people: of those who subscribe to no doctrine, who do not practise any kind of philosophy, but who, having a leaning towards lust, know no delight except that derived from the pleasure which they receive through the senses. On the other hand, he may suppose that the Stoics, who place man's highest good in the mind, live according to the spirit; for what is man's mind if not spirit? In fact, however, it is clear that all of these live according to the flesh in the sense intended by Divine Scripture when it uses the expression.

For Scripture does not use the term "flesh" to mean only the body of an earthly and mortal creature, as when it says: "All flesh is not the same flesh: but there is one kind of flesh of men, another flesh of beasts, another of fishes, and another of birds." On the contrary, there are many other ways in which it uses the term, to signify different things. And among these various usages is that by which man himself—that is, the nature of man—is designated by "flesh": a manner of speaking in which the whole is represented by a part; for example, "By the deeds of the Law there shall no flesh be justified." For what does the apostle wish us to understand by this if not "no man"? This is made clearer a little later, where he says, "No man is justified by the Law"; and, in the Epistle to the Galatians, he says: "Knowing that a man is not justified by the works of the Law."

According to this, we interpret the words "And the Word was made flesh" to mean that Christ became man. Certain persons who have not rightly understood this passage have supposed that Christ was without a human soul. But just as, when we read in the Gospel the words of Mary Magdalene, "They have taken away my Lord, and I know not where they have laid Him," the whole is signified by the part, for she spoke only of the flesh of Christ, which she thought had been taken away from the sepulchre in which it was buried; so too the whole is signified by the part when the word "flesh" is used but "man" is meant, as in the instances given above.

The ways in which the Divine Scriptures use the word "flesh," then, are very numerous, and it would take too long to examine and collect them all. Our present purpose is to discover the meaning of life "according to the flesh," which is clearly an evil, even though the nature of flesh is not evil in itself. Let us, then, diligently examine that passage in the epistle which the apostle Paul wrote to the Galatians, where he says:

> Now the works of the flesh are manifest, which are these; Adultery, fornication, uncleanness, lasciviousness, idolatry, witchcraft, hatred, variance, emulations, wrath, strife, seditions, heresies, envying, murders, drunkenness, revellings, and such like: of the which I tell you before, as I have also told you in time past, that they which do such things shall not inherit the kingdom of God.

If we give to the whole of this passage of the apostle's epistle as much consideration as our present question is found to require, we shall be able to solve the question of what it is to live according to the flesh. For among the "works of the flesh" which he says are "manifest," and which he enumerates and condemns, we find not only those which pertain to the pleasures of the flesh, such as fornication, uncleanness, lasciviousness, drunkenness and revellings, but also those which demonstrate vices of the mind and which have nothing to do with fleshly pleasure. For when it comes to idolatry, witchcraft, hatred, variance, emulations, wrath, strife, seditions, heresies: who does not see that these are vices of the mind rather than of the body? It may be, indeed, that a man tempers his desire for bodily pleasure out of devotion to an idol, or because of some heretical error. Even such a man as this, though he is seen to restrain and suppress the lusts of the flesh, is still convicted, on the authority of the apostle, of living according to the flesh; yet it is his very abstinence from the pleasures of the flesh that demonstrates that he is engaged in the damnable works of the flesh.

Who can feel hatred except in the mind? Would anyone, speaking to an enemy, or to someone who he thinks is his enemy, say, "Your flesh is ill disposed towards me," rather than "Your mind"? Finally, just as, if anyone heard of "carnalities" (if there were such a word), he would undoubtedly attribute them to the flesh [caro], so no one doubts that "animosities" pertain to the mind [animus]. Why, then, does the "teacher of the Gentiles in faith and verity" give the name "works of the flesh" to all these and similar failings? Simply because, using that figure of speech by which the whole is signified by a part, he intends the word "flesh" to be understood as meaning "man."

3. THE CAUSE OF SIN PROCEEDS FROM THE SOUL, NOT THE FLESH; AND THE CORRUPTION RESULTING FROM SIN IS NOT ITSELF A SIN, BUT A PUNISHMENT

Now someone may say that the flesh is the cause of moral evils of every kind, because it is thanks to the influence of the flesh that the soul lives as it does. But he who says this has not considered the whole nature of man with sufficient care. For "the corruptible body presseth down the soul." Hence also the apostle, speaking of this corruptible body, first says, "Our outward man perisheth," and then goes on to say,

> For we know that if our earthly house of this tabernacle were dissolved, we have a building of God, a house not made with hands, eternal in the heavens. For in this we groan, earnestly desiring to be clothed upon with our house which is from heaven: if so be that being clothed we shall not be found naked. For we that are in this tabernacle do groan, being burdened: not for that we would be unclothed, but clothed upon, that mortality might be swallowed up of life.

We are pressed down by the corruptible body, therefore, yet we know that the cause of our being pressed down is not the nature and substance of the body, but its corruption; and, knowing this, we do not wish to be divested of the body, but to be clothed with its immortality. For there will still be a body then; but, because it will not be corruptible, it will not be a burden. At the present time, therefore, "the corruptible body presseth down the soul, and the earthly tabernacle weigheth down the mind that museth upon many things." Nonetheless, those who suppose that the ills of the soul derive from the body are in error.

Virgil, it is true, seems to be expounding Platonic teaching in his magnificent verse when he says, "The force of those seeds is fiery, and their source is heavenly, to the extent that they are not impeded by harmful bodies nor enfeebled by earthly limbs and dying members." Also, he wishes us to understand that the body is the source of all four of the most notable disturbances of the mind: desire, fear, joy and grief, which are the origin, as it were, of all sins and vices. And so he adds: "Hence come desire and fear, gladness and sorrow; nor do they look up to heaven, but are confined in a dark and sightless cave." Our faith, however, is something very different. For the corruption of the body, which presseth down the soul, was not the cause of the first sin, but its punishment; nor was it corruptible flesh that made the soul sinful, but the sinful soul that made the flesh corruptible.

Thus, though this corruption of the flesh results in some incitements to sin and in sinful desires themselves, we still must not attribute to the flesh all the vices of a wicked life. Otherwise, we should absolve the devil from all such vices, since he has no flesh. Certainly, we cannot say that the devil is a fornicator or a drunkard, or that he commits any other such vice pertaining to the pleasures of the flesh, even though it is he who secretly tempts and incites us to such sins. He is, however, supremely proud and envious; and these vices of pride and envy have so possessed him that he is doomed by them to eternal punishment in the prison of this murky air of ours.

Now those vices which hold sway over the devil are attributed by the apostle to the flesh, even though it is certain that the devil does not have any flesh. For the apostle says that hatred, variance, jealousy, wrath and envy are works of the flesh; and the source and origin of all these evils is pride, which reigns in the devil even though he is without flesh. For who has more hatred for the saints than he? Who is found to be more at variance with them, or more wrathful towards them, or more jealous and envious of them? Yet he has all these faults without having flesh. How, then, can they be the "works of the flesh" other than because they are the works of man, to whom, as I have said, the apostle applies the term "flesh"?

It is not, then, by having flesh, which the devil does not have, that man has become like the devil. Rather, it is by living according to his own self; that is, according to man. For the devil chose to live according to self when he did not abide in the truth, so that the lie that he told was his own, and not God's. The devil is not only a liar; he is "the father of lies": he was, indeed, the first to lie, and falsehood, like sin, began with him.

28. Of the Quality of the Two Cities, the Earthly and the Heavenly

Two cities, then, have been created by two loves: that is, the earthly by love of self extending even to contempt of God, and the heavenly by love of God extending to contempt of self. The one, therefore, glories in itself, the other in the Lord; the one seeks glory from men, the other finds its highest glory in God, the Witness of our conscience. The one lifts up its head in its own glory; the other says to its God, "Thou art my glory, and the lifter up of mine head." In the Earthly City, princes are as much mastered by the lust for mastery as the nations which they subdue are by them; in the Heavenly, all serve one another in charity, rulers by their counsel and subjects by their obedience. The one city loves its own strength as displayed in its mighty men; the other says to its God, "I will love Thee, O Lord, my strength."

Thus, in the Earthly City, its wise men, who live according to man, have pursued the goods of the body or of their own mind, or both. Some of them who were able to know God "glorified Him not as God, neither were thankful; but became vain in their imagination, and their foolish heart was darkened. Professing themselves to be wise" (that is, exalting themselves in their wisdom, under the dominion of pride), "they became fools, and changed the glory of the incorruptible God into an image made like to corruptible man, and to birds, and four-footed beasts, and creeping things" (for in adoring images of this kind they were either the leaders of the people or their followers); "and they worshipped and served the creature more than the Creator, Who is blessed forever." In the Heavenly City, however, man has no wisdom beyond the piety which rightly worships the true God, and which looks for its reward in the fellowship not only of holy men, but of angels also, "that God may be all in all."

Discussion Questions

1. The apostle Paul condemned "the works of the flesh." According to Augustine, what does "the flesh" actually refer to in this context? Why is it difficult to discern what the Bible means when it refers to "the flesh"?

2. Why does Augustine disagree with those who think the soul is corrupted by inhabiting a fleshly body?

3. Augustine writes that "man has become like the devil." What does he mean by this? What do humans have in common with the devil?

The Freedom of a Christian

Martin Luther

Martin Luther published his treatise "The Freedom of a Christian" in 1520. Here, he lays out the idea of "justification by faith," arguing that Christians gain salvation by faith alone and not through "works" or adherence to God's laws. However, Luther clarifies that Christians willingly serve God and others. In 1530 the idea of justification by faith was encoded in the Augsburg Confession, written to explain the Protestant position.

To make the way smoother for the unlearned—for only them do I serve—I shall set down the following two propositions concerning the freedom and the bondage of the spirit:

A Christian is a perfectly free lord of all, subject to none.
A Christian is a perfectly dutiful servant of all, subject to all.

These two theses seem to contradict each other. If, however, they should be found to fit together they would serve our purpose beautifully. Both are Paul's own statements, who says in I Cor. 9, "For though I am free from all men, I have made myself a slave to all," and in Rom. 13, "Owe no one anything, except to love one another." Love by its very nature is ready to serve and be subject to him who is loved. So Christ, although he was Lord of all, was "born of woman, born under the law," and therefore was at the same time a free man and a servant, "in the form of God" and "of a servant."

Let us start, however, with something more remote from our subject, but more obvious. Man has a twofold nature, a spiritual and a bodily one. According to the spiritual nature, which men refer to as the soul, he is called a spiritual, inner, or new man. According to the bodily nature, which men refer to as flesh, he is called a carnal, outward, or old man, of whom the Apostle writes in II Cor. 4, "Though our outer nature is wasting away, our inner nature is being renewed every day." Because of this diversity of nature the Scriptures assert contradictory things concerning the same man, since these two men in the same man contradict each other, "for the desires of the flesh are against the Spirit, and the desires of the Spirit are against the flesh," according to Gal. 5.

First, let us consider the inner man to see how a righteous, free, and pious Christian, that is, a spiritual, new, and inner man, becomes what he is. It is evident that no external thing has any influence in producing Christian righteousness or freedom, or in producing unrighteousness or servitude. A simple argument will furnish the proof of this statement. What can it profit the soul if the body is well, free, and active, and eats, drinks, and does as it pleases? For in these respects even the most godless slaves of vice may prosper. On the other hand, how will poor health or imprisonment or hunger or thirst or any other external misfortune harm the soul? Even the most godly men, and those who are free because of clear consciences, are afflicted with these things. None of these things touch either the freedom or the servitude of the soul. It does not help the soul if the body is adorned with the sacred robes of priests or dwells in sacred places or is occupied with sacred duties or prays, fasts, abstains from certain kinds of food, or does any work that can be done by the body and in the body. The righteousness and the freedom of the soul require something far different since the things which have been mentioned could be done by any wicked person. Such works produce nothing but hypocrites. On the other hand, it will not harm the soul if the body is clothed in secular dress, dwells in unconsecrated places, eats and drinks as others do, does not pray aloud, and neglects to do all the above-mentioned things which hypocrites can do.

Furthermore, to put aside all kinds of works, even contemplation, meditation, and all that the soul can do, does not help. One thing, and only one thing, is necessary for Christian life, righteousness, and freedom. That one thing is the most holy Word of God, the gospel of Christ, as Christ says, John 11, "I am the resurrection and the life; he who believes in me, though he die, yet shall he live"; and John 8, "So if the Son makes you free, you will be free indeed"; and Matt. 4, "Man shall not live by bread alone, but by every word that proceeds from the mouth of God." Let us then consider it certain and firmly established that the soul can do without anything except the Word of God and that where the Word of God is missing there is no help at all for the soul. If it has the Word of God it is rich and lacks nothing since it is the Word of life, truth, light, peace, righteousness, salvation, joy, liberty, wisdom, power, grace, glory, and every incalculable blessing. This is why the prophet in the entire Psalm and in many other places yearns and sighs for the Word of God and uses so many names to describe it. On the other hand, there is no more terrible disaster with which the wrath of God can afflict men than a famine of the hearing of his Word, as he says in Amos. Likewise there is no greater mercy than when he sends forth his Word, as we read in Psalm 107: "He sent forth his word, and healed them, and delivered them from destruction." Nor was Christ sent into the world for any other ministry except that of the Word. Moreover, the entire spiritual estate—all the apostles, bishops, and priests—has been called and instituted only for the ministry of the Word.

You may ask, "What then is the Word of God, and how shall it be used, since there are so many words of God?" I answer: The Apostle explains this in Romans 1. The Word is the gospel of God concerning his Son, who was made flesh, suffered, rose from the dead, and was glorified through the Spirit who sanctifies. To preach Christ means to feed the soul, make it righteous, set it free, and save it, provided it believes the preaching. Faith alone is the saving and efficacious use of the Word of God, according to Rom. 10: "If you confess with your lips that Jesus is Lord and believe in your heart that God raised him from the dead, you will be saved." Furthermore, "Christ is the end of the law, that every one who has faith may be justified." Again, in Rom. 1, "He who through faith is righteous shall live." The Word of God cannot be received and cherished by any works whatever but only by faith. Therefore it is clear that, as the soul needs only the Word of God for its life and righteousness, so it is justified by faith alone and not any works; for if it could be justified by anything else, it would not need the Word, and consequently it would not need faith.

This faith cannot exist in connection with works—that is to say, if you at the same time claim to be justified by works, whatever their character—for that would be the same as "limping with two different opinions," as worshiping Baal and kissing one's own hand, which, as Job says, is a very great iniquity. Therefore the moment you begin to have faith you learn that all things in you are altogether blameworthy, sinful, and damnable, as the Apostle says in Rom. 3, "Since all have sinned and fall short of the glory of God," and, "None is righteous, no, not one; . . . all have turned aside, together they have gone wrong." . . . When you have learned this you will know that you need Christ, who suffered and rose again for you so that, if you believe in him, you may through this faith become a new man in so far as your sins are forgiven and you are justified by the merits of another, namely, of Christ alone.

Since, therefore, this faith can rule only in the inner man, as Rom. 10 says, "For man believes with his heart and so is justified," and since faith alone justifies, it is clear that the inner man cannot be justified, freed, or saved by any outer work or action at all, and that these works, whatever their character, have nothing to do with this inner man. On the other hand, only ungodliness and unbelief of heart, and no outer work, make him guilty and a damnable servant of sin. Wherefore it ought to be the first concern of every Christian to lay aside all confidence in works and increasingly to strengthen faith alone and through faith to grow in the knowledge, not of works, but of Christ Jesus, who suffered and rose for him, as Peter teaches in the last chapter of his first Epistle. . . . No other work makes a Christian. Thus when the Jews asked Christ, as related in John 6, what they must do "to be doing the work of God," he brushed aside the multitude of works which he saw they did in great profusion and suggested one work, saying, "This is the work of God, that you believe in him whom he has sent"; "for on him has God the Father set his seal." Therefore true faith in Christ is a treasure beyond comparison which brings with it complete salvation and saves man from every evil, as Christ says in the last chapter of Mark: "He who believes and is baptized will be saved; but he who does not believe will be condemned." Isaiah contemplated this treasure and foretold it in chapter 10: "The Lord will make a small and consuming word upon the land, and it will overflow with righteousness." This is as though he said, "Faith, which is a small and perfect fulfilment of the law, will fill believers with so great a righteousness that they will need nothing more to become righteous." So Paul says, Rom. 10, "For man believes with his heart and so is justified."

Should you ask how it happens that faith alone justifies and offers us such a treasure of great benefits without works in view of the fact that so many works, ceremonies, and laws are prescribed in the Scriptures, I answer: First of all, remember what has been said, namely, that faith alone, without works, justifies, frees, and saves; we shall make this clearer later on. Here we must point out that the entire Scripture of God is divided into two parts: commandments and promises. Although the commandments teach things that are good, the things taught are not done as soon as they are taught, for the commandments show us what we ought to do but do not give us the power to do it. They are intended to teach man to know himself, that through them he may recognize his inability to do good and may despair of his own ability. That is why they are called the Old Testament and constitute the Old Testament. For example, the commandment "You shall not covet" is a command which proves us all to be sinners, for no one can avoid coveting no matter how much he may struggle against it. Therefore, in order not to covet and to fulfil the commandment, a man is compelled to despair of himself, to seek the help which he does not find in himself elsewhere and from someone else, as stated in Hosea: "Destruction is your own, O Israel: your help is only in me." As we fare with respect to one commandment, so we fare with all, for it is equally impossible for us to keep any one of them.

Now when a man has learned through the commandments to recognize his helplessness and is distressed about how he might satisfy the law—since the law must be fulfilled so that not a jot or tittle shall be lost, otherwise man will be condemned without hope—then, being truly humbled and reduced to nothing in his own eyes, he finds in himself nothing whereby he may be justified and saved. Here the second part of Scripture comes to our aid, namely, the promises of God which declare the glory of God, saying, "If you wish to fulfil the law and not covet, as the law demands, come, believe in Christ in whom grace, righteousness, peace, liberty, and all things are promised you. If you believe, you shall have all things; if you do not believe, you shall lack all things." That which is impossible for you to accomplish by trying to fulfil all the works of the law—many and useless as they all are—you will accomplish quickly and easily through faith. God our Father has made all things depend on faith so that whoever has faith will have everything, and whoever does not have faith will have nothing. "For God has consigned all men to disobedience, that he may have mercy upon all," as it is stated in Rom. 11. Thus the promises of God give what the commandments of God demand and fulfil what the law prescribes so that all things may be God's alone, both the commandments and the fulfilling of the commandments. He alone commands, he alone fulfils. Therefore the promises of God belong to the New Testament. Indeed, they are the New Testament.

Since these promises of God are holy, true, righteous, free, and peaceful words, full of goodness, the soul which clings to them with a firm faith will be so closely united with them and altogether absorbed by them that it not only will share in all their power but will be saturated and intoxicated by them. If a touch of Christ healed, how much more will this most tender spiritual touch, this absorbing of the Word, communicate to the soul all things that belong to the Word. This, then, is how through faith alone without works the soul is justified by the Word of God, sanctified, made true, peaceful, and free, filled with every blessing and truly made a child of God, as John 1 says: "But to all who . . . believed in his name, he gave power to become children of God."

From what has been said it is easy to see from what source faith derives such great power and why a good work or all good works together cannot equal it. No good work can rely upon the Word of God or live in the soul, for faith alone and the Word of God rule in the soul. Just as the heated iron glows like fire because of the union of fire with it, so the Word imparts its qualities to the soul. It is clear, then, that a Christian has all that he needs in faith and needs no works to justify him; and if he has no need of works, he has no need of the law; and if he has no need of the law, surely he is free from the law. It is true that "the law is not laid down for the just." This is that Christian liberty, our faith, which does not induce us to live in idleness or wickedness but makes the law and works unnecessary for any man's righteousness and salvation.

✦ ✦ ✦

Let this suffice concerning the inner man, his liberty, and the source of his liberty, the righteousness of faith. He needs neither laws nor good works but, on the contrary, is injured by them if he believes that he is justified by them.

Now let us turn to the second part, the outer man. Here we shall answer all those who, offended by the word "faith" and by all that has been said, now ask, "If faith does all things and is alone sufficient unto righteousness, why then are good works commanded? We will take our ease and do no works and be content with faith." I answer: not so, you wicked men, not so. That would indeed be proper if we were wholly inner and perfectly spiritual men. But such we shall be only at the last day, the day of the resurrection of the dead. As long as we live in the flesh we only begin to make some progress in that which shall be perfected in the future life. For this reason the Apostle in Rom. 8 calls all that we attain in this life "the first fruits of the Spirit" because we shall indeed receive the greater portion, even the fulness of the Spirit, in the future. This is the place to assert that which was said above, namely, that a Christian is the servant of all and made subject to all. Insofar as he is free he does no works, but insofar as he is a servant he does all kinds of works. How this is possible we shall see.

Although, as I have said, a man is abundantly and sufficiently justified by faith inwardly, in his spirit, and so has all that he needs, except insofar as this faith and these riches must grow from day to day even to the future life; yet he remains in this mortal life on earth. In this life he must control his own body and have dealings with men. Here the works begin; here a man cannot enjoy leisure; here he must indeed take care to discipline his body by fastings, watchings, labors, and other reasonable discipline and to subject it to the Spirit so that it will obey and conform to the inner man and faith and not revolt against faith and hinder the inner man, as it is the nature of the body to do if it is not held in check. The inner man, who by faith is created in the image of God, is both joyful and happy because of Christ in whom so many benefits are conferred upon him; and therefore it is his one occupation to serve God joyfully and without thought of gain, in love that is not constrained.

Discussion Questions

1. How is it possible that Christians are simultaneously "subject to none" and "subject to all?" What is Luther's basis for claiming that both these statements must be true?

2. According to Luther, what is the purpose of the commandments in the Old Testament if Christians are not justified by obeying these commandments?

3. After saying that Christians are not justified by works, Luther goes on to say that Christians must use fasting and other techniques to discipline their bodies. Is this a contradiction or not?

Exemplar 1

Apartheid's "Final Solution"
NOBEL LECTURE 1984
Desmond Tutu

Desmond Tutu was born to a Xhosa family in South Africa in 1931. He was ordained an Anglican priest in 1960 and went on to become the archbishop of Cape Town, becoming the first black head of the Anglican Church in South Africa. Tutu was a fierce opponent of apartheid—South Africa's institutionalized system of racial segregation. He was also a central figure in reconciliation between black and white South Africans after this system ended. The following selection is from his speech about receiving a Nobel Peace Prize in 1984.

Your Majesty, members of the Royal Family, Mr. Chairman, ladies and gentlemen:

Before I left South Africa, a land I love passionately, we had an emergency meeting of the executive committee of the South African Council of Churches with the leaders of our member churches. We called the meeting because of the deepening crisis in our land, which has claimed nearly two hundred lives this year alone. We visited some of the trouble spots on the Witwatersrand. I went with others to the East Rand. We visited the home of an old lady. She told us that she looked after her grandson and the children of neighbors while their parents were at work. One day the police chased some pupils who had been boycotting classes, but they disappeared between the township houses. The police drove down the old lady's street. She was sitting at the back of the house in her kitchen, while her charges were playing in the yard in front of the house. Her daughter rushed into the house, calling out to her to come quickly. The old lady dashed out of the kitchen into the living room. Her grandson had fallen just inside the door, dead. He had been shot in the back by the police. He was six years old. A few weeks later, a white mother, trying to register her black servant for work, drove through a black township. Black rioters stoned her car and killed her baby of a few months old, the first white casualty of the current unrest in South Africa. Such deaths are two too many. These are part of the high cost of apartheid.

Every day in a squatter camp near Cape Town called KTC, the authorities have been demolishing flimsy plastic shelters which black mothers have erected because they were taking their marriage vows seriously. They have been reduced to sitting on soaking mattresses, with their household effects strewn round their feet, and whimpering babies on their laps, in the cold Cape winter rain. Every day the authorities have carried out these callous demolitions. What heinous crime have these women committed, to be hounded like criminals in this manner? All they have wanted is to be with their husbands, the fathers of their children. Everywhere else in the world they would be highly commended, but in South Africa, a land which claims to be Christian and which boasts a public holiday called Family Day, these gallant women are treated so inhumanely. Yet all they want is to have a decent and stable family life. Unfortunately, in the land of their birth it is a criminal offense for them to live happily with their husbands and the fathers of their children. Black family life is thus being undermined, not accidentally but by deliberate government policy. It is part of the price human beings, God's children, are called to pay for apartheid. An unacceptable price.

I come from a beautiful land, richly endowed by God with wonderful natural resources, wide expanses, rolling mountains, singing birds, bright shining stars out of blue skies, with radiant sunshine, golden sunshine. There is enough of the good things that come from God's bounty, there is enough for everyone, but apartheid has confirmed some in their selfishness, causing them to grasp greedily a disproportionate share, the lion's share, because of their power. They have taken 87 percent of the land, though being only about 20 percent of our population. The rest have had to make do with the remaining 13 percent. Apartheid has decreed the politics of exclusion: 73 percent of the population is excluded from any meaningful participation in the political decision-making processes of the land of their birth. The new constitution, making provision for three chambers, for whites, Coloreds and Indians, mentions blacks only once and thereafter ignores them completely. Thus this new constitution, lauded in parts of the West as a step in the right direction, entrenches racism and ethnicity. The constitutional committees are composed in the ratio of four whites to two Coloreds to one Indian—zero black. . . . Hence this constitution perpetuates by law and entrenches white minority rule.

Blacks are expected to exercise their political ambitions in unviable, poverty-stricken, and bantustan homelands, ghettos of misery, inexhaustible reservoirs of cheap black labor, bantustans into which South Africa is being balkanized. Blacks are systematically being stripped of their South African citizenship and being turned into aliens in the land of their birth. This is apartheid's final solution, just as Nazism had its final solution for the Jews in Hitler's Aryan madness. The South African government is smart. Aliens can claim but very few rights, least of all political rights.

In pursuance of apartheid's ideological racist dream, over three million of God's children have been uprooted from their homes, which have been demolished, while they have been dumped in the bantustan homeland resettlement camps. I say dumped advisedly: only rubbish or things are dumped, not human beings. Apartheid has, however, ensured that God's children, just because they are black, should be treated as if they were things and not as of infinite value as being created in the image of God. These dumping grounds are far from where work and food can be procured easily. Children starve, suffer from the often irreversible consequences of malnutrition. This happens to them not accidentally but by deliberate government policy. They starve in a land that could be the bread basket of Africa, a land that normally is a net exporter of food.

The father leaves his family in the bantustan homeland, there eking out a miserable existence, while he, if he is lucky, goes to the so-called white man's town as a migrant, to live an unnatural life in a single-sex hostel for eleven months, being prey there to drunkenness, prostitution and worse. This migratory labor policy is declared government policy and has been condemned as a cancer in our society even by the white Dutch Reformed Church—not noted for being quick to criticize the government. This cancer, eating away at the vitals of black family life, is deliberate government policy. It is part of the cost of apartheid, exorbitant in terms of human suffering.

✦ ✦ ✦

Once a Zambian and a South African, it is said, were talking. The Zambian boasted about their Minister of Naval Affairs. The South African asked, "But you have no navy, no access to the sea. How then can you have a Minister of Naval

Affairs?" The Zambian retorted: "Well, in South Africa you have a Minister of Justice, don't you?"

It is against this system that our people have sought to protest peacefully since 1912 at least, with the founding of the African National Congress. They have used the conventional methods of peaceful protest—petitions, demonstrations, deputations and even a passive resistance campaign. A tribute to our people's commitment to peaceful change is the fact that the only South Africans to win the Nobel Peace Prize are both black. Our people are peace-loving to a fault. The response of the authorities has been an escalating intransigence and violence, the violence of police dogs, tear gas, detention without trial, exile, and even death. Our people protested peacefully against the pass laws in 1960, and 69 of them were killed on March 21, 1960, at Sharpeville, many shot in the back running away. Our children protested against inferior education, singing songs and displaying placards and marching peacefully. Many in 1976, on June 16 and subsequent times, were killed or imprisoned. Over 500 people died in that uprising. Many children went into exile. The whereabouts of many are unknown to their parents. At present, to protest that self-same discriminatory education and the exclusion of blacks from the new constitutional dispensation, the sham local black government, rising unemployment, increased rents and General Sales Tax, our people have boycotted and demonstrated. They have staged a successful two-day stay-away. Over 150 people have been killed. It is far too high a price to pay. There has been little revulsion or outrage in the West at this wanton destruction of human life.

✦ ✦ ✦

There is no peace in Southern Africa. There is no peace because there is no justice. There can be no real peace and security until there be first justice enjoyed by all the inhabitants of that beautiful land. The Bible knows nothing about peace without justice, for that would be crying, "Peace, peace, where there is no peace." God's shalom, peace, involves inevitably righteousness, justice, wholeness, fullness of life, participation in decision making, goodness, laughter, joy, compassion, sharing and reconciliation.

I have spoken extensively about South Africa, first because it is the land I know best, but because it is also a microcosm of the world and an example of what is to be found in other lands in differing degree—when there is injustice, invariably peace becomes a casualty. In El Salvador, in Nicaragua and elsewhere in Latin America, there have been repressive regimes which have aroused opposition in those countries. Fellow citizens are pitted against one another, sometimes attracting the unhelpful attention and interest of outside powers, who want to extend their spheres of influence. We see this in the Middle East, in Korea, in the Philippines, in Kampuchea, in Vietnam, in Ulster, in Afghanistan, in Mozambique, in Angola, in Zimbabwe, behind the Iron Curtain.

Because there is global insecurity, nations are engaged in a mad arms race, spending billions of dollars wastefully on instruments of destruction, when millions are starving. And yet, just a fraction of what is expended so obscenely on defense budgets would make the difference in enabling God's children to fill their stomachs, be educated and given the chance to lead fulfilled and happy lives. We have the capacity to feed ourselves several times over but we are daily haunted by the spectacle of the gaunt dregs of humanity shuffling along in endless queues, with bowls to collect what the charity of the world has provided, too little too late. When will we learn, when will the people of the world get up and say, enough is enough? God created us for fellowship. God created us so that we should form the human family, existing together because we were made for one another. We are not made for an exclusive self-sufficiency but for interdependence, and we break that law of our being at our peril. When will we learn that an escalating arms race merely escalates global insecurity? We are now much closer to a nuclear holocaust than when our technology and our spending were less.

Unless we work assiduously so that all of God's children, our brothers and sisters, members of our one human family, enjoy the basic human rights, the right to a fulfilled life, the right of movement, the freedom to be fully human within a humanity measured by nothing less than the humanity of Jesus Christ himself, then we are on the road inexorably to self-destruction, we are not far from global suicide. And yet it could be so different.

When will we learn that human beings are of infinite value because they have been created in the image of God, that it is blasphemy to treat them as if they were less than this, and to do so ultimately recoils on those who do this? In dehumanizing others, they are themselves dehumanized. Perhaps oppression dehumanizes the oppressor as much as, if not more than, the oppressed. They need each other to become truly free, to become human. We can be human only in fellowship, in community, in koinonia, in peace.

Let us work to be peacemakers, those given a wonderful share in our Lord's ministry of reconciliation. If we want peace, so we have been told, let us work for justice. Let us beat our swords into plowshares.

God calls us to be fellow workers with him so that we can extend his kingdom of shalom, of justice, of goodness, of compassion, of caring, of sharing, of laughter, joy and reconciliation, so that the kingdoms of this world will become the Kingdom of our God and of his Christ, and he shall reign for ever and ever. Amen. Then there will be fulfillment of the wonderful vision in the Revelation of St. John the Divine [Revelation 7:9ff].

1. How does it change the way we think about social problems if we think of humans as children of God and human beings as made in God's image?

2. Desmond Tutu invokes the book of Jeremiah, where God accuses Israel of saying, "Peace, peace, where there is no peace." What do people not understand about peace, according to Tutu?

3. Christianity is sometimes described as an otherworldly religion that emphasizes the afterlife and kingdom of God, rather than the world we currently inhabit. For Tutu, what is the relationship between the kingdoms of this world and the kingdom of God?

Exemplar 2

From *The Duty of Delight*
Dorothy Day

Dorothy Day (1897–1980) was born to an Episcopalian family in New York City but converted to Catholicism in 1927. In 1933 she and Peter Maurin cofounded the Catholic Worker Movement, a group that promoted Catholic teaching on social justice as well as pacifism. Day's group operated houses of hospitality that served the poor and published a newspaper, the *Catholic Worker*, that was sold for the symbolic price of one penny. In 2000 Pope John Paul II allowed Day to be declared "a servant of God," the first step toward becoming canonized as a saint. Day kept a diary throughout her life. In the following excerpt she ponders Christian attitudes toward money and government after her paper had to pay taxes on a $55,000 donation. (The Catholic Worker Movement chose not to register as a charitable organization.)

Money, a topic of vital interest to man. Like sex or food, it can be made subject of intense interest. How to get it, how to spend it. Men at highest level—enormous salary, enormous expenses. Tales of corruption in high places always involve money. [Abe] Fortas takes retaining fees to protect a client and is disgraced publicly. Disgraced and discredited.

Dwight Macdonald wrote once that a foundation was a large body of money surrounded by people, all of whom were trying to get some of it.

Foundations are tax-free, and the less powerful are now being investigated.

When gangsters, now called Mafiosi, are being convicted it is often on charge of evading income tax—not on charge of extortion, murder, blackmail, drug trafficking, white slave traffic. The love of money is the root of all evil. Whence come wars among you? Each one seeking his own. People are secretive about money—how much they have, where it came from, inherited, earned? How closely it is tied up to work—hard work, work that is for the common good.

What are students learning in colleges and universities? To work for the common good, to contribute to the common good, or to get the degrees which will entitle them to enter ever-higher fields of learning and recompense.

What vast fields of knowledge there are which relate to man's need for a good life, for the food, clothing, and shelter man needs to lead a good life.

"A certain amount of goods is necessary to lead a good life," St. Thomas Aquinas writes. How much goods? How much land does a man need? What do men live for?

These are questions which preoccupied Tolstoy and about which he wrote so much.

What was the attitude of Jesus toward money? (Judas was the one who held the purse, who betrayed him for money and then threw the money away. He was playing for greater stakes—power, world domination perhaps.)

"Take no thought for what ye shall eat or drink or wear. Your Father knows you have need of these things. Be like little children. Trust. Ask and you shall receive. If a child ask for bread will his father give him a stone? If he ask for fish, will he hand him a scorpion? Take no money on your journey. Do not lay up for yourselves treasures on earth." Do you need money for paying taxes? And here Jesus does something fantastic, like something out of a fairytale. He doesn't tell Peter to go to Judas to get the money. He tells him to go fishing and open the mouth of the first fish he catches and take out the coin he will find there and pay the tribute "lest thou should offend them."

Render to Caesar the things that are Caesar's but the less you have of Caesar the less you have to give him. Jesus was living in an occupied country. At the moment it was peacetime, a Pax Romana. It was Law and Order, Roman law and order, with a standing army to keep the peace. Jesus was not concerned with joining the resistance. He was laying down principles that made for true peace. They could take it or leave it. He forced no man. But he did try to arouse in man that hunger and thirst for "living water," for the abundant life, for the joy that no man can take from you, for the "unspeakable gift" which so many have caught a vision of and have tried to communicate to others.

All this ruminating is because the Catholic Worker has been left $55,000 in a will. People are so cautious and secretive about money that I cannot write about the other legatees, just about ourselves. There were many claims to the will. Servants, friends, isolated missionaries were all left gifts, furniture was given to museums, pets were given to friends to care for, together with money to support them, and the residue of the estate was to be divided between Catholic institutions, charitable institutions, of which we are one.

And now it is a question of taxes to be paid on this inheritance. Are we, or are we not a charitable institution? There was no question about the 4 others. They were accredited institutions, money that came to them could not be taxed. Accredited by the State. The State agreed that money for the poor was exempt from taxation. It was holy. It was on another plane, another level, on another dimension. You entered another realm when you dealt with this money. You dealt with a fairyland. You had gone thru the looking glass like Alice, or thru the wardrobe like the children in the C. S. Lewis stories.

But we—the lawyers of the State decided—were living in this world as well as in the next. When we acted as tho all men were really brothers, as though "all the way to heaven is heaven" because Jesus Christ had said "I am the Way" and we were trying to "put on Christ" as St. Paul advised, and "put off the old man," and really act "as if we loved one another," "as if" our brother, our loved one, was the man on the Bowery, Skid Row, or prison, or prison camp, or battlefield; "as if" the Chinese, Soviets, North and South Vietnamese, Cubans, are truly our brothers, children of one Father, one Creator, maker of Heaven and earth, the moon and stars which we are exploring now—Oh God how wonderful are all Thy works.

Discussion Questions

1. In her diary entry, Day conflates and paraphrases a number of statements Jesus makes in the Bible regarding money. Jesus instructs his disciples not to worry about material needs but also emphasizes that everyone must feed their own child. Do Jesus's teachings contain coherent instructions for how Christians should think about money? Or are they contradictory?

2. Does Day seem resentful that her newspaper the *Catholic Worker* must pay taxes to the government or not?

3. What does Day mean when she says that her organization operates in two worlds simultaneously, while normal, tax-exempt religious organizations operate in only one?

Controversy

Weird Babel of Tongues

Although speaking in tongues is still considered strange by many Christians in North America, roughly a quarter of the world's 2 billion Christians are either Pentecostals or charismatics. The birth of Pentecostalism is sometimes traced to a church at 312 Azusa Street in Los Angeles, where in 1906 a black preacher named William J. Seymour began holding marathon services that involved speaking in tongues, divine healing, and other "gifts of the holy spirit." Seymour's congregation was racially mixed during the height of segregation in America. The "Azusa Street Revival" foreshadowed contemporary trends in Christianity: Christianity is booming in the Global South and Pentecostalism is becoming increasingly mainstream. However, these trends are still met with resistance by those who do not recognize speaking in tongues as "real" Christianity and who may be reluctant to accept that the future of Christianity is being forged in Africa, Asia, and South America. The article below is a famous "hit piece" that seeks to paint the Azusa Street revival as a parody of Christianity and invokes racist attitudes toward the congregation.

New Sect of Fanatics Is Breaking Loose.

✦ ✦ ✦

Wild Scene Last Night on Azusa Street.

✦ ✦ ✦

Gurgle of Wordless Talk by a Sister.

Breathing strange utterances and mouthing a creed which it would seem no sane mortal could understand, the newest religious sect has started in Los Angeles. Meetings are held in a tumble-down shack on Azusa street, near San Pedro street, and the devotees of the weird doctrine practice the most fanatical rites, preach the wildest theories and work themselves into a state of mad excitement in their peculiar zeal.

Colored people and a sprinkling of whites compose the congregation, and night is made hideous in the neighborhood by the howlings of the worshipers, who spend hours swaying forth and back in a nerve-racking attitude of prayer and supplication. They claim to have "the gift of tongues," and to be able to comprehend the babel.

Such a startling claim has never yet been made by any company of fanatics, even in Los Angeles, the home of almost numberless creeds. Sacred tenets, reverently mentioned by the orthodox believer, are dealt with in a familiar, if not irreverent, manner by these latest religionists.

Stony Optic Defies

An old colored exhorter, blind in one eye, is the major-domo of the company. With his stony optic fixed on some luckless unbeliever, the old man yells his defiance and challenges an answer. Anathemas are heaped upon him who shall dare to gainsay the utterances of the preacher.

Clasped in his big fist the colored brother holds a miniature Bible from which he reads at intervals one or two words—never more. After an hour spent in exhortation the brethren present are invited to join in a "meeting of prayer, song and testimony." Then it is that pandemonium breaks loose, and the bounds of reason are passed by those who are "filled with the spirit," whatever that may be.

"You-oo-oo gou-loo-loo come under the bloo-oo-oo boo-loo," shouts an old colored "mammy," in a frenzy of religious zeal. Swinging her arms wildly about her she continues with the strangest harangue ever uttered. Few of her words are intelligible, and for the most part her testimony contains the most outrageous jumble of syllables, which are listened to with awe by the company.

"Let Tongues Come Forth"

One of the wildest of the meetings was held last night, and the highest pitch of excitement was reached by the gathering, which continued in "worship" until nearly midnight. The old exhorter urged the "sisters" to let the "tongues come forth" and the women gave themselves over to a riot of religious fervor. As a result a buxom dame was overcome with excitement and almost fainted.

Undismayed by the fearful attitude of the colored worshiper, another black woman jumped to the floor and began a wild gesticulation, which ended in a gurgle of wordless prayers which were nothing less than shocking.

"She's speakin' in unknown tongues," announced the leader, in an awed whisper. "Keep on, sister." The sister continued until it was necessary to assist her to a seat because of her bodily fatigue.

Gold among Them

Among the "believers" is a man who claims to be a Jewish rabbi. He says his name is Gold, and claims to have held positions in some of the largest synagogues in the United States. He told the motley company last night that he is well known to the Jewish people of Los Angeles and San Francisco, and referred to prominent local citizens by name. Gold claims to have been miraculously healed and is a convert of the new sect.

Another speaker had a vision in which he saw the people of Los Angeles flocking in a mighty stream to perdition. He prophesied awful destruction to this city unless its citizens are brought to a belief in the tenets of the new faith.

Discussion Questions

1. The author of the article makes heavy use of adjectives such as "weird," "fanatical," "peculiar," and so on to shape how the reader thinks about the church on Azusa Street. What other word choices or rhetorical devices are used to create the impression that this group is not really what it purports to be—a Christian church?

2. The author reports that Los Angeles has "almost numberless creeds." Why, then, is this one church worth reporting on? What about this church might make it especially upsetting to the author?

3. By reading this article critically, can you make an educated guess as to what was *actually* going on at this church?

Islam

In Islam the human problem is not sin, but pride. Pride entails not only a failure to submit to God and God's laws but also a failure to remember that God alone is self-sufficient. While the Arabic word *shirk* is often translated as idolatry, it conveys an idea of treating anything as if it were equal to God, including one's own desires and ambitions. Ibn Al-Kalbi's *The Book of Idols* represents an attempt by a classical Muslim historian to understand how the Arabs first forgot how to submit to God and became idolaters, resulting in the age of *Jahiliyah* or "the time of ignorance" before Islam.

The solution to pride is submission, including following the traditions of Islam and the laws of the Quran. In a letter sent from Saudi Arabia in 1964, Malcolm X describes going on the hajj, one of the five pillars of Islam and a requirement of the religion. For Malcolm X, a recent convert to "orthodox" Islam, the experience of the hajj offered hope that Islam was the answer to the problem of racism that he had spent his career combating.

Muhammad is the prime exemplar in Islam as the ideal human and the seal of the prophets. While Islam is clear that Muhammad was only a man, the story of his life is rendered more extraordinary in the *hadith*, or the tradition of sayings attributed to the Prophet. A key example of the hadith concerns Muhammad's mystical "night journey," in which he was taken first to Jerusalem and then through the seven layers of heaven where he met the prophets who preceded him, including Adam, Jesus, and Moses. These figures are also Muslim exemplars in that they submitted to God's will.

Sufism is a mystical tradition within Islam. While Sufis also follow Islamic law, the emphasis is shifted from legal, theological, and political considerations in favor of ascetic traditions intended to cultivate a profound love for God. Sufi exemplars include sheiks who have attained a degree of mystical understanding that can be transmitted to their disciples. Rabia of Basra was a Sufi mystic who was praised for her mystical connection to God that often manifested as seemingly outrageous statements and actions. Rabia's piousness was admired enough that sayings attributed to her were collected by the Muslim writer Abu 'Abd ar-Rahman as-Sulami.

Western critics of Islam often claim that Islam is oppressive to women, citing laws of women in nations such as Saudi Arabia and a passage from the Quran (4:34) that appears to condone beating one's wife under certain circumstances. Muslim feminists have countered that Islam expanded the rights of women of Arabia, citing such reforms as recognizing marriage as a contract between husband and wife and allowing women to inherit property. Furthermore, they have argued that misogynistic practices within Islam are essentially a corruption of Muhammad's original message. Shedding some light on this controversy is an excerpt from *The Veil and the Male Elite* by Muslim feminist author Fatima Mernissi. Mernissi examines how Muhammad received some of his most important revelations concerning gender during a period when the fledgling Muslim community was still at war with Mecca and the daily realities of warfare influenced early discussions about the equality of women.

Problem/Solution

From *The Book of Idols*

The period in the Arabian Peninsula before the time of Muhammad is remembered in Islam as *Jahiliyah*, or "the time of ignorance." Before Islam, Arabs made pilgrimages to Mecca not to honor Allah, but a pantheon of tribal gods. The traditional Muslim view is that the rituals of the hajj were first practiced by Abraham and Ishmael, but that the Arabs slowly forgot about monotheism and became idolaters until Muhammad restored worship to its original state. The three goddesses described here—Allāt, al-'Uzza, and Manat—were particularly beloved in pagan Mecca. Ibn Al-Kalbi, an eighth-century Arab historian, delved into Arabia's pagan past. His account depicts a Muslim concern that it is possible to gradually replace the worship of God with idolatry through such simple practices as keeping a stone to remind one of Mecca. There is also a sense here that idolatry is related to the problem of pride. Al-Kalbi cites the Quran where God says of the three goddesses: "These are mere names; ye and your fathers named them thus." If idols are just human creations, then worshipping them amounts to a form of human self-reliance that ignores God. This view was echoed by the poet Rumi, who stated that "the idol of your self is the mother of idols."

Hisham ibn-Muhammad al-Kalbi said: I was informed by my father and others, and I personally checked and ascertained their report, that when Ishmael, the son of Abraham, settled in Mecca, he begot many children. [Their descendants] multiplied so much that they crowded the city and supplanted its original inhabitants, the Amalekites. Later on Mecca became overcrowded with them, and dissension and strife arose among them, causing them to fight among themselves and consequently be dispersed throughout the land where they roamed seeking a livelihood.

The reason which led them to the worship of images and stones was the following: No one left Mecca without carrying away with him a stone from the stones of the Sacred House (al-Haram) as a token of reverence to it, and as a sign of deep affection to Mecca. Wherever he settled he would erect that stone and circumambulate it in the same manner he used to circumambulate the Ka'bah[1] [before his departure from Mecca], seeking thereby its blessing and affirming his deep affection for the Sacred House. In fact, the Arabs still venerate the Ka'bah and Mecca and journey to them in order to perform the pilgrimage and visitation, conforming thereby to the time-honored custom which they inherited from Abraham and Ishmael.

In time this led them to the worship of whatever took their fancy, and caused them to forget their former worship. They exchanged the religion of Abraham and Ishmael for another. Consequently they took to the worship of images, becoming like the nations before them. They sought and determined what the people of Noah had worshipped of these images and adopted the worship of those which were still remembered among them. Among these devotional practices were some which came down from the time of Abraham and Ishmael, such as the veneration of the House and its circumambulation, the pilgrimage, the visitation or the lesser pilgrimage (al-'umrah), the vigil (al-wuquf) on 'Arafah and [al-]Muzdalifah,[2] sacrificing she-camels, and raising the voice in the acclamation of the name of the deity (tahlil) at the pilgrimage and the visitation, introducing thereinto things not belonging to it. Thus whenever the Nizar[3] raised their voice in the tahlil, they were wont to say:

"Here we are O Lord! Here we are! Here we are!
Thou hast no associate save one who is thine.
Thou hast dominion over him and over what he possesseth."

---

1 Also spelled Kaaba. Literally, "the Cube," a stone shrine in Mecca—according to tradition, built by Abraham—that became the most important site in Islam (Muslims around the world face it when they pray). It is also called "the Sacred House," and as part of the required pilgrimage to Mecca, worshippers walk around it seven times.
2 Two locations near Mecca. Muslim pilgrims stand on the plain of 'Arafah during the second day of the pilgrimage, praying to God for forgiveness, and next stop in Muzdalifah for a night to perform other rites of the pilgrimage.
3 A tribal group in northern Arabia.

They would thus declare His unity through the talbiyah,[4] and at the same time associate their gods with Him, placing their affairs in His hands. Consequently, God said to His Prophet, "And most of them believe not in God, without also associating other deities with Him."[5] In other words, they would not declare His unity through the knowledge of His rightful dues, without associating with Him some of His own creatures.

✦ ✦ ✦

Manah

The most ancient of all these idols was Manah. The Arabs used to name [their children] ʿAbd-Manah and Zayd-Manah.[6] Manah was erected on the seashore in the vicinity of al-Mushallal in Qudayd, between Medina and Mecca. All the Arabs used to venerate her and sacrifice before her. [In particular] the Aws and the Khazraj,[7] as well as the inhabitants of Medina and Mecca and their vicinities, used to venerate Manah, sacrifice before her, and bring unto her their offerings.

The children of the Maʿadd were followers of a faith which still preserved a little of the religion of Ishmael. The Rabiʿah and the Mukar,[8] too, were followers of a similar faith. But none venerated her more than the Aws and the Khazraj.

Abu-al-Mundhir Hisham ibn-Muhammad said: I was told by a man from the Quraysh,[9] on the authority of abu-ʿUbaydah ʿAbdullah ibn-abi-ʿUbaydahibn-ʿAmmar ibn-Yasir[10] who was the best informed man on the subject of the Aws and the Khazraj, that the Aws and the Khazraj, as well as those Arabs among the people of Yathrib[11] and other places who took to their way of life, were wont to go on pilgrimage and observe the vigil at all the appointed places, but not shave their heads. At the end of the pilgrimage, however, when they were about to return home, they would set out to the place where Manah stood, shave their heads, and stay there a while. They did not consider their pilgrimage completed until they visited Manah. Because of this veneration of Manah by the Aws and the Khazraj, ʿAbd-al-ʿUzza ibn-Wadiʿah al-Muzani, or some other Arab, said:

"An oath, truthful and just, I swore
By Manah, at the sacred place of the Khazraj."

---

4 A prayer of greeting to the deity.
5 Quran 12:106.
6 Literally, Servant of Manah and Abundance of Manah.
7 Two tribes of southern Arabia.
8 Three northern Arabian tribes.
9 The tribe that ruled Mecca in Muhammad's time.
10 A *hadith* relater (d. 785).
11 Former name of Medina.

During the Jahiliyah[12] days, the Arabs were wont to call both the Aws and the Khazraj by the single generic name, al-Khazraj. For this reason the poet said, "at the sacred place of the Khazraj."

This Manah is that which God mentioned when He said, "And Manah, the third idol besides."[13] She was the [goddess] of the Hudhayl and the Khuza'ah.[14]

The Quraysh as well as the rest of the Arabs continued to venerate Manah until the Apostle of God set out from Medina in the eighth year of the Hijrah, the year in which God accorded him the victory.[15] When he was at a distance of four or five nights from Medina, he dispatched 'Ali[16] to destroy her. 'Ali demolished her, took away all her [treasures], and carried them back to the Prophet. Among the treasures which 'Ali carried away were two swords which had been presented to [Manah] by al-Harith ibn-abi-Shamir al-Ghassani, the king of Ghassan.[17] The one sword was called Mikhdham and the other Rasub. They are the two swords of al-Harith which 'Alqamah[18] mentions in one of his poems. He said:

> "Wearing two coats of mail as well as
> Two studded swords, Mikhdham and Rajub."

The Prophet gave these two swords to 'Ali. It is, therefore, said that dhu-al-Faqar, the sword of 'Ali, was one of them.

It is also said that 'Ali found these two swords in [the temple of] al-Fals, the idol of the Tayyi',[19] whither the Prophet had sent him, and which he also destroyed.

Allāt

They then adopted Allāt as their goddess. Allāt stood in al-Ta'if,[20] and was more recent than Manah. She was a cubic rock beside which a certain Jew used to prepare his barley porridge (sawiq). Her custody was in the hands of the banu-'Attab ibn-Malik of the Thaqif,[21] who had built an edifice over her. The Quraysh, as well as all the Arabs, were wont to venerate Allāt. They also used to name their children after her, calling them Zayd-Allāt and Taym-Allāt.[22] She stood in the place of the left-

---

12 The age of ignorance (the literal meaning of *Jahiliyah*); that is, the time before Islam.
13 Quran 53:20.
14 Two tribes living near Mecca.
15 That is, the conquest of Mecca in 630.
16 'Ali ibn Abi Talib (ca. 599–661), the Prophet's cousin and son-in-law, who became the fourth caliph.
17 An Arab Christian kingdom in present-day Syria and Jordan, conquered by the Muslims in the seventh century.
18 Pre-Islamic Arab poet (sixth century), associated with the Ghassanid court.
19 A prominent pre-Islamic Arab tribe.
20 A city fifty miles east of Mecca. Some scholars think that the name al-Lat is derived from a verb for the mixing of barley and that mixing barley was part of a pre-Islamic ritual that took place near the "cubic rock" mentioned here, which eventually took on the name al-Lat.
21 The main tribe of al-Ta'if, who opposed Muhammad. "Banu": children of.
22 Servant of Allāt.

hand side minaret of the present-day mosque of al-Ta'if. She is the idol which God mentioned when He said, "Have you seen Allāt and al-'Uzza?"[23] It was this same Allāt which 'Amr ibn-al-Ju'ayd[24] had in mind when he said:

"In forswearing wine I am like him who hath abjured Allāt,
    although he had been at one time her devotee."

Likewise it was the same idol to which al-Mutalammis alluded in his satire of 'Amr ibn-al-Mundhir[25] when he said:

"Thou hast banished me for fear of lampoon and satire.
    No! By Allāt and all the sacred baetyls[26] (anjab), thou
        shalt not escape."

Allāt continued to be venerated until the Thaqif embraced Islam, when the Apostle of God dispatched al-Mughirah ibn-Shu'bah,[27] who destroyed her and burnt her [temple] to the ground.

In this connection, when Allāt was destroyed and burnt to the ground, Shaddad ibn-'Arik al-Jushami[28] said warning the Thaqif not to return to her worship nor attempt to avenge her destruction:

"Come not to Allāt, for God hath doomed her to destruction;
How can you stand by one which doth not triumph?
Verily that which, when set on fire, resisted not the flames,
Nor saved her stones, is inglorious and worthless.
Hence when the Apostle in your place shall arrive
And then leave, not one of her votaries shall be left."

Aws ibn-Hajar,[29] swearing by Allāt, said:

"By Allāt and al-'Uzza and those who in them believe,
And by Allah, verily He is greater than both."

---

23 Quran 53:19.
24 A pre-Islamic poet considered to be a soothsayer; he was known as the sayyid (chief) of the Rabi'a tribe.
25 King of the Lakhmids (r. 554–569), Christian Arabs of southern Arabia, whom the poet al-Mutalammis left to join their rivals, the Ghassanids.
26 Stones that are worshipped.
27 A Thaqafi from al-Ta'if (d. 670).
28 A pre-Islamic poet; his poetry is quoted in *Life of the Prophet* by Ibn Hisham (d. 833).
29 Pre-Islamic panegyrist (sixth century).

From Al-'Uzza they then adopted al-'Uzza as their goddess. She is, in point of time, more recent than either Allāt or Manah, since I have heard that the Arabs named their children after the latter two before they named them after al-'Uzza. Thus I have found that Tamim ibn-Murr had called his son[s] Zayd-Manah.

Discussion Questions

1. Ibn Al-Kalbi was a bit strange in his day for trying to research pre-Islamic paganism. Most classical Muslim scholars preferred to erase awareness of paganism. Why might Ibn Al-Kalbi write such a book?

2. Ibn Al-Kalbi offers an explanation of how a city settled by Abraham's son Ishmael and his descendants gradually forgot monotheism and became idolaters. Does this explanation seem plausible? And if it happened once, could it happen again in the future?

3. Some of the pagan tribes mentioned here, such as the Aws and Khazraj, welcomed Muhammad as a mediator and joined the early Muslim community. What are some reasons why pagan tribes might have rejected their idols for Islam?

Technique

From *Malcolm X Speaks*

Malcolm X

The controversial civil rights leader Malcolm X first encountered Islam in prison, where he joined the black nationalist movement the Nation of Islam, led by Elijah Muhammad. On his release, Malcolm X became the official spokesperson for the Nation of Islam. He left in 1964 after a falling out with Muhammad. Malcolm X became an orthodox Muslim, traveled the world, and went on the hajj. He was assassinated in 1965 less than a year after the letter below was written. The hajj is one of the pillars of Islam. Performing the various rituals of the hajj is an act of submission to God and a rejection of pride. Historians have noted the prophet Muhammad's ability to unite the warring tribes of Arabia and, at least in Malcolm X's experience, the rewards for submitting to God are brotherhood and racial harmony.

Jedda, Saudi Arabia
April 20, 1964

Never have I witnessed such sincere hospitality and the overwhelming spirit of true brotherhood as is practiced by people *of all colors and races* here in this ancient holy land, the home of Abraham, Muhammad and all the other prophets of the Holy Scriptures. For the past week I have been utterly speechless and spellbound by the graciousness I see displayed all around me by people *of all colors.*

Last night, April 19, I was blessed to visit the Holy City of Mecca, and complete the "Omra" part of my pilgrimage. Allah willing, I shall leave for Mina tomorrow, April 21, and be back in Mecca to say my prayers from Mt. Arafat on Tuesday, April 22. Mina is about twenty miles from Mecca.

Last night I made my seven circuits around the Kaaba, led by a young Mutawif named Muhammad. I drank water from the well of Zem Zem, and then ran back and forth seven times between the hills of Mt. Al-Safa and Al-Marwah.

There were tens of thousands of pilgrims from all over the world. They were *of all colors*, from blue-eyed blonds to black-skinned Africans, but were all participating in the same ritual, displaying a spirit of unity and brotherhood that my experiences in America had led me to believe could never exist between the white and non-white.

America needs to understand Islam, because this is the one religion that erases the race problem from its society. Throughout my travels in the Muslim world, I have met, talked to, and even eaten with, people who would have been considered "white" in America, but the religion of Islam in their hearts has removed the "white" from their minds. They practice sincere and true brotherhood with other people irrespective of their color.

Before America allows herself to be destroyed by the "cancer of racism" she should become better acquainted with the religious philosophy of Islam, a religion that has already molded people of all colors into one vast family, a nation or brotherhood of Islam that leaps over all "obstacles" and stretches itself into almost all of the Eastern countries of this earth.

The whites as well as the non-whites who accept true Islam become a changed people. I have eaten from the same plate with people whose eyes are the bluest of blue, whose hair was the blondest of blond, and whose skin was the whitest of white—all the way from Cairo to Jedda and even in the Holy City of Mecca itself—and I felt the same sincerity in the words and deeds of these "white" Muslims that I felt among the African Muslims of Nigeria, Sudan and Ghana.

True Islam removes racism, because people of all colors and races who accept its religious principles and bow down to one God, Allah, also automatically accept each other as brothers and sisters, regardless of differences in complexion.

You may be shocked by these words coming from me, but I have always been a man who tries to face facts, and to accept the reality of life as new experiences and knowledge unfold it. The experiences of this pilgrimage have taught me much, and each hour here in the Holy Land opens my eyes even more. If Islam can place the spirit of true brotherhood in the hearts of the "whites" whom I have met here in the Land of the Prophets, then surely it can also remove the "cancer of racism" from the heart of the white American, and perhaps in time to save America from imminent racial disaster, the same destruction brought upon Hitler by his racism that eventually destroyed the Germans themselves.

Discussion Questions

1. Many religions have pilgrimages. How does travel change the way people understand their religion and, very often, understand themselves?

2. Based on Malcolm X's experience of the hajj, what does the hajj do for the global Muslim community? How does it shape the way Muslims understand their religion and themselves?

3. Malcolm X states, "True Islam removes racism." Does this mean that forms of Islam that do not remove racism are therefore "false Islam"? Is this a "No True Scotsman" argument, in which the things Muslims say and do are ignored when they conflict with our ideas or prejudices about "true Islam"?

Exemplar 1

The Story of the Night Journey
FROM THE HADITH

Although Muhammad is never worshipped in Islam, he is an exemplar as an ideal human being and the seal of God's prophets. The so-called night journey—a mystical experience in which Muhammad travels from Jerusalem through seven layers of heaven and meets the prophets who preceded him—is only hinted at in the Qur-an. Instead, this story is found in the *hadith* or sayings of the Prophet. Muhammad ibn Isma'il al-Bukhari was famous for collecting, codifying, and compiling hadith. Hadith are normally accompanied by a chain of transmission called an *isnad* that relates who Muhammad allegedly said the message to and how it came to be recorded.

The Word of God, exalted be He: Glory be unto Him Who transported His servant by night from the Sacred Temple to the Farthest Temple . . . [1]

> Yabyâ ibn Bukayr related to us: Al-Layth related to us, on the authority of 'Uqayl, on the authority of Ibn Shihâb [who said]: Abû Salamah ibn 'Abd ar-Rabmân related to me: I heard Jâbir ibn 'Abd Allâh [say] that

---

1 Quran 17:1.

He heard the Apostle of God say: When the Quraysh accused me of lying, I remained [praying] in the enclosure of the Ka'bah.[2] Thereupon God displayed Jerusalem before me, and I began describing it to them while I was still looking at it.

The Ascension

Hudbah ibn Khâlid related to us: Hammâm ibn Yabyâ related to us: Qatâdah related to us, on the authority of Anas ibn Mâlik, on the authority of Mâlik ibn Ja'ja'ah [who said]:

The Prophet of God related to them the story of his Night Journey, and said: While I lay on the ground in the Hafim,[3]

—or perhaps he said: in the Hijr—

lo, someone came and cut open

—[Qatâdah] said: I also heard him say: split open—

[my breast] from here to here.

[Qatâdah said:] Then I asked al-Jârûd, who was sitting by my side: What is meant thereby?—He answered: From the pit at the top of his breast to below his navel. I also heard him say: . . . from the uppermost part of his breast to below his navel.

Then he took my heart out. And a golden basin full of faith was brought unto me, and my heart was washed [therein] and was filled [with faith]; then it was restored to its place. Thereupon a white steed, smaller than a mule and larger than an ass, was brought unto me.

—Al-Jârûd asked: Was this the Burâq, O Abû Hamzah?[4]—Anas answered: Yea.—

Its stride was as long as the eye could reach. And I was mounted on it, and Gabriel took me with him to the nearest heaven, and demanded that it be opened. [A voice] asked: Who is it?—[Gabriel] answered: Gabriel.—And who is with thee?—Muhammad.— And hath he received the Message?—Yea.—Welcome unto him! His is a blessed arrival!—And [the heavenly gate] was opened. When I entered [the heaven], lo! there was Adam; and [Gabriel] said: This here is thy father, Adam; offer him thy

---

2 The Ka'bah (also spelled Kaaba) (literally, "the Cube"), a stone shrine in Mecca—according to tradition, built by Abraham—that became the most important site in Islam (Muslims around the world face it when they pray). "Quraysh": the tribe that ruled Mecca.
3 A semicircular wall located about seven feet from the northwest face of the Ka'bah. The space between the Ka'bah and this low-lying wall is often referred to as the *Hijr*.
4 Anas's kunya, or familiar name derived from his son's name. "Burâq": in Islamic mythology, a winged steed.

greeting.—And I greeted him, and he answered my greeting and said: Welcome unto the righteous son, the righteous Prophet!

Then [Gabriel] ascended with me still higher, and [we] reached the second heaven; and he demanded that it be opened. [A voice] asked: Who is it?—[My guide] answered: Gabriel.—And who is with thee?—Muhammad.—And hath he received the Message?—Yea.—Welcome unto him! His is a blessed arrival!—And [the gate] was opened. When I entered, lo! [I saw] John and Jesus, the two cousins. [Gabriel] said: These here are John and Jesus; offer them thy greeting.—And I greeted [them], and they answered [my greeting] and said: Welcome unto the righteous brother, the righteous Prophet!

Then [Gabriel] ascended with me to the third heaven, and demanded that it be opened. [A voice] asked: Who is it?—Gabriel answered: Gabriel.—And who is with thee?—Muhammad.—And hath he received the Message?—Yea. Welcome unto him! His is a blessed arrival!—And [the gate] was opened. When I entered, lo! [I saw] Joseph. Gabriel said: This here is Joseph; offer him thy greeting.—And I greeted him, and he answered [my greeting] and said: Welcome unto the righteous brother, the righteous Prophet!

Then [Gabriel] ascended with me still higher, and [we] reached the fourth heaven; and he demanded that it be opened. [A voice] asked: Who is it?—[My guide] answered: Gabriel.—And who is with thee?—Muhammad.—And hath he received the Message?—Yea.—Welcome unto him! His is a blessed arrival!—And [the gate] was opened. When I entered, lo! I saw Idrîs.[5] Gabriel said: This here is Idrîs; offer him thy greeting.—And I greeted him, and he answered [my greeting] and said: Welcome unto the righteous brother, the righteous Prophet!

Thereafter [Gabriel] ascended with me still higher, and [we] reached the fifth heaven; and he demanded that it be opened. [A voice] asked: Who is it?—[Gabriel] answered: Gabriel.—And who is with thee?—Muhammad.—And hath he received the Message?—Yea.—Welcome unto him! His is a blessed arrival!—And when I entered, lo! [I saw] Aaron. [Gabriel] said: This here is Aaron; offer him thy greeting.—And I greeted him, and he answered [my greeting] and said: Welcome unto the righteous brother, the righteous Prophet!

Then [my guide] ascended with me still higher, and [we] reached the sixth heaven; and he demanded that it be opened. [A voice] asked: Who is it?—[My guide] answered: Gabriel.—Who is with thee?—Muhammad:—And hath he received the Message?—Yea.—Welcome unto him! His is a blessed arrival!—And when I entered, lo! [I saw] Moses. [Gabriel] said: This here is Moses; offer him thy greeting.—And I greeted him, and he answered [my greeting] and said: Welcome unto the righteous brother, the righteous Prophet!—And when I passed [by him], he wept. Someone asked him: What maketh thee weep?—[Moses] answered: I weep because after me

---

5 This prophet is sometimes identified with the biblical Enoch.

there hath been sent [as Prophet] a young man whose followers will enter Paradise in greater numbers than my followers.

Thereafter Gabriel went up with me to the seventh heaven, and demanded that it be opened. [A voice] asked: Who is it?—[Gabriel] answered: Gabriel.—And who is with thee?—Muhammad.—And hath he received the Message?—Yea.—Welcome unto him! His is a blessed arrival!—And when I entered, lo! [I saw] Abraham. [My guide] said: This here is thy father; offer him thy greeting.—And I greeted him, and he returned my greeting, saying: Welcome unto the righteous son, the righteous Prophet!

Thereafter I was made to see the Lote-Tree of the Farthest Limit[6]: its drupes were like the jars of Hajar,[7] and its leaves like elephant-ears. [Gabriel] said: This is the Lote-Tree of the Farthest Limit.—And lo! [I saw] four rivers—two hidden rivers and two manifest rivers. I said: What are these two [kinds of rivers], O Gabriel?—He answered: As to the two hidden ones, they are rivers of Paradise; and as to the two manifest ones, they are the Nile and the Euphrates.—Then I was made to see the Much-Frequented House[8]; and then a vessel full of wine, a vessel full of milk, and a vessel full of honey were brought to me; and I took the milk. Thereupon [Gabriel] said: This is [a symbol of] the inclination toward all that is natural in life; and it is this that thou and thy community stand for.

Thereafter prayers were elevated to a duty of fifty prayers a day. When I was returning, I passed by Moses, and he said: What hath been enjoined upon thee?—I answered: Fifty prayers a day have been enjoined upon me.—[Moses] said: Behold, thy community cannot bear fifty prayers a day. By God! I have tested men before thee, and I exerted myself to the utmost with the Children of Israel. Go back, then, unto thy Sustainer, and beg of Him to lighten thy community's burden.—So I went back, and [God] granted me a remission of ten [prayers]. Then I came again to Moses, but he repeated what he had said [before]. I went back, and [the Lord] granted me a remission of ten [more]. Then I came again to Moses, but he repeated what he had said [before]. And I went back, and [the Lord] granted me a remission of ten [more]. Then I came again to Moses, but he repeated what he had said [before]. And I went back, and ten prayers a day were enjoined upon me. Then I came again [to Moses], but he repeated what he had said [before]. And I went back, and five prayers a day were enjoined upon me. Then I came again to Moses, and he asked: What hath been enjoined upon thee?—I answered: Five prayers a day have been enjoined upon me.—He said: Behold, thy community cannot bear [even] five prayers a day. I have tested men before thee, and I exerted myself to the utmost with

---

6 Quran 53:14. The lote-tree, or jujube, is a shade tree whose single-stoned fruit is usually small.
7 A town in ancient Arabia noted for producing large jars.
8 Quran 52:4.

the Children of Israel. Go back, then, unto thy Sustainer, and beg of Him to lighten thy community's burden.—I answered: I have begged so much of my Sustainer that I feel ashamed. But I am content now, and I shall submit [to God's will].—And when I left, I heard a voice: I have confirmed My injunction, and have lightened the burden of My worshippers!

> Al-Humaydî related to us: Sufyân related to us: 'Amr related to us, on the authority of 'Ikrimah,

On the authority of Ibn 'Abbâs. Concerning His Word, exalted be He, *We ordained the vision which We shewed thee but as a temptation for mankind*,[9] he said: This is [an allusion to] that which the Apostle of God was shewn in his vision on the night when he was transported to Jerusalem.

> ['Ikrimah] added:

[Concerning] the Accursed Tree in the Qur'ân, [Ibn 'Abbâs] said: This is the tree of az-Zaqqûm.[10]

Discussion Questions

1. Al-Bukhari went to great lengths to collect the testimony about Muhammad's night journey so that the reader can know the provenance of these accounts and whether the witnesses and transmitters were reliable. What is the purpose of giving the reader this information? Aren't stories like this normally just accepted on faith?

2. Muhammad meets such figures as Jesus and Moses and is welcomed as a brother. Moses weeps because Muhammad will send more followers to Paradise than he had. Does this story show tolerance toward Judaism and Christianity by acknowledging the status of these figures in heaven, or does it serve to demonstrate Islam's superiority over these traditions?

3. What do you make of Moses advising Muhammad to negotiate God's demand of praying fifty times a day down to only five? What could the purpose of this story be? Is it problematic to portray Muhammad questioning God in this way?

---

9 Quran 17:60.
10 Quran 17:60.

From *Early Sufi Women*

Abu 'Abd ar-Rahman as-Sulami

While Islam is largely concerned with submission to God's will as expressed in the Qur-an, the Sufi tradition emphasizes connection with God through love and mystical experience. Sufi sheiks and saints are revered for their mystical understanding of God, and this is sometimes expressed in ways that resemble drunkenness or even madness. Such is the case of Rabia of Basra (714–801), who was known for her provocative statements and actions that seemed designed to shock audiences into a deeper understanding of God. The following account of Rabia's statements was compiled by Abu 'Abd ar-Rahman as-Sulami (937–1021), a prolific writer and Sufi.

I. Rabi'a Al-'Adawiyya[1]

Rabi'a was from Basra and was a client (mawlat) of the clan of Al 'Atik. Sufyan ath-Thawri[2] (may God have mercy upon him) sought her advice on legal matters and referred such issues to her. He also sought her spiritual advice and supplications. Both ath-Thawri and Shu'ba [ibn al-Hajjaj][3] transmitted Rabi'a's words of wisdom.

Muhammad ibn 'Abdallah b. Akhi Mimi personally reported from Abmad ibn Isbaq b. Wahb that his father [Wahb al-Bazzaz] reported through 'Abdallah ibn Ayyub al-Muqri' (the Qur'an Reciter) through Shayban ibn Farrukh, that Ja'far ibn Sulayman related: Sufyan ath-Thawri took me by the hand and said about Rabi'a: "Take me to the mentor. For when I am apart from her, I can find no solace." When we entered her abode, Sufyan raised his hand and said, "Oh God, grant me safety!" At this, Rabi'a wept. "What makes you weep?" he asked. "You caused me to weep," she replied. "How?" he asked. She answered, "Have you not learned that true safety from the world is to abandon all that is in it? So how can you ask such a thing while you are still soiled with the world?"

Abu Ja'far Muhammad ibn Abmad b. Sa'id ar-Razi reported from al-'Abbas ibn Hamza through Abmad ibn Abi al-Hawari through al-'Abbas ibn al-Walid al-Mashriqi that Shayban al-Ubulli related: I heard Rabi'a say: "For everything there is a fruit (thamara), and the fruit of the knowledge of God (ma'rifa) is in orienting oneself toward God at all times (iqbal)."

---

1 Born ca. 714 and died in 801.
2 Best known as a collector of traditions (ca. 715–778), but also an influential commentator on the Qur-an and on religious law.
3 A Basran transmitter of hadith (d. 776/77).

Also on his authority, Rabi'a said: "I ask God's forgiveness for my lack of truthfulness in saying, 'I ask God's forgiveness.'"

Also on his authority, Rabi'a was asked: "How is your love for the Prophet (may God bless and preserve him)?" To which she replied, "Verily, I love him. But love for the Creator has turned me away from love for created things."

[Shayban al-Ubulli] also said: One day, Rabi'a saw Rabab [al-Qaysi]⁴ kissing a young boy. "Do you love him?" she asked. "Yes," he said. To which she replied, "I did not imagine that there was room in your heart to love anything other than God, the Glorious and Mighty!" Rabab was overcome at this and fainted. When he awoke, he said, "On the contrary, this is a mercy that God Most High has put into the hearts of His slaves." I heard Abu Bakr ar-Razi report from Abu Salama al-Baladi that Maymun ibn al-Ajbagh related through Sayyar from Ja'far [ibn Sulayman]: Mubammad ibn Wasi'⁵ came upon Rabi'a while she was staggering like one inebriated. "What causes you to stagger?" he asked. "Last night I became intoxicated with love for my Lord and woke up inebriated from it," she replied.

In a quarter of Baghdad named Qafi'at ad-Daqiq, I heard Muhammad ibn 'Abdallah b. Akhi Mimi report from Abmad ibn Isbaq b. Wahb al-Bazzaz (the Cloth Merchant) through 'Abdallah ibn Ayyub al-Muqri' through Shayban ibn Farrukh that Ja'far ibn Sulayman said: I heard Rabi'a al-'Adawiyya say that Sufyan ah-Thawri asked her, "What is the best way for the slave ('abd) to come close to God, the Glorious and Mighty?" She wept and replied: "How can the likes of me be asked such a thing? The best way for the slave to come close to God Most High is for him to know that he must not love anything in this world or the Hereafter other than Him."

Also on [Ja'far ibn Sulayman's] authority it is reported that ath-Thawri said in Rabi'a's presence, "How sorrowful I am!" "Do not lie!" she said. "Say instead, 'How little is my sorrow!' If you were truly sorrowful, life itself would not please you." Also on his authority Rabi'a said: "My sorrow is not from feeling sad. Rather, my sorrow is from not feeling sad enough."

Also on his authority: In Basra, Rabi'a came across a man who had been arrested and crucified for immorality. She said: "Upon my father! With that tongue you used to say, 'There is no god but God!'" Sufyan said: "Then she mentioned the good works that the man had done."

Also on his authority: Jalib al-Murri⁶ said in her presence, "He who persists in knocking at the door will have it opened for him." "The door is already open," she replied. "But the question is: Who wishes to enter it?"

---

4 A Sufi ascetic (d. 796).
5 A Sufi ascetic and judge (d. ca. 735).
6 A preacher, Quran reciter, and transmitter of early Muslim traditions (d. 792/93) [translator's note, edited].

1. Rabia chides another Muslim for saying, "Oh God, grant me safety!" Why does she do this?

2. What could Rabia have meant when she said, "I ask God's forgiveness for my lack of truthfulness in saying, 'I ask God's forgiveness'"?

3. Rabia's statements seem to celebrate being sad. Why is this? Why might a mystic think feeling sad is desirable or praiseworthy?

Controversy

From *The Veil and the Male Elite*

Fatima Mernissi

Western critics of Islam often claim that Islam denigrates women as second-class citizens. By contrast, Muslim feminists have argued that Islam led to advances for women. Some Muslim feminists, such as Fatima Mernissi (1940–2015), argue that the earliest message of Islam was one of equality between men and women, but that patriarchal agendas quickly intervened, even within Muhammad's own lifetime. Later, sacred texts were manipulated to create "false traditions" that ensured male dominance in society. The passage below is from Mernissi's book *The Veil and the Male Elite*, which explores the three-year period in which the traditions of veiling and separating men and women were first revealed to Muhammad.

The Muslim God is the only monotheistic God whose sacred place, the mosque, opens on to the bedroom, the only one to have chosen a Prophet who does not keep silent about his concerns as a man, but who, on the contrary, voices his thoughts about sexuality and desire.

Clearly, the imams were able to take advantage of our ignorance of the sacred texts to weave a hijab—a screen—to hide the mosque/dwelling. But everyone knows that, as the Koran tells us, "of use is the reminder,"[1] and all we have to do is pore over the yellowed pages of our history to bring to life 'A'isha's[2] laughter, Umm Sala-

---

1 Quran 87:9.
2 Regarded by many Muslims as Muhammad's favorite wife (d. 678).

ma's[3] fiery challenges, and to be present to hear their political demands in a fabulous Muslim city—Medina open to the heavens.

The Wives of the Prophet: The Happy Years

When the Prophet asked for the hand of Umm Salama in year 4 of the Hejira (AD 626), 'A'isha was very jealous because she had heard about Umm Salama's beauty. When she saw her for the first time, she caught her breath: "She is more beautiful than they led me to believe!" The author of *Al-Isaba*[4] describes Umm Salama as "a woman of uncommon beauty, very sound judgment, rapid powers of reasoning, and unparalleled ability to formulate correct opinions."

Umm Salama, like Muhammad, belonged to the Quraysh[5] aristocracy. She had four children by her first marriage when the Prophet asked for her hand. At first she refused, for, she said, "I already have children, and I am very jealous." To persuade her, the Prophet told her that he was going to ask God to rid her of her jealousy, and as for the question of age, in any case he was much older than she was. It was Umm Salama's son who gave her in marriage to the Prophet. The bride was nursing her last-born, Zaynab, when she joined the Prophet's household, and he used to greet her when he came to her apartment by saying, "Where is Zunab?," the affectionate nickname of Zaynab.

Umm Salama was one of those women of the Quraysh aristocracy in whom physical beauty and intelligence assured them as they grew older a special ascendancy over their entourage, and the privilege of being consulted on matters of vital concern to the community. The Prophet's first wife, Khadija, was also typical of such women, full of initiative in public life as well as private life. Khadija had had two husbands before the Prophet and had borne a child by each. It was she who "asked for the hand of the Prophet," because she found that he had the qualities she most appreciated in a man. She was also, as we have seen, the heiress of a large fortune left to her by her previous husband, a fortune that she augmented by investing it in wide-ranging trading operations. Tradition stresses the difference in age at the time of marriage between Muhammad (25) and Khadija (40), but one may question whether she really was that old, since in 15 years of marriage together she bore seven children to the Prophet.

A typical example of the dynamic, influential, enterprising woman in public as well as private life is Hind bint 'Utba, who played such a central role in the Meccan opposition to Muhammad that, when he conquered Mecca, her name was on the list of the few Meccans condemned to death by the Prophet. He never forgave her the

---

3 Another of Muhammad's wives (d. ca. 679), whom he married in 626.
4 A biographical dictionary of the Companions of the Prophet, by Ibn Hajar al-'Asqalani (1372–1449), an Egyptian Sunni historian and scholar of traditions. It is the source of the quotations in this and the following paragraph.
5 The tribe that ruled Mecca in Muhammad's time.

songs and dances she performed among the dead Muslims on the battlefield of Uhud[6]: "The women, coming down from the mountain, stood behind the army, beating their tambourines to spur on the soldiers. Hind, the wife of Abu Sufyan, skipped and danced as she sang this verse:

> We are daughters of the morning star.
> We trample cushions underfoot.
> Our necks are adorned with pearls.
> Our hair is perfumed with musk.
> If you battle us, we will crush you in our arms.
> If you retreat, we will let you go.
> Farewell to love."[7]

One of women's roles in pre-Islamic Arabia was to spur men on during war to fight to the end, to not flinch, to brave death on the battlefield. This role obviously has nothing to do with the image of the nurturing woman who bandages wounds and comforts the dying. Hind and her war song express, on the contrary, an image of woman as exhorter to death. In addition, Hind is described as a cannibal, because she is supposed to have eaten the liver of Hamza, the Prophet's uncle, whom she particularly detested. Al-'Asqalani justifies Hind's excessive behavior on the battlefield of Uhud by recalling that she had a grudge against the Prophet's uncle because he had killed *her* uncle, Shayba, and taken part in the intrigues that led to the death of her father, 'Utba. Her hatred of Islam was not just simply acknowledged, but considered justified because Islam had decimated her clan.

So it is understandable that the Prophet demanded her head upon his triumphal entry into Mecca in year 8 of the Hejira (AD 630). But she was the wife of Abu Sufyan, the chief of the city, who pleaded mercy for her from Muhammad. Once it was granted, she had to appear before Muhammad with a delegation of the female population of Mecca to swear the oath of allegiance, after, of course, having recited the declaration of faith. Hind's oath of allegiance, which has been transcribed word for word by the historians, is a masterpiece of humor and political insolence by a woman forced to submit, but in no way renouncing her right to self-expression. When the Prophet commanded her to swear to "not commit adultery," Hind replied: "A free woman never commits adultery." The Prophet is supposed to have thrown an amused glance at 'Umar, "because he was aware of Hind's love affairs and her relations with 'Umar before his conversion to Islam." The historians have been so fascinated by Hind's personality that they have devoted pages and pages to her. How do they speak

---

6 A mountain near Medina; in the battle by its side (624/25), the Meccan forces (led by Abu Sufyan) defeated the Muslims and wounded Muhammad.
7 Quoted from *History of the Prophets and Kings*, by the Muslim historian al-Tabari (ca. 839–923).

about Hind, that woman who accepted Islam with so much reluctance? As strange as it may seem today, and to the great honor of the Muslim historians, Hind's personality emerges in all its complexity, with her excessive hate and her cannibalism on the one hand, but also with her undeniable gifts on the other: "Hind became Muslim the day of the conquest of Mecca. She was one of the women most gifted in judgment."

The Prophet then was not surprised to hear a woman like Umm Salama, in contrast to the still adolescent 'A'isha, raise very political questions that only mature women were in a position to do: "'Why,' she asked the Prophet one day, 'are men mentioned in the Koran and why are we not?'"[8] Once her question was asked, she awaited the reply from Heaven.

One day when she was calmly combing her hair, worried about her question still not having been answered (in those days God used to respond when a woman or a man asked a question about his or her status and position in the new community), she heard the Prophet recite in the mosque the latest verse that had been revealed to him and that concerned her:

> I had asked the Prophet why the Koran did not speak of us as it did of men. And what was my surprise one afternoon, when I was combing my hair, to hear his voice from the *minbar*.[9] I hastily did up my hair and ran to one of the apartments from where I could hear better. I pressed my ear to the wall, and here is what the Prophet said:
>
> "O people! Allah has said in his book: 'Men who surrender unto Allah, and women who surrender, and men who believe and women who believe,'" etc. And he continued in this vein until he came to the end of the passage where it is said: "Allah hath prepared for them forgiveness and a vast reward."[10]

The answer of the Muslim God to Umm Salama was very clear: Allah spoke of the two sexes in terms of total equality as believers, that is, as members of the community. God identifies those who are part of his kingdom, those who have a right to his "vast reward." And it is not sex that determines who earns his grace; it is faith and the desire to serve and obey him. The verse that Umm Salama heard is revolutionary, and reading it leaves no doubt about it:

> Lo! Men who surrender unto Allah, and women who surrender, and men who believe and women who believe, and men who obey and women who obey, and men who speak the truth and women who speak the truth, and men who persevere (in righteousness) and women who persevere, and men who are humble and women who are humble, and men who give

---

8 Quoted from al-Tabari's Quran commentary, or *tafsir*.
9 Pulpit (Arabic).
10 Quran 33:35.

alms and women who give alms, and men who fast and women who fast, and men who guard their modesty and women who guard (their modesty), and men who remember Allah much and women who remember— Allah hath prepared for them forgiveness and a vast reward.[11]

✦ ✦ ✦

Women and Booty

After Umm Salama's success and the verses affirming women's equality and especially their right to inheritance, a critical period followed. Other verses came, which temporized on the principle of equality of the sexes and reaffirmed male supremacy, without, however, nullifying the dispositions in favor of women. This created an ambiguity in the Koran that would be exploited by governing elites right up until the present day. In fact, women's triumph was of very short duration. Not only did Heaven no longer respond to their pleas, but every time they formulated a new demand, revelations did not, as before, come to their rescue.

Encouraged by the fact that Allah considered them to be believers just like men, women were emboldened to claim the right to go to war in order to gain booty and the right to have a say with regard to the sex act. These claims were surely going to be perceived by men for what they were: a challenge to the very foundations of male supremacy. The heads of family, realizing that what women were demanding was eminently political, mobilized a veritable opposition movement with an elite leader: 'Umar Ibn al-Khattab,[12] a military chief without peer. His courage had always galvanized the Muslim troops, and the Prophet himself recognized that "the conversion of 'Umar to Islam was a conquest and a triumph in itself." 'Umar had boundless admiration for the Prophet and his projects for change, for the creation of an Arab society. He was prepared to go far with the Prophet, to follow him in his desire to change society in general. But the point at which he was no longer prepared to follow him came when it was a question of relations between the sexes. 'Umar could not imagine an Islam that overturned the traditional—that is, pre-Islamic—relations between men and women. Women's demands to bear arms and to participate actively in military operations instead of passively waiting to be taken prisoner, as the *jahiliyya*[13] tradition required, seemed absurd to him. He was ready to destroy the gods of polytheistic Mecca that his ancestors had worshipped and thus to upset the equilibrium of the heavens. But to envisage that the Arab woman could claim a different status on earth seemed an intolerable change to him.

This was happening at the moment when the women, in a triumphant mood, were taking action. The most virulent of them became openly provocative by declar-

---

11 Quran 33:35.
12 The second caliph (ca. 586–644), who was also a close companion of Muhammad.
13 Literally, "ignorance" (Arabic); that is, pre-Islamic.

ing that the Koranic verse that said that "a man's share is double that of a woman"[14] did not apply only to inheritance, but also to sin. At the last judgment, they said, every man would have the surprise of seeing the number of his sins multiplied by two: "Since they have two shares of inheritance, let them have the same for sins!" The situation was heating up!

To the great surprise of women, Heaven intervened this time on the side of men and affirmed their privileges. Verse 32 of the sura on women[15] is divided into two arguments and responds to two requests that must be carefully distinguished: women's desire to have the same privileges as men, and their declaration that real equality is achieved in terms of wealth. So, for them to be really the equals of men, Allah had to give them the right to go to war and thus to gain booty. Allah answered in terms of the obvious: since the rights of each are proportional to what they earn, women, who are exempted from going to war, cannot claim to be treated equally: "Unto men a fortune from that which they have earned, and unto women a fortune from that which they have earned."[16] This part of the verse, al-Tabari tells us, is an answer to women's demand to bear arms. They then pushed the reasoning about equality to its logical limit. Since the share of each person is equal to what he or she acquires, and since men only grow rich through war, they demanded the right to this privilege.

To understand women's insistence on this point, we have to have some appreciation of the mechanisms of war and booty and their importance to Medina's economy. *Al-ghazawa*, according to the *Lisan al-'Arab* dictionary,[17] were "raids on an enemy to strip him of his possessions." The dictionary says that a "failed raid is one in which no booty is seized." *Al-ghazawa* were one of the most common means of "creating" wealth. They were intertribal forays, extremely ritualized, whose primary aim was to capture "the wealth of the other," camels most of the time, while avoiding bloodshed. Causing bloodshed was a very serious act which was to be avoided at all costs, because the *ghazi* (attacker) would then be exposed to revenge by the tribe of the person killed. Bloodshed unleashed a chain of reprisals with interminable vendettas governed by the law of an eye for an eye. Nevertheless, two kinds of *ghazawa* coexisted, one that we have just discussed for possessions, and the other for war, in which no quarter was given. War with access to booty, along with the trading of the Meccans and the agriculture of the Medinese, was one of the possible and important sources of revenue. Muhammad himself engaged in it, while using it, however, for an objective that went beyond the traditional *ghazawa*. If he had done otherwise, he would have become just one of the many small tribal chieftains of Arabia whom history would have forgotten or noted only briefly. However, the Prophet quickly

---

14 See Quran 4:11.
15 Sura 4.
16 Quran 4:32.
17 *The Tongue of the Arabs* (Arabic), by the Tunisian lexicographer Ibn Manzur (1232–1311).

discovered the limits and contradictions of such an activity. The laws of *ghazawa* were implacable and left to the victor only a choice between two equally inhumane alternatives with regard to the defeated: kill the men and reduce the women (occasionally the men too) to slavery, or, if the men and women were of aristocratic origin, exchange them for a large ransom. But the question Muslims had to face was: What should be done with prisoners who declare themselves converts to Islam? Although one gains a believer, one also loses booty, which was the original aim of the enterprise.

The women took advantage of the new questions that arose to slip in their own demands. "During the pre-Islamic period, men excluded women and children from inheriting, because, they said, they did not go on raids and did not share in booty." Umm Salama, in her usual clear and concise way, formulated in a petition the essential point of women's new claim: "Messenger of God, men make war, and we do not have the right to do it although we have the right to inheritance!" In another version Umm Salama is supposed to have said: "Messenger of God, why do men make war and we do not?"

Discussion Questions

1. Historians have fairly detailed accounts of Muhammad's wives and their relationships with him. How does this information affect discussions about the status of women in Islam?

2. The early Muslim community lived in Medina and was at war with the Quraysh tribe that controlled Mecca. How did this condition of war create new opportunities for Muslim women? How did it give leverage to Muslim men who were resistant to granting new rights to women?

3. As a historian, Mernissi seems to admire Hind bint 'Utba. Hind's father, son, uncle, and brother were all killed in a battle with Muhammad's forces and she allegedly retaliated by eating the liver of Hamza, one of Muhammad's best warriors. But she later joined the Muslims, supported them in battle, and her son founded the Umayyad dynasty. Is Hind an icon of the independence of Muslim women, a cannibalistic villainess, or something else entirely?

Confucianism

From a Confucian perspective, the fundamental problem with the world is social chaos brought about by humanity's neglect of their public obligations, filial responsibilities, and appropriate ritual behavior. The solution to this particular problem is the development of social harmony through ritual propriety (*li*), humaneness (*ren*), and other methods of self-cultivation. To reflect this problem/solution, we have an excerpt from the Book of History (Shujing, 书经). One of the Five Classics edited by Confucius, the Book of History relates the governmental deeds of the Xia, Shang, and Zhou dynasties. It also includes details on the reign of Yu the Great, the legendary originator of the Xia dynasty who is said to have created irrigation channels and controlled floods. Reflected in its detailed collection of historical documents is a fundamentally Confucian vision of both the preservation and the breakdown of social order: on one hand, just rulers who model appropriate care for their subjects and the prosperous society that results; on the other, inappropriate rulers who mete out overly harsh punishments while indulging in a reckless pursuit of their own desires and the resulting social chaos and disharmony. Through Confucius's heavy editorial hand in selecting and compiling these documents, we see the beginnings of Confucian philosophies, including the first textual appearance of both the paradigmatic representative of Confucian philosophy, the Duke of Zhou, and the developing concept of the mandate of heaven. The Analects (Lunyu, 论语) provides insight into the techniques necessary to bring about the ideal society portrayed by Confucius in the Book of History. Initially compiled by Confucius's students and edited heavily in the centuries following his death, the Analects collects brief aphorisms and specific moments of teaching from Confucius's life to paint the picture of an ideal sage, as well as the political and social philosophy that will return China to the glory of the Zhou dynasty seen in the Book of History. As a text over two thousand years old and lacking the narrative through line common to European and American religious literature, the Analects can sometimes be a difficult text to understand because of its often far distant cultural context; the selections, therefore, below are arranged thematically to help guide the reader.

Confucianism celebrates as the ideal exemplar the profound person (*junzi*, 君子) and the sage (*shengren*, 圣人). Initially framed as a largely unobtainable ideal, "sage-hood" became framed as something within reach through inner contemplation and personal development with the development of Neo-Confucianism in the twelfth to fifteenth centuries. Many of these Confucian contemplative practices represented adaptations of Buddhist practices and concepts. Here, we see Neo-Confucian luminary Wang Yangming (1472–1529) developing the idea of the internal "heart-mind" that intuitively understands the truth of Confucianism and acts out of a recognition of one's social connections with the entire universe. To argue this, Wang Yangming rejects the belabored contemplative strategies of his Neo-Confucian predecessor Zhu Xi (1130–1200) and instead emphasizes humanity's innate goodness and ability to perceive Confucian truth.

Despite its sometimes stodgy reputation, Confucianism is an evolving tradition that continues to exert an important influence today as seen in the reading selection composed by the second exemplar, Yu Dan. Professor of Media Studies at the prestigious Beijing Normal University, Yu Dan has become the face of China's contemporary revival of interest in Confucianism. In this selection from her bestseller *Confucius from the Heart*, we see a modern transformation of Confucian principles, focusing on personal fulfillment and happiness to make the "best version of ourselves possible." While critics note that Yu Dan's Confucianism is largely defanged of its political and social commentary, she remains an important voice in understanding contemporary manifestations of Confucian ideals.

As explored by scholars like Anna Sun, Confucianism has long held an uncomfortable seat at the world's religions' table. Oftentimes it is excluded because of its disinterest in an afterlife, a creator god, and other supernatural elements frequently considered essential to how the term "religion" is applied in the West. A selection from scholar Tu Weiming argues for a reappraisal of our term "religious" through highlighting Confucianism's commitment to communal self-transformation as a response to the transcendent, what he calls "becoming fully human." Tu Weiming's interpretation of Confucianism has been so influential that many credit him as ushering in a third development in Confucian history, or "New Confucianism," which presents Confucianism as a "humanistic religion" and spiritual tradition.

From the Book of History

Considered threatening by some Chinese leaders, the Book of History was almost destroyed during the 213 BCE Burning of Books and Burying of Scholars, during which hundreds of Confucian scholars and thousands of texts were supposedly destroyed to cement support for the Qin dynasty's Legalist ruling philosophy. While many historians doubt some of the more dramatic elements of this story, it speaks to the potential political threat represented by Confucianism for its ability to hold rulers responsible for society's well-being through their moral actions—a trait not always highlighted in Western discussions of the tradition. In the selection below, we see two chapters extolling the virtues and vices of rulers in various times, each detailing how their behavior affects the social harmony of their subjects. A clear pattern emerges, in which an unjust and licentious ruler leads to a disorderly and immodest populace, affirming Confucianism's fundamental belief that society and the individual are deeply interwoven. This relationship is further reflected in the discussion of social ills in *The Marquis of Lü on Punishments*, in which we see a rejection of local divinatory practices to spirits in favor of social work and caring for the poor and widowed.

Document 15

The Duke of Zhou said, "Oh! The superior man rests in this; that he will indulge in no luxurious ease. He first understands how the painful toil of sowing and reaping conducts to ease, and thus he understands how the lower people depend on this toil for their support. I have observed among the lower people that where the parents have diligently labored in sowing and reaping, their sons often do not understand this painful toil but abandon themselves to ease, and to village slang, and become quite disorderly. Or where they do not do so, they still throw contempt on their parents, saying, 'Those old people have heard nothing and know nothing.'"

The Duke of Zhou said, "Oh! I have heard that aforetime Dai Wu, one of the kings of Yin, was grave, humble, reverent, and timorously cautious. He measured himself with reference to the decree of Heaven and cherished a reverent apprehension in governing the people, not daring to indulge in useless ease. It was thus that he enjoyed the throne seventy and five years.

"If we come to the time of Wu Ding, he toiled at first away from the court and among the lower people. When he came to the throne and occupied the mourning shed,[1] it may

---

1 The mourning shed was a temporary structure built next to the tomb of one's deceased parent so that they may ritually grieve them. Though the mourning period was officially supposed to be three years, reflecting the period of time during which a child is completely dependent on their parents, it was often shortened for emperors and other high-level officials due to their bureaucratic duties.

be said that he did not speak for three years. Afterwards he was still inclined not to speak; but when he did speak, his words were full of harmonious wisdom. He did not dare to indulge in useless ease but admirably and tranquilly presided over the regions of Yin until throughout them all, small and great, there was not a single murmur. It was thus that he enjoyed the throne fifty and nine years. In the case of Zu Jia, he refused to be king unrighteously, and was at first one of the lower people. When he came to the throne, he knew on what they must depend for their support and was able to exercise a protecting kindness toward their masses. He did not dare to treat with contempt the wifeless men and widows. Thus it was that he enjoyed the throne thirty and three years.

"The kings that arose after these from their birth enjoyed ease. Enjoying ease from their birth, they did not know the painful toil of sowing and reaping, and had not heard of the hard labors of the lower people. They sought for nothing but excessive pleasure; and so not one of them had a long life. They reigned for ten years, for seven or eight, for five or six, or perhaps only for three or four."

The Duke of Zhou said, "Oh! There likewise were King Tai and King Ji of our own Zhou, who were humble and reverently cautious. King Wen dressed meanly, gave himself to the work of tranquilization and to husbandry. Admirably mild and beautifully humble, he cherished and protected the inferior people and showed a fostering kindness to the wifeless men and widows. From morning to midday, and from midday to sundown, he did not allow himself leisure to eat; thus seeking to secure the happy harmony of the myriads of the people. King Wen did not dare to go to excess in his excursions or his hunting, and from the various states he would receive only the correct amount of contribution. The appointment of Heaven came to him in the middle of his life, and he enjoyed the throne for fifty years."

The Duke of Zhou said, "Oh! From this time forward, let you who have succeeded to the throne imitate Wen's avoiding of excess in sightseeing, indulgence in ease, excursions, hunting; and from the myriads of the people receive only the correct amount of contribution. Do not allow yourself the leisure to say, 'Today I will indulge in pleasure.' This would not be holding out a lesson to the people, nor the way to secure the favor of Heaven. Men will on the contrary be prompt to imitate you and practice evil. Become not like Shou the King of Yin, who went quite astray and became abandoned to drunkenness."

The Duke of Zhou said, "Oh! I have heard it said that, in the case of the ancients, their ministers warned and admonished them, protected and loved them, taught and instructed them; and among the people there was hardly one who would impose on them by extravagant language or deceiving tricks. If you will not listen to this and profit by it, your ministers will imitate you and the correct laws of the former kings, both small and great, will be changed and disordered. The people, blaming you, will disobey and rebel in their hearts; yea, they will curse you with their mouths."

Document 27

In reference to the charge to the marquis of Lü: when the king had occupied the throne until he reached the age of a hundred years, he gave great consideration to the appointment of punishments in order to deal with the people of the four quarters.

The king said, "According to the teachings of ancient times, Chi Yu was the first to produce disorder—which spread among the quiet, orderly people until all became robbers and murderers, owl-like and yet self-complacent in their conduct, traitors and villains snatching and filching, dissemblers and oppressors.

"Among the people of Miao, they did not use the power of goodness but the restraint of punishments. They made the five punishments engines of oppression, calling them the laws. They slaughtered the innocent and were the first also to go to excess in cutting off the nose, cutting off the ears, castration, and branding. All who became liable to those punishments were dealt with without distinction, no difference being made in favor of those who could offer some excuse. The people were gradually affected by this state of things and became dark and disorderly. Their hearts were no more set on good faith; they violated their oaths and covenants. The multitudes who suffered from oppressive terrors and were in danger of being murdered declared their innocence to Heaven. God surveyed the people, and there was no fragrance of virtue arising from them, but the rank smell of their cruel punishments.

"The great Shun was compassionate to the innocent multitudes that were in danger of being murdered and made the oppressors feel the terrors of his majesty. He restrained and finally extinguished the people of Miao, so that they should not continue to future generations. Then he commissioned Chong and Li to make an end of the communications between earth and heaven; and the descents of spirits ceased. From the princes down to the inferior officers, all helped with clear intelligence the spread of the regular principles of duty; the solitary and widows were no longer overlooked. The great Shun with an unprejudiced mind carried his enquiries down among the people, and the solitary and widows laid before him their complaints against the Miao. He awed the people by the majesty of his virtue and enlightened them by its brightness."

The king said, "Oh! Lay it to heart. My uncles, and all ye, my brethren and cousins, my sons and my grandsons, listen all of you to my words in which, it may be, you will receive a most important charge. You will only tread the path of satisfaction by being daily diligent; do not have occasion to beware of the want of diligence. Heaven, in its wish to regulate the people, allows us for a day to make use of punishments. Whether crimes have been premeditated, or are unpremeditated, depends on the parties concerned. Let you deal with them to accord with the mind of Heaven and thus serve me, the One Man. Though I would put them to death, do not you therefore put them to death; though I would spare them, do not you therefore spare them. Reverently apportion the five punishments so as fully to exhibit the three virtues. Then shall I, the One Man, enjoy felicity; the people will look to you as their sure dependence; the repose of such a state will be perpetual."

Discussion Questions

1. Likely edited with a heavy hand, the Book of History owes as much to Confucius's composition as it does to historical texts that preceded it. Why might Confucius describe his ideal society as existing in the distant past, rather than laying out a vision of it in the present?

2. Of Confucianism's Five Relationships, the Book of History focuses almost exclusively on the ruler/subject relationship. What would a Confucian say about applying these ideas to the other relationships? From a Confucian perspective, how is the ruler/subject relationship similar to and different from the relationship between a husband and wife or an elder brother and younger brother?

3. Later Chinese histories claim that this text was almost destroyed by the Qin dynasty—why might a ruler find this text threatening?

Technique

From the Analects

The love Confucius's students had for him is legendary; after his death, each student supposedly brought a tree from their hometown and planted it at his estate in Qufu—a grove that can still be seen to this day. Unlike the widespread aristocratic schools of his time, Confucius believed that everyone could benefit from education and welcomed students regardless of their social background or ability to pay. The Analects, gathered together by his students after his death, consists of brief moments of teaching from Confucius's life. While later thinkers would continue to develop, extend, and elaborate Confucius's ideas, the Analects remains the foundation of his philosophy. The selections here are organized by thematic content.

Confucius's Character

The master said, "How delightful it is to study and to review from time to time what one has studied! How pleasant to have friends visit from afar!"

[1.1.1–2]

The master said, "At fifteen I was intent on study, at thirty I had established myself, at forty I had no uncertainty, at fifty I knew the mandate of heaven, at sixty I was in consonant accord with things, and at seventy I could follow my heart's desires without overstepping convention."

[2.4]

The master said, "One can still find happiness if one has only simple food to eat, water to drink, and a bent arm for a pillow. Wealth and high rank attained unrighteously are to me but floating clouds."

[7.15]

Zigong said, "The master is congenial, pleasant, courteous, good tempered, and complaisant. Thus does he engage the world, and his way of engaging it is quite different from that of other people."

[1.10.2]

There were four things he was completely free of. He never showed a lack of forethought, he was not opinionated, he was not hidebound, and he was not egoistic.

[9.4]

The master offered instruction concerning four things: cultural refinement, proper conduct, loyalty, and good faith.

[7.24]

When the master was eating next to someone who was in mourning, he never ate to the full. He never sang on a day in which earlier he had been crying.

[7.9]

The master fished, but not with a net. When hunting he did not shoot at roosting birds.

[7.26]

Human Nature

Zigong said, "One can apprehend the master's disquisitions on culture and refinement, but not his discussions of human nature or the way of heaven."

[5.12]

The master said, "In terms of human nature, people are much alike. But in terms of practice and effort, they are quite different."

[17.2]

Confucius said, "Those who are possessed of understanding from birth are the highest type of people. Those who understand things only after studying them are of the next lower type, and those who learn things from painful experience are yet the next. Those who have painful experiences but do not learn from them are the lowest type of people."

[16.9]

The Honorable Person

The master said, "Isn't one truly an honorable person if one is not acknowledged by others yet still does not resent it!"

[1.1.3]

The master said, "Honorable people are modest in what they say but surpassing in what they do."

[14.29]

The master said, "There are three aspects to the way of the honorable person, but I am incapable of them: to be possessed of humanity and have no anxieties, to be wise and have no doubts, and to be strong and have no fears." Zigong said, "Master, those are your own ways."

[14.30]

The master said, "Honorable persons seek things within themselves. Small-minded people, on the other hand, seek things from others."

[15.20]

Confucius said, "There are three things of which the honorable person is in awe: the mandate of heaven, great people, and the words of the sages. Small-minded people do not understand the mandate of heaven and are not in awe of it; they are insolent toward great people and ridicule sages."

[16.8]

Humanity, Virtue, and Consideration

The master rarely spoke of profit, of one's mandated fate, or of humanity.

[9.1]

The master said, "Persons possessed of humanity are like this: wanting to develop themselves, they also develop others; wanting to achieve things themselves, they also allow others to achieve what they want. This is the direction humanity takes: to use what is close to oneself as an analogy to be extended to others."

[6.28.2–3]

Zhonggong asked about humanity. The master said, "In your social affairs behave as if you are meeting with important guests, and treat people as if you were participating in a great sacrificial offering. Do not impose on other people anything you yourself dislike. Let there be no animosity either in the state or in the family." Zhonggong said, "Even though I am not gifted, I will try to practice what you have just said."

[12.2]

Fan Chi asked about humanity. The master said, "Be solicitous of others." Fan Chi asked about understanding. The master said, "Be understanding toward others."

[12.22]

The master said, "Only persons possessed of humanity can truly like other people or truly dislike them."

[4.3]

The master said, "Is humanity something far away? If I want to be humane, then humanity has already been attained."

[7.29]

Someone asked, "What of repaying animosity with virtue?" The master said, "How could one repay that with virtue? Repay animosity with directness, and repay virtue with virtue."

[14.36]

Zigong asked, "Is there one word by which one may live one's entire life?" The master said, "Isn't that word 'consideration'? Do not impose on other people anything you yourself dislike."

[15.23]

Governance

The master said, "Someone who governs with virtue is like the northern polar star, which stays in one place while all the other stars pay their respects to it."

[2.1]

Ji Kangzi asked Confucius about governance. Confucius replied, "To govern means to rectify. If you start by rectifying yourself, how would anyone else not do the same?"

[12.17]

The master said, "If you rectify your own self, then even if you give no orders they will still be carried out. If you don't rectify yourself, then even if you do give orders they will still not be followed."

[13.6]

The master said, "If one adopts administrative measures and implements punishments in a consistent fashion, the people will comply with them but will have no shame. But if one follows the Way of virtue and implements ritual consistently, the people will have a sense of shame and moreover will correct themselves."

[2.3]

Fan Chi asked to study farming with him. The master said, "Better to ask an old farmer about it." He then asked to study gardening. "Better to ask an old gardener." When Fan Chi left, the master said, "Fan Chi is such a small-minded person. If a superior loves ritual, then the people will be reverent. If a superior loves righteousness, the people will oblige him, and if he loves good faith, the people will respond to him. If he can be like this, then people from all directions will come to him, bearing their children on their backs. Why should he need to study farming?"

[13.4]

Heaven

The master said, "No one understands me." Zigong said, "How can you say that no one understands you?" The master said, "I bear no animosity toward heaven and no ill-will toward human beings. My studies, while lowly, attain certain heights. It is heaven that understands me."

[14.37]

The master said, "I don't want to say anything." Zigong said, "If you don't say anything, then what should we write down?" The master said, "Does heaven say anything? The four seasons proceed and all things are generated, but does heaven say anything?"

[17.19]

A great minister asked Zigong, saying, "Can't your master be considered a sage? He is a man of many different abilities." Zigong replied, "Heaven has granted that he has very nearly become a sage, and, moreover, he is a man of many skills." The master heard this, and said, "The great minister understands me. When I was young, I was of very humble background, and hence I am capable at many different but nevertheless common things. But does the honorable person need this diversity? No."

[9.6]

Sima Niu lamented, "All people have brothers, but only I do not." Zixia said, "I have heard it said that 'Death and life are mandated, and wealth and high honor lie with heaven.' If the honorable person is reverential and well mannered, is respectful of others and follows ritual, then within the four seas all people will be brothers. How could the honorable person be worried that he have no brothers?"

[12.5]

Ritual

The master said, "People say 'ritual this' and 'ritual that.' But is ritual just jades and silks? They say 'music this' and 'music that.' But is music just bells and drums?"

[17.11]

Yan Yuan asked about humanity. The master said, "If one can prevail over the self and turn toward ritual, that is humanity. If one can do this for just a single day, the whole world will incline toward humanity. But is it that humanity just comes from one's own self alone, or from interacting with other people!" Yan Yuan said, "I would like to ask about the specific details of this." The master said, "Look at nothing contrary to ritual; hear nothing contrary to ritual, speak nothing contrary to ritual, do nothing contrary to ritual." Yan Yuan said, "Even though I am not gifted, I will try to practice what you have just said."

[12.1]

The master said, "What does someone not possessed of humanity have to do with ritual? What does someone not possessed of humanity have to do with music?"

[3.3]

Lin Fang asked about the fundamental basis of ritual. The master replied, "That is a good question! In performing rituals it is better to be simple rather than extravagant. For rites of mourning it is better to be sorrowful rather than casual."

[3.4]

When Fan Chi was Confucius's charioteer, the master said, "Meng Sun asked me what filiality was and I said, 'Not being disobedient.'" Fan Chi asked, "What did you mean by that?" The master replied, "I meant to serve one's parents with ritual when they are alive, to bury them with ritual when they die, and thereafter to sacrifice to them with ritual."

[2.5.2–3]

Zigong wanted to eliminate the offering of the sacrificial sheep at the beginning of the lunar month. The master said, "Zigong, you are concerned about the sheep, but I am concerned about the ritual."

[3.17]

The master said, "Honorable people, widely studied in cultured things and guided by ritual, will not overstep themselves."

[6.25]

The master said, "Respect without ritual becomes tiresome, circumspection without ritual becomes timidity, bold fortitude without ritual becomes unruly, and directness without ritual becomes twisted."

[8.2.1]

Sacrifice

The master was very circumspect about observing the vigils before sacrificing, about warfare, and about illness.

[7.12]

When observing the vigils before sacrifice, Confucius wore immaculately clean clothing. He altered his diet, and he moved from the place where he commonly sat.

[10.7]

Spirits

When he sacrificed to the ancestral spirits, he did so as if they were actually present; when he sacrificed to other spirits, he did so as if they were actually present. The master said, "If I do not really take part in the sacrifice, it is as if I did not sacrifice at all."

[3.12]

Fan Chi asked about wisdom. The master said, "To perform the obligations properly due to the people; and to pay reverence to ghosts and spirits, while keeping a distance from them—this may be called wisdom."

[6.20]

The master did not talk about strange marvels, the use of force, chaos and disorder, or spirits.

[7.20]

Shamanism, Divination, and Exorcism

The master said, "The people of the south say that unless someone is a steady person, they cannot become either a shaman or a healer. That is an excellent saying! Unless one is of steady virtue, one will invite disgrace. This would come simply from not divining properly."

[13.22]

When the villagers were performing the Nuo exorcism, he donned court dress and stood on the eastern steps.

[10.10.2]

Recluses

Once when Chang Ju and Jie Ni were out plowing their fields together, Confucius passed by and had Zilu ask them where the ford was. Chang Ju asked, "Who is that there in the carriage?"

"Confucius."

"Confucius from Lu?"

"Yes," Zilu replied.

"Well, if that's who it is," Chang added, "then he knows where the ford is."

Zilu then asked Jie Ni, who said, "Who are you?"

"I am Zilu."

"You're a disciple of Confucius from Lu?"

"That is so."

"The whole world is flooded," Jie stated, without interrupting his raking, "and who can change it? It's better to be a follower of someone who withdraws from the whole world than of someone who withdraws only from certain people."

When Zilu got back he told Confucius what they said. Surprised, the master said, "One cannot flock together with birds and beasts. If I do not associate with human beings, then with whom should I associate? If the Way prevailed within the world, then I would not try to change it."

[18.6]

Zilu, following at some distance behind the master, encountered an elderly man carrying a bamboo basket slung over his shoulder on a pole. Zilu asked, "Have you seen my master?" The old man replied, "You don't look too hardworking, and you probably can't even tell one kind of grain from another. Just who might your master be?" The man stuck his staff in the ground and started weeding, but Zilu just stood there respectfully with his hands clasped in front of his chest. In the end the old man invited Zilu to stay over; he killed a chicken and prepared some millet to feed him, and he introduced him to his two children. The next day, Zilu went on his way, and when he caught up with the master he told him what had happened. The master said, "He is a recluse." He had Zilu go back so that he might meet him, but when they arrived, he had already gone out. Zilu said, "Not to serve in office is not right. The proper customs between old and young cannot be set aside, but how much less can one set aside the righteousness between ruler and minister? By wanting to make himself pure, this man has thrown greater human relationships into disarray. When honorable persons serve in office, they enact this righteousness. When the Way is not enacted, they also know it of themselves."

[18.7]

Discussion Questions

1. Does Confucius deny the existence of supernatural forces? What relationship does he think one should have with them?

2. What do Confucius's statements on ritual (especially 17.11 and 3.3) reveal about how one should do it? Is it something to be done simply out of routine or should one have a particular state of mind?

3. Based on these passages, what is Confucius's opinion of those who live in solitude or intentionally retreat from social interactions? What does this tell us about individual improvement in Confucius's philosophy?

Exemplar 1

From Inquiry on the *Great Learning*

Wang Yangming

With the Han dynasty's establishment of the imperial academy to study Confucian classics in 124 BCE, Confucianism became an important part of the Chinese state ideology. However, as Daoist institutions strengthened and Buddhist missionaries arrived from India, Confucianism began to encounter rivals poised to threaten its imperial patronage. Beginning in the twelfth century CE, Confucian thinkers responded by developing a range of new contemplative practices that borrowed heavily from Buddhist and Daoist elements to emphasize internal development and an "original principle" shared by all humanity. Out of this movement, which Western scholars call Neo-Confucianism, arose Wang Yangming (1472–1529). Whereas earlier Neo-Confucian thinker Zhu Xi (1130–1200) had argued for a lengthy, belabored "investigation of things" to attain moral knowledge, Wang Yangming emphasized humans' intuitive understanding of Confucian principles through their heart-mind, which exists in unity with all heaven and earth. In making his argument, Wang Yangming pulled heavily on the philosophies of classical Confucian thinker Mencius (371–289 BCE) and his argument that man is naturally incapable of bearing another's suffering; Wang Yangming, however, extended this natural disinclination toward suffering to all the world, including animals, plants, and even broken tiles. In this fictitious question-and-answer passage found in his commentary on the Confucian classic the *Great Learning*, Wang Yangming demonstrates how the heart-mind and the natural expression of cosmic unity between humanity and the world naturally achieve the three main principles that underlie social harmony: (1) manifesting a clear character, (2) loving the people, and (3) abiding in the highest good.

QUESTION: The *Great Learning* was considered by a former scholar [Zhu Xi] as the learning of the great man. I venture to ask why the learning of the great man should consist in "manifesting the clear character"?

MASTER WANG SAID: The great man regards Heaven and Earth and the myriad things as one body. He regards the world as one family and the country as one person. As to those who make a cleavage between objects and distinguish between the self and others, they are small men. That the great man can regard Heaven, Earth, and the myriad things as one body is not because he deliberately wants to do so, but because it is natural to the humane nature of his mind that he do so. Forming one body with Heaven, Earth, and the myriad things is not only true of the great man. Even the mind of the small man is no different. Only he himself makes it small. Therefore when he sees a child about to fall into a well, he cannot help a feeling of alarm and commiseration. This shows that his humanity (*ren*) forms one body with the child. It may be objected that the child belongs to the same species. Again, when he observes the pitiful cries and frightened appearance of birds and animals about to be slaughtered, he cannot help feeling an "inability to bear" their suffering. This shows that his humanity forms one body with birds and animals. It may be objected that birds and animals are sentient beings as he is. But when he sees plants broken and destroyed, he cannot help a feeling of pity. This shows that his humanity forms one body with plants. It may be said that plants are living things as he is. Yet even when he sees tiles and stones shattered and crushed, he cannot help a feeling of regret. This shows that his humanity forms one body with tiles and stones. This means that even the mind of the small man necessarily has the humanity that forms one body with all. Such a mind is rooted in his Heaven-endowed nature, and is naturally intelligent, clear, and not beclouded. For this reason it is called the "clear character." Although the mind of the small man is divided and narrow, yet his humanity that forms one body can remain free from darkness to this degree. This is due to the fact that his mind has not yet been aroused by desires and obscured by selfishness. When it is aroused by desires and obscured by selfishness, compelled by greed for gain and fear of harm, and stirred by anger, he will destroy things, kill members of his own species, and will do everything. In extreme cases he will even slaughter his own brothers, and the humanity that forms one body will disappear completely. Hence, if it is not obscured by selfish desires, even the mind of the small man has the humanity that forms one body with all as does the mind of the great man. As soon as it is obscured by selfish desires, even the mind of the great man will be divided and narrow like that of the small man. Thus the learning of the great man consists entirely in getting rid of the obscuration of selfish desires in order by his own efforts to make manifest his clear character, so as to restore the condition of forming one body with Heaven, Earth, and the myriad things, a condition that is originally so, that is all. It is not that outside of the original substance something can be added.

QUESTION: Why, then, does the learning of the great man consist in loving the people?
ANSWER: To manifest the clear character is to bring about the substance of the state of forming one body with Heaven, Earth, and the myriad things, whereas loving the people is to put into universal operation the function of the state of forming one body. Hence manifesting the clear character consists in loving the people, and loving the people is the way to manifest the clear character. Therefore, only when I love my father, the fathers of others, and the fathers of all men can my humanity really form one body with my father, the fathers of others, and the fathers of all men. When it truly forms one body with them, then the clear character of filial piety will be manifested. Only when I love my brother, the brothers of others, and the brothers of all men can my humanity really form one body with my brother, the brothers of others, and the brothers of all men. When it truly forms one body with them, then the clear character of brotherly respect will be manifested. Everything from ruler, minister, husband, wife, and friends to mountains, rivers, spiritual beings, birds, animals, and plants should be truly loved in order to realize my humanity that forms one body with them, and then my clear character will be completely manifested, and I will really form one body with Heaven, Earth, and the myriad things. This is what is meant by "manifesting the clear character throughout the empire." This is what is meant by "regulation of the family," "ordering the state," and "bringing peace to the world." This is what is meant by "full development of one's nature."

QUESTION: Then why does the learning of the great man consist in "abiding in the highest good"?
ANSWER: The highest good is the ultimate principle of manifesting character and loving people. The nature endowed in us by Heaven is pure and perfect. The fact that it is intelligent, clear, and not beclouded is evidence of the emanation and revelation of the highest good. It is the original substance of the clear character

which is called innate knowledge of the good. As the highest good emanates and reveals itself, we will consider right as right and wrong as wrong. Things of greater or less importance and situations of grave or light character will be responded to as they act upon us. In all our changes and movements, we will stick to no particular point, but possess in ourselves the Mean that is perfectly natural. This is the ultimate of the normal nature of man and the principle of things. There can be no consideration of adding to or subtracting from it. If there is any, it means selfish ideas and shallow cunning, and cannot be said to be the highest good. Naturally, how can anyone who does not watch over himself carefully when alone, and who has no refinement and singleness of mind, attain to such a state of perfection? Later generations fail to realize that the highest good is inherent in their own minds, but exercise their selfish ideas and cunning and grope for it outside their minds, believing that every event and every object has its own peculiar definite principle. For this reason the law of right and wrong is obscured; the mind becomes concerned with fragmentary and isolated details and broken pieces; the selfish desires of man become rampant and the Principle of Nature is at an end. And thus the learning of manifesting character and loving people is everywhere thrown into confusion. In the past there have, of course, been people who wanted to manifest their clear character. But simply because they did not know how to abide in the highest good, but instead drove their own minds toward something too lofty, they thereby lost them in illusions, emptiness, and quietness, having nothing to do with the work of the family, the state, and the world. Such are the followers of Buddhism and Taoism. There have, of course, been those who wanted to love their people. Yet simply because they did not know how to abide in the highest good, but instead sank their own minds in base and trifling things, they thereby lost them in scheming strategy and cunning techniques, having neither the sincerity of humanity nor that of commiseration. Such are the followers of the Five Despots and the pursuers of success and profit. All of these defects are due to a failure to know how to abide in the highest good. Therefore abiding in the highest good is to manifesting character and loving people as the carpenter's square and compass are to the square and the circle, or rule and measure to length, or balances and scales to weight. If the square and the circle do not abide by the compass and the carpenter's square, their standard will be wrong; if length does not abide by the rule and measure, its adjustment will be lost; if weight does not abide by the balances, its exactness will be gone; and if manifesting clear character and loving people do not abide by the highest good, their foundation will disappear. Therefore, abiding in the highest good so as to love people and manifest the clear character is what is meant by the learning of the great man.

1. What might Mencius say about Wang Yangming's interpretation of his ideas? Would he agree with Wang Yangming's extension of his ideas into the nonhuman world of plants and animals? Or might he see this as an inappropriate application of a human-centered philosophy onto a nonhuman world?

2. How does Wang Yangming use classical Confucian ideas about the Five Relationships to promote his unique interpretation of humanity sharing one body with all things? Is this a logical extension of the Five Relationships, or is Wang Yangming doing something more revolutionary?

3. How might creatively incorporating elements of Buddhism and Daoism make Neo-Confucianism more fit to compete with these traditions?

Exemplar 2

From *Confucius from the Heart*

Yu Dan

Teaching at one of the foremost universities in China, Yu Dan has become among the leading representatives of "popular" Confucianism in contemporary China. Born in 1965, she came to public attention in 2006 for her popular lecture series on the Analects. Her lectures were transcribed and edited into the book *Confucius from the Heart*, which has since sold over 4 million copies worldwide. Scholars and other cultural interpreters have generally understood Yu Dan's popularity as fueled by the growing middle class in China, who crave a spiritual practice that connects them to China's ancient culture. Her interpretation of Confucianism reflects that desire, focusing almost exclusively on individual personal fulfillment, while excluding much of the outwardly political aspects of Confucianism that the governing Communist Party may find threatening. In this selection, Yu Dan contemplates Confucian insight on the type of social character one should develop for personal and professional success.

In the modern world, with e-mail and messaging, we can be constantly in touch with people thousands of miles away, yet we make no effort to get to know our neighbors.

More than ever before, the way we deal with other people is crucial.

In this confused and complicated social environment, how should we treat others?

When someone treats us unfairly, how should we react? What are the principles we should adopt when dealing with the people closest to us?

Confucius gives us many rules on how to conduct ourselves in society and so be a decent person. These rules may at first appear fixed, even rigid, but in fact they contain a surprising flexibility.

Put simply, he gives us the principles that should govern our actions and the degree to which we should follow those principles.

We often ask ourselves what we should do and what we shouldn't; what is good and what is bad.

Actually, when it comes to asking these questions, it very often happens that things cannot be divided according to simple ideas of right and wrong, good and bad, yes and no. When we do something, and the extent to which we do it, will also have a direct influence on how we should act. Confucius particularly stressed how far we should go in doing anything. Acting to excess or not doing enough are both to be avoided, as far as possible.

So, although Confucius advocated benevolence and charity, he did not believe that we should pardon the faults of everybody we meet with indiscriminate benevolence.

Somebody asked him: "What do you think of the saying 'Repay an injury with a good turn'?"

Confucius replied: "You repay an injury with straightness but you repay a good turn with a good turn." This may not be quite what we would have expected to hear, but an awareness of the limits of what is acceptable in others is one key hallmark of the true *junzi*.

What Confucius is advocating here is respect for human dignity.

Of course, he did not suggest repaying one grievance with another grievance. If we constantly confront wrongs done to us with ill will and spite, then we will be caught up in a vicious circle that can never cease. We will sacrifice not only our own happiness, but our grandchildren's, too.

Repaying a grievance with virtue is not practicable, either. If you are too free with your goodness and mercy, treating those who have done you wrong with unnecessary kindheartedness, this, too, is a waste.

But there is a third attitude, which is to face all of this calmly, with fair-mindedness, justice, openness, and uprightness, that is to say, to approach it with a high moral character. By extension, Confucius stressed that we must keep our feelings and our talents for the places where they are needed.

These days everyone is trying to avoid wasting resources, yet we have overlooked the desolation of spirit and waste of energy that occurs within our bodies every day.

Today's material prosperity and the increasing speed of the rhythms of life require us to make very swift judgments. We have to choose the best way to live, a way that is truly our own.

In our lives, we often see the following perplexing situations:

A father and mother who are good to their child, yet this only drives the child away.

Friends who are as close as close can be, but always seem to end up hurting each other.

A person who schemes with all their might for a closer relationship with superiors and colleagues, yet who frequently achieves the very opposite.

How can this be?

Confucius believed that neither excessive aloofness nor excessive intimacy was ideal. For him "going too far is as bad as not going far enough." Extreme intimacy is not the ideal situation for two people who want to get along.

So how do we achieve "good" relationships?

Confucius's student Ziyou said: "To be importunate with one's lord will mean humiliation. To be importunate with one's friends will mean estrangement." In other words, if you are always hanging around your superiors whether you have any business with them or not, although you are making a show of closeness you will soon bring humiliation upon yourself. Equally, if you are always sticking close to your friend's side, although it appears that you are inseparable, estrangement will not be far away.

There is a fable that illustrates this. There once was a group of porcupines, all covered in sharp spines, huddling together to keep warm over the winter. They could never work out how far apart they should be. Just a little bit too far away and they couldn't keep each other warm, so they crowded closer; but as soon as they squeezed closer together, the sharp spines would prick them, so they started to move farther apart, but once they did, they felt the cold. It took a good deal of trial and error for the porcupines to finally find the right degree of separation, so that they could retain the warmth of the group without hurting each other.

In China today, especially in the big cities, the old multifamily courtyards have all been pulled down and blocks of flats built in their place. Gone are the days when one family would make dumplings and give some to all the neighbors, and we no longer see all the inhabitants of a courtyard celebrate New Year together, one table for the adults, another for the children. Often neighbors who have lived for three or four years on the same staircase don't really know each other.

Because our relationships with the people who live around us have become colder, it is harder for us to communicate with one another.

This then increases the burden on the few friends we do rely on.

You might think: My best friend should treat me a bit better; then I will go out of my way to be a bit nicer to him. You might think: If you're having family problems, an argument with your partner, for example, why don't you tell me? I can step in and mediate for you!

A lot of us think in this way. But we should listen to Ziyou; excessive closeness is bound to harm other people.

So how should we get on with our friends?

Zigong once asked his teacher this question and Confucius told him: "Advise them to the best of your ability and guide them properly, but stop when there is no hope of success. Do not ask to be snubbed." When you see a friend doing something wrong, you should do your best to warn them off, and guide them with goodwill, but if they really don't listen, let it go. Don't say any more; otherwise you're just making a rod for your own back.

So with good friends you also need boundaries. More is not always better.

Confucius warns us that, whether with friends or leaders, we must keep a certain distance, and know where the boundaries lie between intimacy and estrangement.

So, with our family, who are dearer to us than anyone else, should we be as close as close can be?

Or should we also maintain a certain distance between parents and children, husband and wife, or between lovers?

Psychologists have a term for the kind of behavior that we often see in modern people's interactions – "nonloving behavior." It describes, very accurately, what happens when, in the name of love, people behave in a grasping, coercive way toward those dearest to them. It often happens between husband and wife, between lovers, between mother and son, or father and daughter – in other words, between the people who are closest to one another.

A husband or wife might say to the other: "Just look what I have given up for love of you. I did this or that just for the sake of this family, so now you must treat me a certain way."

Lots of mothers say to their children: "Look – after I had you, I fell behind at work, I lost my looks, I sacrificed everything for you, so why can't you do a bit better at school?"

All of this is nonloving behavior: a sort of coercion in the name of love, to make other people behave the way we want them to.

I once read a book on parenting by a British psychologist who had some very wise things to say:

Love is almost always about bringing people closer together. But there is one kind of love, and one only, whose aim is separation: the love of parents for their children. Truly successful parental love means letting the child become independent and separate from your lives as early as possible; the earlier this separation, the more successful you have been as parents.

Seen like this, independence and a respectful distance are essential to an individual's personal dignity, and this respect should be maintained, even between the people we are closest to.

Whether between fathers and sons, mothers and daughters, or long-married husbands and wives, once that respectful distance is breached, once you have overstepped the mark, and reached the stage that Confucius calls "importunate," so that you are no longer properly independent of each other, there will be problems. Hidden damage, estrangement, or even a total breakdown in relations will not be far away.

Confucius shows us that we must respect every person equally and rationally, maintain a tactful distance, and give each other breathing space.

1. How does Yu Dan's vision of Confucianism compare with other interpretations you have seen in this class? Do you think Confucius or Wang Yangming would agree with her interpretation? Why or why not?

2. Reading this selection, what type of audience does Yu Dan seem to be speaking to? What clues in the text lead you to this conclusion?

3. Having read Yu Dan's interpretation, how do non-Confucian, North American cultures handle intimacy differently than those influenced by Confucianism? Do most Americans believe you should maintain a distance between husband and wife or between friends?

Controversy

From *Centrality and Commonality: An Essay on Confucian Religiousness*

Tu Weiming

Born in 1940 in Yunnan, China, and raised in Taiwan, Tu Weiming has become a leading voice in the contemporary revival of Confucian philosophies known as New Confucianism. New Confucianism traces its roots to the reformation of Confucian ideas that began after the 1919 May Fourth Movement, which blamed Confucianism for China's international decline. As a result, Confucian thinkers—who were often forced to flee mainland China—constructed a new vision of Confucianism in dialogue with Western philosophical traditions like rationalism and humanism. Today, New Confucianism emphasizes traditions of self-cultivation, the sacredness of the relationship between self and society, and the possibility for shared wisdom between the West and China. In this selection of his commentary on the *Doctrine of the Mean* (Zhongyong), Tu Weiming defends the religiosity of Confucianism through its belief in the fundamentally interrelated nature of the individual, the community, and the transcendent, which he defines as opening oneself up to a dimension of reality that exists beyond human rationality.

Being religious, in the Confucian perspective, informed by sacred texts such as *Zhongyong*, means being engaged in the process of learning to be fully human. We can define the Confucian way of being religious as *ultimate self-transformation as a communal act and as a faithful dialogical response to the transcendent*. This is also the

Confucian prescription for learning to be fully human. We can say that Confucian religiosity is expressed through the infinite potential and the inexhaustible strength of each human being for self-transcendence. Three interrelated dimensions are involved here: the person, the community, and the transcendent.

The Confucian conviction that a person's self-cultivation is the root of social order and that universal peace depends on social order has far-reaching implications for our perception of the linkage between the person and the community on the one hand and the community and the transcendent on the other. For example, the private, psychological management of one's emotive state is not separate from the well-being of the public; social responsibility and religious faith are not conflicting demands. The movement from the self via the community to Heaven is predicated on a holistic vision of human self-transcendence that the compartmentalized methods of psychology, sociology, or theology, which are characteristic of academic "disciplines" in modern universities, are grossly inadequate to grasp.

The conviction that what we do as ordinary citizens within the confines of our private homes is socially and politically important and what we do as public servants performing our roles and functions in the mundane world is religiously significant reflects a deep Confucian concern for "the secular as sacred." In the post-Machiavellian, Hobbesian, Marxian and Freudian age, it is extremely difficult to imagine that there is or can ever be an organismic unity that underlies the person, the community and the transcendent. Indeed, any insinuation that these connections are still whole may give the impression of a prelapsarian worldview, a worldview that can still be imagined but is no longer viable as a spiritual and intellectual option for the sophisticated modern mind.

The Confucians do not glorify a utopia that historically has never existed but describe what we naturally and inevitably are as human beings. As the Confucians argue, it is more difficult to imagine ourselves as isolable individuals than as centers of relationships constantly interacting with one another in a dynamic network of human-relatedness. Similarly, it is more difficult to believe in an omnipotent God who violates rules of nature for mysterious reasons, than in enduring cosmic patterns discoverable by human rationality. I do not mean to challenge the doctrine of individualism which has inspired generation after generation to search for autonomy, independence and dignity, or the concept of an all-mighty God which continues to be informed by sophisticated theological argumentation. I simply want to note that, despite its apparent naiveté, the concept of organismic unity is predicated on an inclusive humanist vision. The Confucian way of being religious is a means of understanding of that vision.

"Ultimate self-transformation" implies that the process of learning to be human never ends (even though the Confucians do not subscribe to the "existentialist" belief that since our existence precedes our essence we can shape our nature according to our own independent action through conscious living). Our inescapable humanity specifies the minimum condition, the lowest common denominator, "ultimate" refers to the greatest possible realization of that humanity. Self-transformation suggests that although we are not what we ought to be, we can reach the highest state of humanity through personal cultivation. Learning to be fully human is to learn to become a sage (an authentic manifestation of our nature, indeed our essence as ordained by Heaven). Since the sage is genuinely human, the aim of self-transformation is not to go beyond humanity but to realize it as completely as possible. We can never embody our humanity in its all-embracing fullness.

The statement that we are naturally and inescapably human and that we must endeavor to learn to be fully human may appear paradoxical. If we are already human, why must we try to learn to be human? It seems easier to comprehend the thesis that to transcend the state of being human is to become superior to what is still human, to become superhuman or divine. However, the Confucian insistence that ultimate self-transformation does not go beyond humanity but realizes it is a substantive ethicoreligious claim. The minimum requirement—that one is human—serves as the basis for the maximum realization of humanity, just as a tiny stream serves as the beginning of the mighty Yangtze. We cannot deny that there is water in the tiny stream, but we must admit that the greatness of the water in the Yangtze has given it a qualitatively different significance.

The metaphor that humanity, like water, must reach a high enough level for it to flow suggests that the Confucians conceive of humanity as dynamic. Self-transformation, symbolized by an ever-broadening and ever-deepening stream of humanity, is a process of "establishing" and "enlarging." It is radically different from one's quest for inner spirituality as an isolable individual. In this context, "ultimate" connotes the full realization of humanity, its maximum fulfillment as well as its highest point of attainment.

If we envision the ultimate self-transformation of a fellow human being as a stream gushing forth from its springs, then as that stream establishes and enlarges itself, it will meet other streams. The confluence of two or more streams is what we refer to as *the communal act*. To the Confucians, one cannot establish and enlarge oneself through spiritual transformation without encountering like-minded people. Even if we imagine a subterranean stream making its way alone to the ocean, we must assume that it benefits from other sources. A defining characteristic of Confucian religiousness is its emphasis on the fiduciary community as an irreducible reality in ultimate self-transformation.

One becomes fully human within a community. The Confucians believe that normally it is desirable to establish fruitful communication with the transcendent through communal participation. Only in extraordinary circumstances, such as the case of Chu Yuan, who was the only sober person in a drunken multitude, can we appeal to heaven directly. Such an action—facing Heaven alone as an isolated individual without reference to one's community—has grave consequences for the community as a whole as well as for the individual. It must be undertaken with extreme care and even a sense of tragedy. The preferred course of action is to integrate all levels of the community (family, neighborhood, clan, race, nation, world, universe, cosmos) into the process of self-transformation. The Confucians believe that this gradual process of inclusion is inherent in the project of learning to be fully human.

The Confucians advocate a humanism that neither denies nor slights the transcendent. I use the term "inclusive humanism" to underscore the comprehensiveness of the concept of humanity in the Confucian perspective and to differentiate it from the familiar forms of exclusive secular humanism. In light of Confucian inclusive humanism, the process of learning to be fully human entails not only communal participation but also a *faithful dialogical response to the transcendent*. The willingness—which implies one's ability—to open up to the dimension of reality that can never be completely apprehended by human rationality, is not only an imagination but also an action. This opening up is a fulfillment of humanity as well as an answer to the mandate of heaven. The mutuality of Heaven and the man (in the gender neutral sense of humanity) makes it possible to perceive the transcendent as immanent. To suggest that the full meaning of Heaven can be embodied in our humanity would be blasphemous. Rather, our inborn ability to respond to the bidding of heaven impels us to extend our human horizon continuously so that the immanent in our nature assumes a transcendent dimension.

To become fully human, in this sense, one must establish a dialogical relationship with Heaven. The Confucian faith in the perfectibility of human nature through self-effort is, strictly speaking, a faith in self-transcendence. The godlike sage is the co-creator of the universe not because the transcendent is totally humanized but because the human is ultimately transformed by means of a faithful dialogical response to the transcendence. The fiduciary community, as a defining characteristic of Confucian religiosity, is not governed by social ethics devoid of reference to the transcendent. On the contrary, the community based on trust rather than on contract is itself a sacred confirmation that human nature is ordained by Heaven. It may not be farfetched to suggest that in the Confucian sense our "covenant" with Heaven is the full realization of humanity as Heaven's own ultimate transformation.

Discussion Questions

1. What is at stake in Tu Weiming's claim that Confucianism is a religion? What would it mean, for example, if the United States Supreme Court either recognized Confucianism as a religion or officially declared that it is not a religion?

2. Does Tu Weiming understand self-transformation as something done to benefit oneself or to benefit society?

3. A central tenet of New Confucianism is that Confucian philosophies can address the excesses of the modern West. Reading this passage, do you agree? Who might benefit from Confucian ideas and how? Are there any elements of Confucianism that could be potentially unhelpful?

Daoism

Daoism defies easy description, containing more philosophical texts, health practices, esoteric rituals, and traditions of worship than can be covered here. The Daoist perspective is also informed by Confucianism, which has traditionally served as a foil for Daoist thought. Where Confucianism sees the human problem as social chaos, Daoism sees the problem as "lifelessness" caused by humanity falling out of harmony with the rhythms of nature and its mystical source of nature known as the Dao. The result of this separation is unhappiness and, especially, early death. The Daodejing, one of the earliest texts in the Daoist tradition, describes how human efforts to fix society only bring about more problems as we become further alienated from the natural order.

The solution to lifelessness is flourishing. Daoist philosophy posits that the solution to most problems lies not in exerting more force but rather in exerting as little effort as possible, relying on intuition and timing, and allowing the universe to resolve itself. The Daoist writer Zhuangzi presents an anecdote about a master butcher whose knife never becomes dull because he can make an ox carcass come apart "like a clod of earth crumbling to the ground." Zhuangzi invites readers to imagine how the flourishing of the butcher could be adapted into flourishing in their own lives.

Daoist exemplars include people who have obtained extraordinary wisdom or abilities by achieving harmony with the Dao—immortals, sages, or "holy men." Often these exemplars appear extremely humble or even insane because they are no longer bound by the human institutions that separate us from the flow of the universe. Zhuangzi provides a dialogue in which skeptics cannot believe the strange behaviors or abilities attributed to a Daoist master. While exemplars are often men in Daoist tradition, women too can master esoteric techniques such as "inner alchemy" in order to transform their subtle energies and obtain immortality. The folk novel *Seven Taoist Masters* tells the story of Sun Buer, a woman who sacrificed her beauty and her social station in order to pursue the highest path toward immortality.

Daoism celebrates change and Daoist tradition continues to evolve, incorporating new elements and resulting in strange new forms. The most controversial iteration of Daoist tradition is Falun Gong, a group the Chinese government has condemned as "a cult." The controversy surrounding Falun Gong demonstrates that even in a tradition that celebrates detachment from society, religion is not easily separated from politics.

Problem/Solution

The More Taboos under Heaven
FROM THE DAODEJING

In Daoism the human problem has been described as "lifelessness." Among other things, this means that humans find themselves cut off from the natural rhythms of nature that make flourishing possible. This separation from the Dao was not a divine punishment: it is self-created by imposing norms and rules on ourselves in what some misguidedly perceive as the march of civilization. The Daodejing is a Daoist text, attributed to Laozi, that was likely composed in its current form around the third century BCE. The passage below lays out how humanity's efforts to control nature and each other have only worsened the very problems they were intended to solve. Daoism advises the opposite approach, known as *wuwei* or "nonaction," in which problems are allowed to resolve themselves. The Daodejing is particularly concerned with statecraft and the behaviors of rulers, but the philosophy of wuwei also applies to ordinary people and daily problems.

Govern the state by the proper norm,
Conduct warfare with surprise,
Win the world without meddling.
How do I know it is so?
Because of this:

The more inhibitions the world has,
The more impoverished the common people become.
The more weapons the ruler has,
The more disorderly the state becomes.
The more cunning the ruler uses,
The more untoward things happen.

The more laws and decrees are issued,
The more bandits and thieves come forth.

Therefore the sage says:
I do nothing,
And the common people change of themselves.
I stay still,
And the common people get things right for themselves.
I do not meddle,
And the common people make themselves prosperous.
I have no desires,
And the common people keep themselves simple.

Discussion Questions

1. The advice in this passage seems counterintuitive. For example, we normally think of laws as stopping bandits and thieves, not causing more to come forth. Can you think of a specific example where attempts to combat a problem actually make it worse?

2. Do you think it is really possible to "win the world without meddling"? Are there no situations where direct action is necessary to improve society and help people?

3. Some might reasonably argue that this passage is not religious in nature. Is there a way this could be religious? How would we have to define what "religion" is in order to think about this passage as religious?

Technique

The Secret of Caring for Life
Zhuangzi

Zhuangzi is the second most important thinker in early Daoist literature. The book attributed to him took its current form around the third century BCE and consists largely of humorous yet insightful stories. The reader is often left to infer what the larger point of these stories is. In the anecdote below, Lord Wenhui listens to his cook describe how he butchers oxen and declares that he has learned how to care for life. The implication is that the cook's technique, which involves solving problems largely through intuition and relying on what is naturally there instead of exerting effort, serves as a metaphor for human flourishing. But the details of this metaphor are left for the reader to discern.

Your life has a limit but knowledge has none. If you use what is limited to pursue what has no limit, you will be in danger. If you understand this and still strive for knowledge, you will be in danger for certain! If you do good, stay away from fame. If you do evil, stay away from punishments. Follow the middle; go by what is constant, and you can stay in one piece, keep yourself alive, look after your parents, and live out your years.

Cook Ding was cutting up an ox for Lord Wenhui. At every touch of his hand, every heave of his shoulder, every move of his feet, every thrust of his knee—zip! zoop! He slithered the knife along with a zing, and all was in perfect rhythm, as though he were performing the Dance of the Mulberry Grove or keeping time to the Jingshou music.[1]

"Ah, this is marvelous!" said Lord Wenhui. "Imagine skill reaching such heights!"

Cook Ding laid down his knife and replied, "What I care about is the Way, which goes beyond skill. When I first began cutting up oxen, all I could see was the ox itself. After three years I no longer saw the whole ox. And now—now I go at it by spirit and don't look with my eyes. Perception and understanding have come to a stop and spirit moves where it wants. I go along with the natural makeup, strike in the big hollows, guide the knife through the big openings, and follow things as they are. So I never touch the smallest ligament or tendon, much less a main joint.

"A good cook changes his knife once a year—because he cuts. A mediocre cook changes his knife once a month—because he hacks. I've had this knife of mine for nineteen years and I've cut up thousands of oxen with it, and yet the blade is as good as though it had just come from the grindstone. There are spaces between the joints, and the blade of the knife has really no thickness. If you insert what has no thickness into such spaces, then there's plenty of room—more than enough for the blade to play about in. That's why after nineteen years the blade of my knife is still as good as when it first came from the grindstone.

"However, whenever I come to a complicated place, I size up the difficulties, tell myself to watch out and be careful, keep my eyes on what I'm doing, work very slowly, and move the knife with the greatest subtlety, until—flop! the whole thing comes apart like a clod of earth crumbling to the ground. I stand there holding the knife and look all around me, completely satisfied and reluctant to move on, and then I wipe off the knife and put it away."

"Excellent!" said Lord Wenhui. "I have heard the words of Cook Ding and learned how to care for life!"

---

1 While it is difficult to say anything with certainty, the Dance of the Mulberry Grove may have been a ritual dance performed to inspire rainfall. Similarly, Jingshou music was fast-paced music performed at the time.

1. Have you ever, like Cook Ding, mastered a skill in which a task that initially seems very difficult gradually becomes effortless? What changed?

2. What does this story about how to butcher oxen have to do with the Daoist goals of longevity and immortality?

3. Cook Ding says that sometimes there are "complicated places" where he has to stop and think about what he is doing. If butchering is a metaphor for life, what do these complicated places represent?

Exemplar 1

The Superior Man

Zhuangzi

Daoist literature is replete with fantastic stories about sages, immortals, and perfected people who have obtained superhuman abilities through their connection to the Dao. For Zhuangzi, the ideal person was a holy man (*shen jen*, literally, "spirit person"). In the reading below, a skeptic relates stories of a holy man with amazing powers who is unbound from the government and the Five Relationships (both deeply valued by Confucians). Were these powers meant to be literally true or a metaphor?

Chien Wu said to Lien Shu, "I was listening to Chieh Yu's talk—big and nothing to back it up, going on and on without turning around. I was completely dumbfounded at his words—no more end than the Milky Way, wild and wide of the mark, never coming near human affairs!"

"What were his words like?" asked Lien Shu.

"He said that there is a Holy Man living on faraway Ku-she Mountain, with skin like ice or snow, and gentle and shy like a young girl. He doesn't eat the five grains, but sucks the wind, drinks the dew, climbs up on the clouds and mist, rides a flying dragon, and wanders beyond the four seas. By concentrating his spirit, he can protect creatures from sickness and plague and make the harvest plentiful. I thought this was all insane and refused to believe it."

"You would!" said Lien Shu. "We can't expect a blind man to appreciate beautiful patterns or a deaf man to listen to bells and drums. And blindness and deafness are not confined to the body alone—the understanding has them too, as your words just now have shown. This man, with this virtue of his, is about to embrace the ten thousand things and roll them into one. Though the age calls for reform, why should he wear himself out over the affairs of the world? There is nothing that can harm this man. Though flood waters pile up to the sky, he will not drown. Though a great drought melts metal and stone and scorches the earth and hills, he will not be burned. From his dust and leavings alone you could mold a Yao or a Shun![1] Why should he consent to bother about mere things?"

Discussion Questions

1. Does the holy man have no worries because he has extraordinary powers? Or does he have extraordinary powers because he has no worries?

2. From this text, do you think people in ancient China really believed in holy men who ride flying dragons and eat only wind and dew? Do you think Zhuangzi wanted or expected readers to believe in such things?

3. Why is the holy man described as being "gentle and shy like a young girl"? This is not how we normally imagine people with superpowers acting.

Exemplar 2

From *Seven Taoist Masters*

Sun Buer (Sun Pu-erh) (1119–1182 CE) was the only female of the Seven Perfected, the greatest disciples of Wang Chongyang (Wang Ch'ung-yang) who founded the Complete Perfection school of Daoism. Her religious name, Pu-erh, literally means "not two," conveying both an understanding of mystical unity and the single-minded determination that she brought to her training. This selection from the novel *Seven Taoist Masters* (c. 1500 CE) describes Sun Buer's willingness to sacrifice everything to travel to the city of Luoyang, the ancient capital of China, where she later acquired many followers. It also describes her secret practice of inner alchemy: techniques used to attain immortality by turning the body into an alchemical crucible. A work titled *The Codified Sayings of the Primordial Goddess Sun Pu-erh* describes meditation practices for women and may have been written by one of her disciples.

Sun Buer felt as if she had awakened from a bad dream. Everything now seemed clear. She sighed and said to Ma Tanyang, "Brother, if not for your help I would have remained in the depth of illusion and ruined myself. Usually I am more intelligent in dealing with daily matters, but when it comes to learning Taoist knowledge you sur-

---

1 Yao and Shun are the last two of the so-called Five Emperors of ancient China. These revered, semidivine figures supposedly ruled China in the centuries before the Xia dynasty (2205–1766 BCE) and helped to introduce the art of civilization to the Chinese people.

pass me by far." Ma TanYang said, "It is not because I grasp the instructions of our teacher better, but because for a long time you closed your mind to learning new things. You thought you had learned all there was to learn. Your intelligence became an obstacle to your training. Learning is limitless. Not many can fully grasp this idea." Sun Buer thanked Ma Tanyang and said, "From now on I shall be humble and learn whatever there is to learn." Ma Tanyang returned to his room, happy that Sun Buer had realized her mistakes and was now ready to progress again.

A few days later Ma Tanyang prepared to attend the birthday celebration of an aunt in a nearby town. He asked Sun Buer to accompany him, but she pleaded sick and said she could not make the journey. So Ma Tanyang packed the gifts, loaded them on a mule, and set out alone.

Sun Buer sat in her room and thought once more about Ma Tanyang's words. She especially remembered his saying that she had lost her motivation to learn. Left alone in the mansion, she thought things through. Ma Tanyang would be away for a few days, and the servants were busy. This would be a good opportunity for her to go to Wang Chongyang and humbly ask for instructions.

She went to the meditation hall and found Wang Chongyang sitting quietly in meditation. She knelt at the doorway and said respectfully, "Sir, your student Sun Buer has been stupid and did not appreciate your teachings. Now that Ma Tanyang has explained everything to me, I am ashamed of myself and what I have done. I would like to ask for forgiveness and hope that you will instruct me again." She bowed low several times. Wang Chongyang beckoned her in and said, "You may stand up now. I shall describe to you three vehicles of the Taoist path. Listen well and then tell me which vehicle you aspire toward. Those who seek that Tao are nonattached to life and death. The heart is void of form and free from dust. There are no thoughts or feelings that tie one to the material plane. Their being is like the bright moon in a cloudless sky. With the spark of original nature they intuit the mystery of heaven and earth. They understand the principles behind the union of *yin* and *yang*, and, using the methods of internal alchemy, they return to the void and emerge with the Tao. They are at one with the sun and moon, they age with the heaven and earth and achieve the highest rank of immortality in heaven. This is the Great Vehicle. It is the fastest and most direct path to immortality. Those who cultivate the Middle Vehicle observe the festivals of the gods and immortals with veneration, chant regularly the names of the gods and refrain from meat on designated vegetarian days. By immersing themselves in chanting, they purify the heart and let the original nature shine. In due time their spirit ascends to the heavens, and they become immortals of the middle rank. Those who cultivate the Lower Vehicle do good deeds, and by so doing their original nature is prevented from being tainted. They are contented and are at peace with themselves, living a long and healthy life. In due time, when they have accumulated enough good works, they will ascend to heaven and become immortals of the lower ranks." Wang Chongyang finished speaking, smiled, and asked Sun Buer, "To which vehicle do you aspire?" Sun

Buer replied, "Your student aspires to the Great Vehicle." Wang Chongyang said, "You have ambitious aspirations, but I don't know whether you have the discipline and perseverance to pursue that path." Sun Buer said, "Sir, my aspirations are not ambitious, but my will is strong. I am willing to sacrifice everything to attain the Great Vehicle."

Wang Chongyang then said, "Those who cultivate the Tao must find a place that is conducive to training. Certain places are filled with power, and training at these power places will enhance one's progress. There is a power hidden in the city of Luoyang, and the gods have ordained that an immortal will emerge from there. One need merely cultivate oneself there for ten to twelve years, and immortality will be attained. Are you willing to go?" Sun Buer said, "I am willing to go anywhere if that is what is required to cultivate the Great Vehicle." Wang Chongyang looked at Sun Buer and then shook his head. "You cannot go." Sun Buer said, "I am willing to do anything. I am willing to die, if necessary." Wang Chongyang said, "Dying is a waste if it achieves no purpose. To simply throw your life away is to rob yourself of the chance to become an immortal. Luoyang is more than a thousand miles away. You will meet with perils along the way. You will be the target of men who desire your beauty. They will rape you and molest you. And rather than be shamed, you would take your own life before they touch you. Now, is that not wasting your life to no purpose? Not only will you not achieve immortality but you will throw away what was given to you by Heaven. That is why I said you cannot go."

Sun Buer left the meditation hall and went directly to the kitchen. Telling the servants to leave, she filled a wok with cooking oil, heated the oil until it was hot, and then poured in cold water. The oil sizzled, and sparks of hot liquid shot out of the wok. Sun Buer closed her eyes and let the liquid hit her face, burning the skin in numerous places; even after healing, the burns would leave scars and marks all over her face. She then returned to Wang Chongyang and said, "Look at my ugly face. Now will you allow me to travel to Luoyang?" Wang Chongyang clapped his hands and said, "I have never seen one as determined as you are or willing to sacrifice so much. I did not come to Shantung Province in vain. You shall go to Luoyang."

Wang Chongyang then taught Sun Buer the methods of internal alchemy. He showed her how to immerse fire in water, how to unite *yin* and *yang*, and how to conceive and nourish the spirit. When he was satisfied that Sun Buer remembered and understood the instructions, he said, "Remember, hide your knowledge. Do not let people know you are a seeker of the Tao. After you have finished the Great Alchemical Work, then you may reveal yourself and teach others. In the meantime, let your face heal. Do not even let your servants know of your plans. Leave as soon as you are ready. You need not come to say farewell to me. We shall meet again soon at the celebration of the ripening of the immortal peach."

Sun Buer thanked Wang Chongyang and left the meditation hall. On her way back to her room, she ran into a servant, who screamed when she saw the lady's face. When the servant recovered her wits, she asked Sun Buer, "Lady, what has happened to your face?" Sun Buer said, "I was cooking a snack for the teacher, and by mistake I added water to the cooking oil. I did not get out of the way in time, and the sizzling liquid shot into my face. It is nothing serious." Sun Buer locked herself in her room for the next few days and reviewed Wang Chongyang's instructions.

When Ma Tanyang returned home, the servants at once told him about his wife's accident in the kitchen. Ma Tanyang went to Sun Buer's room, saw her face, and consoled her. Gently he said, "You should have been more careful. Let the servants do the cooking. The lady of the house should not be working in the kitchen. Now your beautiful face is ruined with scars." Sun Buer stared at Ma Tanyang and cackled madly. "Are you the messenger of the Empress of Heaven? Have you come to invite me to attend the celebrations in heaven? If so, let's get going!" She opened the window and jumped out. Pretending to slip, she deliberately fell and lay on the ground, groaning. Ma Tanyang ran out, put his arms around her and helped her up. Sun Buer laughed and cried like a mad woman. Ma Tanyang escorted her back to her room and then went to Wang Chongyang.

Seeing his teacher, Ma Tanyang said, "Sir, my wife has gone mad. She has lost her mind. She is talking nonsense, and she laughs and cries for no reason." Wang Chongyang said, "If she is not mad, how can she become an immortal?" Ma Tanyang did not understand Wang Chongyang's remark. He was about to ask his teacher what it meant when Wang Chongyang waved his hand and told him to leave. Sadly, Ma Tanyang went back to his room.

Sun Buer's pretended insanity succeeded in getting Ma Tanyang and everyone else in the mansion to leave her alone. She reviewed Wang Chongyang's instructions repeatedly until she could perform them naturally and effortlessly. A month passed, and Sun Buer looked at her face in the mirror. Scars and pockmarks dotted her face. Since she had not combed her hair for a month, she was no longer the beautiful wife of a wealthy merchant. Sun Buer was delighted. She was now ready to make the journey to Luoyang. With a piece of charcoal she smeared her face and her clothing. Looking like a mad beggar-woman, she ran out into the living room, laughed wildly, and rushed out the front door. A servant tried to stop her, but she bit the girl in the arm. Yelping in pain, the servant let go of her. The other servants alerted Ma Tanyang. He hurried to the living room, but was told that the lady had already left the house. Ma Tanyang and the servants searched the town and the immediate countryside for Sun Buer, but they could not find her.

Knowing that Ma Tanyang would search for her, Sun Buer had hidden herself inside a haystack on a nearby farm. She heard the voices of the servants and her husband and continued to conceal herself until it was dark. When everything was silent, she quietly slipped out and walked toward Luoyang. Along the way, she slept in abandoned temples and caves. She obtained her food from begging, and when peopled asked who she was, she acted insane and uttered nonsense. In this way, people left her alone, and eventually she arrived safely at Luoyang.

✦ ✦ ✦

In Luoyang, Sun Buer found shelter in an abandoned house. Daily she begged in the city. When people tried to communicate with her, she acted insane, and as time went on she became known as the "mad beggar-woman." Because of her ugly face and her madness, the townspeople left her alone and she was able to practice internal alchemy without distraction.

In the city of Luoyang there were two wanderers of seedy character called Zhang San and Li Si. They solicited every woman they saw, and they raped those who refused their company. One day the two men saw Sun Buer begging on a street corner. They noticed that despite her rags and scars on her face Sun Buer was quite attractive. That night, when Zhang San and Li Si were returning home from an evening at the brothels, it occurred to Zhang San that they might finish their evening of fun with the mad beggar-woman. When he voiced his plan to Li Si, the latter said, "We cannot do that. Don't you know the saying 'Those who take advantage of mad people will meet with bad luck all their lives'?" Zhang San said, "I don't care about the superstitious sayings of old women. I am not afraid of the gods of Heaven or earth. I am going to have some fun with that woman." Zhang San strode ahead toward the abandoned house where Sun Buer was living. Li Si followed behind apprehensively.

Just as the abandoned house came into view, ominous storm clouds gathered in the sky. Suddenly there was a flash of lightning and a loud crack of thunder. When Zhang San and Li Si recovered from the deafening sound, they found that they were being struck by enormous hailstones. Since they were on the outskirts of town, they had to run a good distance before they could find shelter from the balls of ice. As they ran, Li Si said to his friend, "You should have listened to me. That was the wrath of heaven coming down on us." Zhang San cursed under his breath and tried to run faster, but he tripped over a pile of logs hidden by the tall grass and fell into a thorny bush. Bruised and bleeding, he got up and staggered toward the gates of the inner city.

By the time Zhang San and Li Si reached the inner city, the sky had cleared and a bright moon shone. Zhang San was bleeding badly. He had been pelted by enormous hailstones and cut by sharp thorns. Li Si, on the contrary, had not received a single scratch. It appeared that only the small hailstones had struck him. Zhang San finally sighed and said, "I am convinced. That mad woman cannot be touched." Li Si replied, "Now you know. I hope that you have learned your lesson well this time and will not try to bother her again." Zhang San said, "The lesson was learned well. From now on I will not even walk in the direction of that abandoned house."

The next day Li Si related the incident to all his friends, and the story spread around the city. From then on in the town no one made fun of her when she begged or went near the abandoned house she was living in. Thus Sun Buer was left in peace for the twelve years that she lived in Luoyang.

1. Why is Sun Buer instructed to "hide her knowledge"? Why is it so important to conceal the fact that she is practicing inner alchemy?

2. What does Wang Zhe mean when he asks, "If she is not mad, how can she become an immortal?" Are immortals insane?

3. In the story, why do you think Heaven appears to protect Sun Buer from rapists? Is this because Sun Buer has started to obtain special powers? Or because Heaven has chosen her to become an immortal? Or simply because rape is wrong?

Controversy

In Beijing: A Roar of Silent Protesters

Seth Faison

Falun Gong (referred to here as Buddhist Law) was founded in 1992 by Li Hongzhi, who combined Buddhist and Daoist teachings with traditional Chinese health practices known as qigong. The Chinese government became alarmed after the group reached as many as one hundred million followers in only a few years. When state-controlled media and the police began to put pressure on Falun Gong, members responded by gathering ten thousand demonstrators in Beijing. This protest—the largest since the 1989 Tiananmen Square uprising—only inspired a further crackdown from the government, which labeled Falun Gong a "cult." Both Falun Gong and the Chinese government have claimed they are being treated unfairly in media stories about this controversy. Does the article below seem tilted? And if so, toward which side?

BEIJING—The most amazing thing about the well-organized protest that occurred here on Sunday was the ease with which more than 10,000 followers of a religious sect materialized at the door of China's leadership and then vanished.

To the authorities, who are nervous about any unsanctioned gathering, it can only be deeply unsettling that so many people assembled without warning, essentially walking up to the secretive compound where China's leaders live and work, and sitting silently for an entire day.

Unlike student protesters who noisily thronged the streets of Beijing with colorful banners and pungent slogans 10 years ago, Sunday's demonstrators drew no attention to themselves and attracted no notice until there were suddenly many thousands of them sitting quietly in one of the most politically sensitive locations in the nation.

They looked like ordinary people from different parts of China, which they were. Here lies a puzzle—and for China's leaders, the scariest thing about the protest.

As followers of a sect of qigong (pronounced chee-goong), a traditional Chinese teaching that human energy can be cultivated by yoga-like disciplines and directed to improve one's own health, to heal others and, when mastered, to achieve powers like flying, the protesters represent an amorphous and hard-to-control body that is deeply confident and far-reaching.

An overwhelming majority of Chinese believe in qigong to some extent, making it hard to know exactly who belongs to the sect called Buddhist Law, which carried out the protest.

Buddhist Law, led by a qigong master named Li Hongzhi, claims to have more than 100 million followers. Even if that is an exaggeration, the government's estimate of 70 million adherents represents a large group in a nation of 1.2 billion.

Throughout Chinese history, mysticism has played a critical role in times of political turmoil, attracting adherents confused by sudden changes in society and becoming explosively violent when the authorities act to suppress them.

Anyone who doubts the potential strength of such a sect need only have witnessed the protest Sunday, when the followers seemed to appear from nowhere, sitting immobile and silent on sidewalks in the heart of Beijing. Even if efforts by many of them to direct mystical energy at the leadership compound fell short, their impressive organization left a significant imprint on Beijing.

Conducting a demonstration in this city is no easy trick. Plainclothes police and informers are everywhere, keeping an eye out for any hint of organized protest. Even lone protesters who tried to unfurl banners on the street during a meeting of China's legislature last month were whisked away, usually within minutes.

Beijing returned to normal Monday, as the police tightened security outside the leadership compound, blocking pedestrians from the street where China's leaders come and go from their compound, Zhongnanhai.

Premier Zhu Rongji met several representatives of the sect on Sunday, and directed government officials Monday to form a clear strategy to handle the group's complaints, the Associated Press reported. The state-run media remained silent about the protest.

Chinese leaders are in a bind: Acting decisively against a qigong sect clearly risks a greater counterreaction; allowing large protests is an invitation to other kinds of demonstrations, including the overtly political.

The government position has so far remained ambiguous. Hundreds of sects of qigong have flourished in recent years as China has become a less regimented society. While officials approve of harmless health exercises, they are alarmed at the appearance of popular qigong masters, some of whom fool followers with crass get-rich-quick schemes, while others like Li command fervent followers who believe their sect is morally superior to any other organization, including the Communist Party.

"The government has never banned qigong and other bodybuilding activities," said a spokesman for China's State Council. "It is understandable that there are different views and opinions. They should be expressed through proper channels."

Buddhist Law, founded by Li in 1992, mixes traditional Chinese teaching with Buddhism and Taoism to urge its followers to be good citizens by leading a moral life, not to smoke or drink or have sexual relations outside marriage, and to resist the consumerism that has swept China.

Sunday's protest was apparently set off by an incident in Tianjin, where practitioners staged a protest last week after a local magazine ran an article maligning Buddhist Law and the police used force to drive away followers.

The group decided that the time had come to demand that the central government clarify its stand on qigong sects so that the group can practice legally, protesters said. They also want the authorities to ease restrictions on publishing books of Buddhist Law teachings.

Those demands sound innocuous. Yet because Buddhist Law commands such a huge following, and has now shown that it can execute well-organized and disciplined demonstrations, it must cause deep concern to Chinese leaders.

Discussion Questions

1. According to the article, what was the scariest thing for the Chinese government about these protests? Does this assessment seem accurate?

2. Why was the Chinese government in a bind with respect to how it responded to this protest? How would you have responded to a protest like this if you were a government official?

3. Three months after this article was published, the Chinese government banned Falun Gong, declaring that it was "a cult" seeking to "spread superstition" and "disrupt social stability." Do these claims seem inaccurate? If not, why make them? Is there a meaningful difference between a religion and a cult?

Navajo

Navajo religion hangs on a profound philosophy of life that is difficult to explain to outsiders or even render in the English language. The central problem in the Navajo way is *hocho*, a word that conveys notions of disease, disharmony, chaos, conflict, and evil. The solution is *hozho*, typically translated as beauty or harmony. Navajo frequently describe the goal of life with the four words "Sa'a Nágháí Bik'e Hózhó" (SNBH). This too, defies simple translation. One anthropologist rendered it, "In old age walking, his trail beautiful." In an essay on Navajo philosophy and the concept of hozho, Vincent Werito attempts to articulate some of the different meanings that hozho has for him personally.

Part of achieving hozho is restoring harmony and health, and a key technique for achieving this involves ceremonies performed by ritual specialists known as singers. Frank Mitchell was a Blessingway singer, and an excerpt from his autobiography offers a glimpse into Navajo ceremonies and their significance as well as the training the singers undergo.

The exemplars of the Navajo religion are the heroes of their myths and stories, especially the Holy People (Diyin Dine'é)—godlike beings who possess superhuman powers and are invoked during ceremonies. Jim Kristofic offers his translation of the story of the Hero Twins—offspring of Changing Woman and her consort the Sun. With the help of the Holy People, they save humanity by defeating a cannibalistic giant. A selection from the Diné Bahane', or the Navajo Creation story, translated by Paul Zolbrod, tells the story of how Changing Woman—one of the most important of the Holy People—departed the world for a special house that she ordered the Sun to construct for her.

The difficulty outsiders have in understanding Navajo religion is not merely a problem for translators, anthropologists, and religion scholars. When a ski resort sought to create artificial snow by spraying processed sewer water onto a mountain sacred to the Navajo, the Navajo Nation sued, claiming it was an unconstitutional burden on their religion and that the government—which legally controlled the mountain—should not allow this. An excerpt from the Ninth Circuit court case *Navajo Nation v. United States Forest Service* (2008) highlights the American legal system's difficulty in understanding a religion so connected to specific geographic locations and with different ideas about how land can be used or experienced.

Problem/Solution

Understanding Hózhǫ́ to Achieve Critical Consciousness

Vincent Werito

Vincent Werito is originally from a Navajo community in New Mexico and is currently a professor at the University of New Mexico, where his research interests include Diné language and pedagogy. In the essay below he attempts to articulate his understanding of hozho—the goal of Navajo religion. Hozho is often translated as "harmony" or "beauty." However, this essay demonstrates that it is much more than this: it is an abstract idea that operates at many levels simultaneously, and the pursuit of hozho informs an entire way of life. Although Werito does not discuss hocho (ugliness and chaos) here, something of the nature of this problem can be inferred here.

Kodóó Hózhǫ́ Dooleeł: It Begins in Beauty, Harmony, and Peace

I awoke to the sweet smell of burning cedar and juniper in the stove, the sound of light footsteps shuffling around in the house, and the whispered voices of my mother and father telling my brothers and me to wake up. Then, I felt a warm strong hand on my shoulder and heard the voice of my father say to me "Nidiidaah shiyázhí, t' į́' tł'óógo ch'ídiikah" (Get up my little one, let's go outside). Slowly I raised my head and started to get up. I felt the cold, brisk morning air in the house as the signs of early light came through the window and the open door. As I put on my shoes, I saw my younger brother still moving around in his *golchǫǫ́n* (quilt blanket) and my older brothers rolling up their *yaat'eeł* (sheepskin bedding). With great effort, my younger brother and I followed suit. Then slowly we filed out behind our mother and father as we walked out to the front of the house toward the early dawn light, with the sound of birds chirping in the distance. As we stood there behind our parents, they began their prayers. I listened intently as they both started praying "Kodóó hózhǫ́'dooleeł" ("It begins in beauty").

Nánitłah dóó biyáhoyee'nidii hózhǫ́ǫ́go naashaa dooleeł diiní means "although it is hard and difficult to aspire to it we want to live our lives in beauty/harmony." In my childhood, I had heard my parents and other elders make this statement on many different occasions. As I grow older I now realize that they were referring to the idea of living according to the Diné philosophy of Sa'ąh Naagháí Bik'eh Hózhǫ́ǫ́n (SNBH), or the lifelong journey of striving to live a long and harmonious life. So what does that really mean in our contemporary lives as Diné peoples? SNBH is a hard concept to understand on a personal level because there are some challenges to understanding what each part of the phrase means, such as the concept of *hózhǫ́*. Oftentimes, for many young people today it is easier and more convenient not to have to think about it, especially now in the contemporary contexts when other things such as the popular media and technology seem to pervade our psyches. For purposes of this chapter, I will discuss what I believe constitutes Diné critical theory and thought by explaining my interpretation of the concept of hózhǫ́ and making some connections to key philosophical aspects of Diné philosophy. Furthermore, I offer these ideas as a way to begin a critical dialogue about consciousness raising, community revitalization, and decolonization by discussing and referring back to the principles of hózhǫ́.

For Diné peoples or Ni'hookáá' Diyiin Dine'é—the five-fingered Earth-surface spiritual beings—SNBH is who we are; it is part of our thought processes and everyday lives. SNBH is what we strive for, hope for, and pray for, because we believe that its essence and meaning lie at the base of our language and cultural identity and traditional cultural knowledge and teachings. Also, SNBH is an intangible idea that is often evoked and referred to in many aspects of our lives, especially in the ceremonial and personal contexts. Thus, as a Diné, whether I am at home, in school, driving on a road, lying awake at night, sitting in a prayer meeting, or out in the early dawn praying, I have to remind myself and think of how I want to live my life in a better and more harmonious and peaceful way.

Hózhǫ́ has been defined and discussed by linguists and anthropologists who have studied Navajos as meaning "in a state of harmony and peace and/or a positive ideal environment." As formulated here, this is already quite a complex idea. However, as a Diné, it means a lot of other things to me as well. For example, my understanding of hózhǫ́ is that it is a part of all traditional Navajo ceremonies and cultural teachings because of its emphasis on harmonious outcomes in most every situation. For example, many Diné prayers start with *"kodóó hózhǫ́ dooleeł"* ("it begins with beauty") and end with "*hózhǫ́ náhasdlį́į́*" ("it is done in beauty"). So while hózhǫ́ could be discussed as a simple idea, it is also multifaceted and difficult to understand. Furthermore, while it could be interpreted as being essential to Diné holistic thought and life, it could also be seen as part of a much larger Diné worldview and the Diné philosophy of SNBH. While these ideas may seem contradictory, they also reveal a dialectical nature in that a synthesis of meanings is necessary.

As a philosophical idea, hózhǫ́ has been described by Navajo scholars as being central to Navajo life and integral to the philosophy of SNBH and the Hózhǫ́ǫ́jí (Blessing Way) and Naayee'jí (Protection Way) teachings. SNBH is our life that we strive to live, yet it is also part of our thoughts, language, prayers, and songs and is integral to our inherent human quality for making sense of our lives and striving for harmony, peace, and justice. For that reason, I believe that understanding the principles of hózhǫ́ is contingent upon how a person interprets and comes to understand SNBH and how the individual wants to live her or his life according to its philosophy. Correspondingly, I have often heard the phrase "*t'áá hó'ají̜t'éego t'éíyá*" ("it is all up to you"). This idea is also captured in the philosophy of SNBH by which individuals internalize how they want their lives to be and what they must do to achieve SNBH. The important aspect of this idea is that it is up to each individual to pursue and live her or his life according to SNBH by recognizing how to live according to the principles of hózhǫ́ as the individual understands it.

Furthermore, the principles of hózhǫ́ are encapsulated in the cognitive (mental), physiological (physical), psychological (emotional), and intuitive (spiritual) aspects of human development and growth—or holistic living and learning—as discussed by philosophers and psychologists. According to Dr. Wilson Aronilth Jr., a prominent Navajo scholar who teaches at Diné College in Tsaile, Arizona, the Diné philosophy of SNBH actively involves and engages these four aspects of human development, which are embedded in and reflective of the natural processes of nature and the cosmos. Specifically, the Diné philosophy is associated with and orientated to the four cardinal directions, starting with the east direction; the four seasons, starting with spring; and the four parts of the day, beginning with early dawn and moving around in a clockwise direction with the path of the sun. This is commonly referred to as the *T'áá shá bik'ehgo na'nitin*, or the Sun Wise Path Teachings. So in relation to human life, this process of orientation for living and learning guides how an individual lives and develops respect and/or reverence for self, his or her relatives, and the natural world. These four aspects of the Diné philosophy of learning and living are Nitsáhákees (Thinking), Nahat'á (Planning), Iiná (Living), and Siihasin (Assurance), in respective order. These four aspects of Diné philosophy are understood to represent life principles that guide our processes of thinking or conceptualization, planning or self-actualization, doing by establishing relationships with others, and reflecting or being self-reflective and aware of others and the natural spiritual world.

Hózhǫ́ Nahásdłį́į,': It Is Fulfilled in Beauty

Over my lifetime until now and continuing into the future, I hope to interpret the principles of hózhǫ́ and internalize them in my life, my education, my worldview, and my vocation. In this final section, I share how I am still learning to interpret and apply the principles of hózhǫ́ to my life today, as in the past.

1. The first principle of hózhǫ́ involves conceptualization: 'ádá nitsídzíkees, or thinking for one's self. This principle helps to define who I am ontologically and metaphysically as Ni'hookáá' Diyiin Dine'é, or Earth-surface spiritual being, and Diné, a child of Earth and the sky. More so, it is part of a deeper humble belief that I am part of a larger and more complex spiritual, natural world. Therefore, these ideas inform my most basic belief as a Diné that I am from and of my mother, Earth, and that I walk with the guidance and protection of my father, the sky. Finally, this knowledge informs my worldview that my family, my language, all my relations (e.g., the Holy People, the winged ones, and the four-legged ones), my prayers, stories, songs, and cultural traditions are central to my survival. All of this is consummated in the principles of living with hózhǫ́ or Hózhǫ́ǫ́go 'Iiná.

2. The second principle is about actualization: ádaa'ákózhniidzíh, or coming to realization about who you are. This principle reinforces the value of my Diné language, philosophy, and pedagogy. With realization begins critical conscientization, which entails a plan to strategize ways to empower myself and other Diné peoples. Also, I realize that I must continue to learn through Western and other paradigms of knowledge to help guide my work and scholarship as an Indigenous (Diné) educator and scholar so that I may counter the language and discourse of oppression. In doing so, it is important to emphasize Diné culture and language and to reaffirm Indigenous thought and worldview in everyday life as a way of decolonizing and transforming colonial structures and notions of Indigenous nationhood, sovereignty, and leadership through the development of an Indigenous intelligentsia. Also, with this principle, I am constantly aware of my life goals to do good and my potential to do good for others. Thus, I am walking a good path of life in search of happiness and fulfillment, or SNBH bik'ehgó yiishaał.

3. The third principle entails action: 't'áá hwó'ajít'éego 'iiná 'ajilééh, or acting to achieve life goals. With this in mind, I begin to understand that the conceptualization and actualization of life goals results in action to achieve new consciousness or new understandings that continuously informs ongoing acts of advocating for self and others in the spirit of peace and justice. This principle helps to remind me about the different ways to advocate for my people, my community, for my students' learning and development of positive self-worth

and self-identity by recognizing individual and group language and cultural strengths in hopes of achieving transformation and change within the process of schooling. My life goals and purpose are intertwined with my vocation as an Indigenous educator with the central goal of helping others (students) to achieve consciousness and to reach their life goals in the process.

4. Finally, there is the principle of reflection: *síísdinídzin*, or having hope, faith, respect, and reverence for life. This principle continuously informs the other principles as well as my lifelong personal and community goals, my faith, and my hope in life as I continue walking on the path of SNBH, or long life and happiness, as a Diné. Also, this principle reinforces my commitment to recognizing and honoring other Indigenous communities, ethnic groups, and forms of knowledge, languages, and cultural traditions that have faith and love for self, others, and the natural world.

In sum, through this creative process of living and learning and engagement with others and my natural surroundings, I am constantly learning and striving to reaffirm myself and embrace my humanity today as a child of Earth and the sky and respect the humanity of others and the natural world around me through the principles of hózhǫ́.

I have shared some of my personal ideas and beliefs about the meaning of hózhǫ́ and how I try to live my life according to its principles as they exist in Diné philosophy, which I partly frame in Western theory using the work of Paulo Freire and other nonindigenous scholars. My hope is that this chapter will help to explain for other Native and nonnative scholars, students, teachers, and researchers how I came to and continue to work to understand and live by the principles of hózhǫ́. I am well aware of how this act of framing the ideas in a Western paradigm is not in line with Indigenous thought, and I am also aware of how as an Indigenous educator I have to be careful not to speak out of place if it is not my place to speak or to pretend to speak out for my community from a privileged position. With that in mind, I think it is important to note that I have only shared what information or knowledge is already out in academia and written about by other Diné scholars. I have not overstepped my boundaries by describing ceremonial knowledge. Instead, I have only tried to explain and share my own interpretation of the principles of hózhǫ́. Also, instead of trying to fit an Indigenous paradigm into a Western framework, I have used the master's tools to make it fit. Furthermore, my intent for framing it in a Western discourse is to avoid essentializing Navajo thought and philosophy and romanticizing Indigenous forms of knowledge. In the end, I hope that I was able to articulate my understanding of hózhǫ́ using my Diné and Western frames of mind as well as the language and theory of academia so that others may gain a new appreciation and understanding of Indigenous intellectual sovereignty.

Since this writing is not primarily for the academy only, I am using this forum to speak out and speak to my relatives, peers, and friends in the Indigenous communities about asserting our intellectual sovereignty, as discussed by Robert Warrior. I hope that we can begin to think of ways to engage in more critical dialogue and praxis with other Diné, Native American, and even nonnative scholars to work for the benefit of all children. All of this work ultimately should be to achieve and realize a transformative educational model for the next generation of Indigenous and other youths. That said, part of my message here is also to give courage and hope to Indigenous youths, families, and communities that we are capable of reclaiming, rearticulating, and reaffirming the value and worth of our cultural knowledge and heritage without having to compromise ourselves, even within a Western framework.

Finally, I maintain that as Indigenous scholars we can utilize Indigenous thought to make sense of Western concepts and vice versa whether they exist in traditional or contemporary forms. Diné philosophy and theoretical frameworks were around for thousands of years before the advent of Euro-Western thought, and these principles or philosophies continue to mean something and everything to our contemporary lives and understandings of ourselves. In this way, the contemporary interpretation of the principles of hózhǫ́ emanate from and continue to reverberate with the traditional Diné philosophical aspects of human growth and development, or human living and learning. As I have described before, these ideas are a conceptualization of the mind and the realization of self for positive outcomes (Nitsáhákees), achieving critical consciousness through the process of achieving and planning life goals (Nahat'á), developing an awareness and responsibility to act for self and others (Iiná), and engaging in an ongoing process of self-awareness and reflection (Siihasin) for the good of self, family, community, and the natural world. In the end, I hope that these kinds of dialogue will help to create and illuminate the need for more discussion, thought, and interpretation about Indigenous life principles, such as the concept of hózhǫ́, that will ultimately lead to a pedagogy of love and hope for all.

Discussion Questions

1. What is hozho? Why is "a state of harmony" not a sufficient definition?

2. In this essay Werito describes four principles of hozho. What is the difference between the four principles? What is each one articulating?

3. Werito is trying to explain Diné ideas using the language and terminology of Western academia. What is the advantage of doing this? What are the potential disadvantages or dangers of talking about Diné ideas in this way?

From *Navajo Blessingway Singer: The Autobiography of Frank Mitchell, 1881–1967*

Frank Mitchell

While the goal of hozho saturates many aspects of Navajo culture, it is perhaps most apparent in religious rituals such as the Blessingway. Frank Mitchell was a Navajo elder and Blessingway singer. His autobiography—which he begins with the history of his family's incarceration at the Bosque Redondo reservation in 1868—was published in 1978. Mitchell's account is important because he describes not only important Navajo rituals such as the Blessingway but also how and why he became a Blessingway singer.

Learning the Blessingway

During the time I was going to school, my brother John was working at Fort Defiance, and his family was living there with him. I already told about how he was married twice; that was his first wife he was living with when he was at Fort Defiance. I lived there with him during the time that I worked at the trader's place as a housekeeper and dishwasher. There was an old man who was some relation to my brother's wife. His name was He Who Seeks War, and he was a singer of the Blessingway.

He used to visit my brother's place a lot, and I guess John learned that he was a Blessingway singer and started picking up some of the songs, learning something about them. That man used to give me some instruction in Blessingway, too, telling me what goes on in the ceremony and how the Blessingway goes. At the same time I listened whenever I could, trying to pick up pieces of it. I began learning some of the songs from here and there in the ceremony, and I remembered them pretty well.

Later on I came back over here because my wife's parents were getting pretty old and sick. I gave up hauling freight and started tending their farm and livestock. Like I have said, my father-in-law was a well-to-do man: he had cattle and sheep and horses. Also, he was a Blessingway singer, and I went out with him whenever he performed his ceremony. I noticed that the songs I had learned from He Who Seeks War were the same as the ones my father-in-law was singing.

Before I began to learn these things, way back before that, I did not even think about life as being an important thing. I did not try to remember things or keep track of what happened at certain times. Nothing seemed to matter to me, I just didn't care about anything, so long as I kept on living. But then when I began to learn the Blessingway, it changed my whole life. I began really thinking about ceremonies. I had heard singing before that, but now I began to take it more seriously because I began to realize what life was and the kind of hardships we have to go through.

Before I started learning the Blessingway, the older people used to tell me that I should think about life more seriously. "If you don't know any songs you have nothing to go by. If a child grows up in a family like that he doesn't know where he is going or what he is doing." That is what the older people told me, that I should have something to live by. It is just like going to school: you are being trained and being told what is wrong and what is right. It was the same way with this ceremony; that is when I began learning about life.

So during that time after I stopped hauling freight and began working more around home, I used to go out with my father-in-law, Man Who Shouts, whenever he was asked to perform the Blessingway. At first I just watched, and then finally I had learned practically everything he was doing, and before I knew it I was helping him with the ceremony. Finally I reached the point where I had learned it well enough so that I had a ceremony of my own.

Man Who Shouts and his wife used to move to the mesa during the winter months. We stayed here because I had a separate home and my own way of making a living. When he got sick I went over to the mesa and took care of him until his end. After he got sick he lived on for about three years. We moved over there during his last days. That is where he called me in to talk to me about the future.

He said he noticed that I was the kind of young man who didn't seem to care about anything. He settled down to talk with me and told me that if I was going to continue being the way I was then, I would never achieve anything in life and would just end up ruining my life, one of these days. He told me that I'd better settle down soon and start living right if I was going to make a living for my children.

If I wanted to get out on the farm and work, if I wanted to be a farmer, he said, it was going to take all my strength, all my heart to do that work. "It takes a lot of work to do that," he told me. "And if you're going to be a farmer, you will probably make a good one if you really put your mind to it. But you can't be a farmer all your life; as soon as your strength starts to go, as soon as you start getting weaker and weaker, that will be the end of your farming life," he said. Then he told me it was the same thing with raising stock. "If you're going to be a cattleman or a sheepherder it's just the same thing; there is a lot of work to it; it takes a lot of energy to do that," he told me. "But then, again, you'll end up just the way a farmer will," he said.

Then he told me, "But if you are a singer, if you remember your ceremonies really well, even if you get old, even if you get blind and deaf, you'll still remember everything by heart, how each part of the ceremony is performed." He said to me, "Even though you are so old you can't ride a horse or you can't even see any more, people will still have a use for you until old age finally finishes you off."

So that is why I chose this way of life. When Man Who Shouts got sick I got seriously interested in learning the ceremony, but I was not too sure yet—my mind was not really made up until just before his death. And now I can see that my father-in-law was right: even as old as I am, unable to get around too much, people still come to have my ceremony done over them. I have it inside my head so well that I remember everything, and even though I can't get around, they come in a wagon or a car for me and take me over to where the ceremony is needed and then bring me back. So I think my father-in-law was right. If I had decided to be a farmer at that time I probably wouldn't have lasted very long.

It was mainly from Man Who Shouts that I learned the Blessingway, by following him whenever he was asked to do some singing. I picked up most of his songs and prayers that way. Whenever he went to Fort Defiance we would go in a buggy. We would stop in Sawmill overnight where there lived He Who Seeks War and his younger brother, who knew the same Blessingway songs. They would practice them, and I would listen. After we would leave there he would explain things to me, and that is how I would learn.

We would spend the night there sitting around talking about the Blessingway until late at night, and then we would go on to Fort Defiance the next day. And then, coming back, we did the same thing. We always stopped there, and I learned a little more again. Just gradually like that I learned all about that ceremony from those two men. He Who Seeks War was related to my wife's father through a niece, or something like that. So they knew each other pretty well.

So I picked up a lot of knowledge like that and finally got to the point where I could do the ceremony all by myself. I did not have a Blessingway bundle of my own, but I was able to help Man Who Shouts and do whatever he asked me to do.

During that last winter we went up there on the mesa with him. He gradually got worse and worse. There were four singers with him all the time towards the end: Red Water Tall Bead Man, Little Many Goats, Noweta̱li and Dził Yé'há. They were doing their ceremonials: Mountainway, Shootingway, Flintway and Big Starway in the Ghost Chasing and Evilway forms. The helpers in all this were all the members of the immediate family and his wife's family. Long Moustache was supervising everything. So was Jake Tom. The young boys were told to do the chores around there.

One day I had a sweat bath with the singers. They were all tired after so many days, and Man Who Shouts told me to fix a sweat bath for them, so they could take that and be refreshed a little bit. I went out and cut wood and fixed a sweathouse, and we all got in there. Then I went to my house to eat, and Man Who Shouts requested that I come in and see him. I sat by him as he was lying in the hogan. He told me he did not think he was going to live much longer the way things were. He told me that all these singers had been here so long performing their ceremonies for him, but he could not see that it was doing any good. He felt that his time was coming, and that is why he called me in.

He wanted me to know that he had been depending on me as a strong young man to look after the livestock and the farm when he was away performing his ceremony. Now the time had come for me to take charge of things because there would be nobody for me to depend on the way I could when he was living and strong. He told me that it was up to me at that moment to make up my mind if I was going to carry on the Blessingway ceremony the way he had. He said he had worked hard and had acquired this farm and livestock and a good deal of property to take care of his children and his grandchildren, too. He told me that from there on it would be up to me to carry it on.

He said, "It appears that I will never recover from this sickness. This is my final talk to you. After I am gone, the burdens you and I have been carrying will be yours alone. If you have patience and strength you can do it. If you are the man I think you are, even though it may mean a lot of hardship, you will continue to carry on the work of the farm the way you have since you first started living with my daughter." He said, "If you aren't, if you are going to be the kind of man that isn't too good at anything, then you might leave the whole thing and go away and just let the women do the work. It's up to you right now to decide."

I think the main reason he talked this way to me was that he wanted me to have this Blessingway bundle that he had been using for so long. Then he told me that I had done the ceremony so many times and had been such a good helper with it that he knew I could carry it on by myself. He said, "If anything happens to me, then that Blessingway is just yours." Before he began talking this way, those four singers had come back into the hogan, and he said to them, "If anybody ever questions my son-in-law's right to this ceremony, you men here have heard me say it. You've heard everything I said to him: that the Blessingway is just his, and he is to use it the right way."

At the same time he told me, "If you use it properly, you may live on to a good old age yourself. But if it does happen that you get too old, if it comes to the time where you can't use your ceremony any more, then whatever you do, do not pass it on to the Two Streams Meet Clan; it should go to the Standing House Clan. That is one wish I have that I want you to respect, that this Blessingway should be kept in the Standing House Clan. In these last three years none of my relatives have visited me. Don't give it to them after I am gone. It is not to go to the Bitter Water Clan or the Near the Water Clan, either, even though those relatives of mine come running in here after my property."

This was said in the presence of those singers from outside the family, so it was binding. He willed his crane bills for the Flintway ceremonial to his grandson, Man with a Yellow Face, who is now dead. Even though he did not know any of the songs, he could just keep the ceremonial bundle and later he might be able to sell it. The bundle for the Cutting Prayersticks ceremony was willed to his stepson, Mr. Cottonwood, half-brother to my wife, Tall Woman. He was named for a lonely cottonwood tree that stood on his property.

He had other sacred bundles, too, like the one that my wife still has. That also used to belong to my father-in-law. I do not know what ceremony that is used for, but she still has it. When Man Who Shouts died, that bundle was given to one of my wife's cousins who just passed away last October. He never learned a ceremony for it, but it was willed to him before my father-in-law died.

Man Who Shouts still had quite a lot of property, even though the family had used up about half of what they had during all that time he was sick. You see, for about three years he had been having ceremony after ceremony, and this was using up all their sheep and cattle and whatever little money they had, too. So the number of cattle went down, but there were still some left, and there were still some sheep. My father-in-law said for me to take care of them, that they all belonged to his wife: "She can do whatever she wants with that, it's all hers. The children should not claim any of it, saying that this or that is theirs. They are just to let their mother take care of it until the day she leaves them, too. It is the same way with the cattle that are left; they are to be in her hands, too." He also had a buckboard, and it was left to my wife. There was another wagon, too, that was used for heavy hauling, and I was to use that for the farm in any way I wanted. But this other buckboard was given to my wife for her use alone. "If she ever wants to go somewhere, make sure she is taken in that. Take care of your wife and take care of your children."

He went on talking like that and gave me a good lecture on how I should live and what I should do and should not do and how I should not mistreat my wife. He talked to me about everything.

Finally he mentioned the jewels he had gotten together during his lifetime. He had every known kind of precious stone: abalone, coral, jet, turquoise, all on one string. He had a set of earloops. He also had carved out two eardrops that were buried with him. The rest of the beads went to his wife.

"Fix me up nicely and put me away in a suitable place. That buckskin horse that I've always like so much, I want that, too, because the saying is that people live after their death, and I may need something to get around on. After I'm gone, don't be afraid of me. I want you still to respect me as you do now. Don't call me a ghost."

I said, "Wait a minute, don't go on talking like this. Tell me why you feel the end is near. What is overtaking you?"

He said, "I haven't urinated for the last twenty-four hours. I am beginning to feel it."

I said, "I know that's dangerous." I thought of the doctor in Chinle right away and how they have a way they can help that trouble. "Well, my father-in-law," I said, "be patient and I'll get something to help you." I came down to Chinle on horseback and got there about nine in the evening.

The doctor said he had no way of getting up on the mesa. "But I'll give you the instruments to use and tell you what to do," he said. This took a little time, and then I rushed right back up there.

When I got near the place where they were living, I saw that the people had built a fire outside the hogan and they were all outside there. And when I got there I realized my father-in-law had already died. They had him all fixed up, covered with blankets. I went over there and pulled the covers off and felt for a pulse, but there was no life. I was too late with those things, even though I tried to help him. So I talked to him: "Well, my father-in-law, I was hoping I would get back before it was too late. But whatever you have asked us to do, we'll follow your instructions." That was how he passed away. He was very old, and old age had a lot to do with it, too.

The next morning we prepared him for burial. We put him on a horse and took him away and dug a grave for him. Those of us who put him in the ground were myself, Man with a Yellow Face and his son-in-law. Whoever carries a body out like that has to make the grave according to our customs. A body is supposed to be buried in a deep hole a long way from the hogan, against a rock wall. First we put the body in, then his saddle and saddle blanket. We killed his horse at the grave, and we left the digging tools there, too. We broke them up so that nothing was left in a whole piece. You are supposed to blindfold the horse first and then kill it with an axe or a club. That is according to the old custom, though in later years people felt it was all right to use a gun. The people doing this burying should not be wearing clothes.

If you are obliged to do a burial, you must prepare yourself. When you remove your clothes you tie your foreskin closed with a strip of yucca leaf but not with a square knot. You build a fire some distance from the hogan where the death took place and have a bucket of water heated there so that you can bathe yourself in soapsuds when you come back. From the time you pick up the body until after the bath you only speak with sign language. If the person is buried some distance away, you then remove the furniture from the hogan and burn it down. If that cannot be done, you can bury the person inside the hogan and then pull it all down over the grave. After the burial, you brush away your tracks as you leave the grave. You can do that with anything that acts as a brush.

After all this had been done and we had eaten, my close friend Long Moustache sat down and told me, "After four days you can go back to normal life; until then you must remain quiet. On the fourth morning you should wash your hair and bathe yourself all over. Then the outsiders can all return and try to arrange things according to what he told us about his property. The reason is that now the different clan relatives will be coming in here to claim all sorts of things. You singers should remain, too. You should wait four days until the members of the family have purified themselves, then you can come and get the things belonging to you and take them away." He told the young boys doing the chores around there to come back to help with the old singer's stock. Just the family and those who helped with the burial were there for the four days. After that everything was done as he said.

We had farmland across the wash there. All that farmland belonged to my father and mother. My father had left us for the second time at this point and was married to that woman down here called Those Who Walk About Woman; he was still with that woman when I married my wife. When we moved to the mesa, my father was still in this area here. So when we moved back over here my father used to come and visit me every now and then, and finally it got to the point where he left that woman. Another man took his wife, that old man, White Sinew, who passed away about two or three years ago. So my father just kind of hung around where I was, down here with my children. He went back and forth from here to Tsaile to visit Slim Man, one of his sons by Red Woman.

My father left his livestock with that cousin of mine who used to wrestle with me—Tall Water Edge Man. He only brought his personal possessions when he came to live at my place. My father came and went while I was working as a freighter. He stayed mainly in Canyon del Muerto. He would also go to visit Redhaired Water Edge Man where Tall Water Edge Man's brother lived. Redhaired Water Edge Man was learning Blessingway from him. These were the same songs that I use. When my father was staying with me, I would ask him about Blessingway prayers and songs—all the things I had learned from Man Who Shouts. This way I filled in the gaps in the two versions and formed my complete ceremony. I learned things this way for quite a long while. Some of the time I would be busy, and my father would be visiting other people like Slim Man, who was always asking him about Blessing-way, too.

We lived like that for some time here, just taking care of the farm, and finally my father decided to go back to Slim Man for another visit. While he was there he got sick. I got word from there that my father was pretty bad, so I saddled up my horse and went up there to Slim Man's place and, sure enough, he was sick, and they were having a five-night ceremonial for him. I got there on the third day. I spent the night there and the next day and the last day of the whole ceremonial I spent there, too. I stayed there until it was all over with, until the next morning. I think it was a fever that he had, some kind of fever that was going around. He was not sick in any partic-ular place.

So he got all right after the singing was over, and he wanted to come home with me. They told him he should not leave right after there had been this singing for him. They said he should spend at least a couple of nights there before he left that place. So he stayed there another night, and then the night after that and then he came back with us. We went by way of the Canyon. Slim Man took him in the wagon, and I came along with the horses. I rode and drove my father's horses and we got to Standing Cow in the Canyon where some of our relatives lived and spent the night there. While we were there we saw a great many people going up the Canyon, and finally we stopped someone and asked where they were going and if there was something going on up that way. They told us there was a Blessingway and that those people were making a new ceremonial bundle. Right then my father told Slim Man and me to go over there and find out exactly how such things were done. He was curious to know if it was done the same way he was taught. This singer we heard about, Cane's Son, was supposed to be very careful with how it was done.

All that time my father knew all about the Blessingway, but he had never performed that ceremony because he was never asked. He had learned it from his father, Man Who Speaks Often, but during that time so many of the singers had their ceremonial bundles already, and there were not many new ones being made for younger singers learning it, so they didn't ask him to perform that ceremony.

We went over there that night, and when we got there we went inside the hogan. All that took place in the early evening was a prayer, nothing else. Just a prayer, and then everybody went to bed. Slim Man spent the night there, but there was another Blessingway just beyond that place, and I went over there. The singer there was a man by the name of Tall Schoolboy; he was the one that was doing this Blessingway there at his place. This ceremony and what I learned from my wife's father were about the same. I was over there for the last night. I stayed all night and helped with the singing until the next morning. Then I got back over to this other place where they were making the Mountain Earth bundle.

That day they brought the yucca soap and performed the regular bathing ritual and all that. They bathed the one they were making the ceremonial bundle for. He was the main one that the ceremony was for. The bundle was going to be his, so he had to be the one-sung-over. So they brought the soapweed, and they started the regular Blessingway rituals. After the bathing and all that goes with it, they started working on the ceremonial bundle, and they didn't sing any songs during that time. There were just short prayers here and there until the bundle was completed, and they told me that was all there was to it. They just made up the bundle, and there were no songs at any point. We were just there to listen and to watch how things were done.

In the afternoon it was all over with, and we got restless and went back to where we had left our father at Standing Cow. When we got back over there, he was a little ways from the house there, under the trees sitting straight up, all ears for what we had learned. Before I even got off my horse he called out, "Open up your pack of news!" So I told him what happened the night before from the time we first got there, and how things went on and then about the next morning too, up until the time we left.

Before we even finished telling him, my father was not interested in hearing any more. He just moved away from us. Later he told us he knew what I had said was true, that there are some singers that will do crazy things like that just to get something out of it. He knew right away that the way this singer Cane's Son did it was all wrong.

Making up the ceremonial bundle was one thing I had not learned from my father-in-law, Man Who Shouts. I just learned the straight Blessingway from him, so right then and there I got interested in how the new ceremonial bundle is made, and I started asking my father all kinds of questions. I asked him how it was done, and that is when my father gave me all the information; he told it all to me. He told me how the story went along with the prayers and the songs, and I got them all put together until I had them learned. The songs used by those two men over where we stopped are the same ones I learned from my father. I guess they came from my grandfather, and all the people in that area learned it from him. There are little differences, but there is no place where the differences are large enough to say that it is a different version of the Blessingway. The prayers and the songs are the same, too.

I really got interested in it from there on. I asked my father all the questions I could think of about the way that ceremony goes, and I started learning it. First he told me all about the story of it and the songs and prayers and all that went along with it. It was just about the same as the way I learned from Man Who Shouts. That was how I came to learn the Blessingway.

After we returned to my place, my father gradually got sick. He started having ceremonies for that, using his own property and livestock to pay for them until finally he was left with nothing. Those Who Walk About Woman had married that old man by then, so he didn't even have a wife. He began to feel that it was hopeless. He said, "This is too much of a burden on you. Go to my relatives in Steamboat and tell them I want to go over there. Let's see what they can do." Red Hair Knot and Tall Water Edge Man would come over here to help while I was sponsoring some of my father's ceremonies. His nieces and nephews would come over, too, and they took him back with them in the fall. He wanted to leave his beads and other things with me, and also his ceremonial bundle, but I said, "Take them, you may need them to hire a singer."

My father passed away early the next summer; I was not there when it happened. When he left here he had called me and Tall Water Edge Man in to talk to us: "I don't think I'll ever get well from this sickness. I want to leave two head of cattle and the horse I always use here." And that is what he did. He said to Tall Water Edge Man, "If I don't take them back for my own use before I die, then they are yours."

After my father died, Redhaired Water Edge Man took his Blessingway bundle; he claimed my father had said it was to go to him. It contained a mirage stone that originally belonged to my mother. John Mitchell, being stingy as he was, went over there and got that stone. When he died it was not mentioned in his will, and so it went to Herbert. Redhaired Water Edge Man is still living at that place, where he is a Blessingway and Shootingway singer. He used to be the best Yeibichai dancer in the country.

I was one of those who helped collect the contents of the Mountain Earth bundle from the four sacred mountains. It started way back in about 1925, when Father Berard was out here and I had a chance to go on some of those trips. He put up the money himself for the gasoline and told us we could use the mission car he had available. We wanted to collect earth from each sacred mountain so that we could each have a Mountain Earth bundle.

We had to furnish our own food while we were out camping on those four mountains. The women around here, especially my wife, got all of the things ready to go on that trip. There were still only a few trading posts out here at that time and very little flour. That is why the bread we took was corn bread rather than fry bread.

When a trip like this was to be undertaken we had to plan everything carefully in advance. We had to take a kind of bread with us that represented all the vegetation that is grown on earth, like wheat, whole wheat, corn—all different kinds of corn— and all different kinds of wheat. You can get flour out of barley, and all those other different kinds of wheat that grow around here, including the wild kinds. You can grind that all up like cornmeal, or make it more like flour.

So we ground all that together, all those kinds of wheat with cornmeal and all the other vegetation that grows. We ground it all together into something like cornmeal and made bread out of that to eat during the journey. It was all right to have other food from the store, too, but we had to have this particular bread that is made out of all different kinds of vegetation. Then, when we were going on our way up the mountain, whenever we would stop to eat, the first thing would be some of this bread. There was some boiled meat that we took that we also had to eat first before any other food was taken—coffee or tea, or anything else. After we ate some of those things, then we could eat what supplies we had brought.

✦ ✦ ✦

When we would get to a mountain, we would not just go up into it in our ordinary clothes. Besides our food we took a new basket, such as we use in a Blessingway when we bathe the person being sung over. And we took a mirage stone in a little ceremonial pouch. We would go up as far as the first waterhole that we could find. And there at the waterhole we all undressed and bathed ourselves. We did that just as they do during the Blessingway. We dried ourselves with cornmeal and then with the powder from grinding the mirage stone. Then, when we were dry, we got into clothing something like you see on the Yeibichai dancers. You know, when the Yeibichai is ready to dance he is all decorated with silver belts and bracelets and beads. That is the way we dressed on the mountain. We had buckskins thrown over our shoulders, too.

Then we started going up the mountain, and there was always one of the men who was picked out to be the leader. He went before the others, and we started singing before we left that waterhole. I was the leader for the trip to Mount Taylor. When we got to the top of the mountain I gave the directions as to where the earth was to be picked up from.

There is something else that we took when we set out on these trips for the mountain earth—little chips of turquoise and other jewels. The leader took this, and he went before the others; we were all singing just as in the Blessingway. We all followed him until we came to a waterfall. That is where we put the jewels as a gift to Mother Earth for what we were going to take from her. We left the jewels there and in return gathered up some of the earth from the mountain. After we gathered up as much as we needed, we smoothed out the place; we did not want to leave it disturbed. We fixed it up so that it looked just as it had been before, and then coming back we sang more songs until we reached our starting place at the bottom. There we finished with the singing and passed the pollen around so that each one of us could bless himself. Then we dressed in our ordinary clothes and started back home.

On those trips we just went up each mountain as far as we had to go in order to find water. On Mount Taylor we did not find any water until we got clear to the top, but the other ones were not like that; we just had to go a little ways. Most of the mountains I went to had spring water here and there all over. After we made the jewel offering to Mother Earth, we said a prayer up there on each mountain to thank her for what we came for and for the protection that we would have because of that. We were praying for the whole Navajo tribe, because the ceremonial singers are the ones the people look up to for protection.

It took about three years to visit all of those mountains. It took so long because a trip like that requires so much preparation. Another thing that had to be prepared was a buckskin especially made to wrap the mountain earth in. This could not be just any deer that you would go out and shoot with a gun or a bow and arrow that would wound it and make it bleed. This deer had to be roped; no kind of weapon could touch it.

That is why it took all that time to visit those mountains: the preparations like hunting a deer for that purpose. It is pretty hard to rope a deer, and then you cannot shoot it; what you do is put a handful of pollen in its mouth, hold the nose and mouth tight and suffocate it. Then you butcher it, and the skin is used for wrapping up the mountain earth. It takes a long time to get that all fixed up. After you get the deer, then somebody has to tan that hide, and it takes quite a while to do that, too. That is a highly valued thing whenever a deer is killed like that.

In wrapping the mountain earth, we put just a bit into each little pouch, about half a teaspoonful. What we do is cut a little piece of the buckskin and, when it is still wet, push a stick right into the middle of it so the skin is stretched out the other side like a nipple. After it dries that way we just put the earth in there and then fold it back and tie it. You can put a lot of these little sacks together and tie them into one bundle just the right size for holding in one hand.

What we do is put the earth from each of the four mountains in a separate sack and then right in the center put a mirage stone, a nice one, for the center piece. Then we put the earth from Blanco Peak on the east side of it, and from Mount Taylor on the south side of it and so on, all around in the same direction as the mountains. Then you know just how this should be so you can hold it facing the right way. Some other mirage stones or other things that are valued can be put in there, too. You tie it all together that way, and there is something on each of those little sacks so you know which earth is from Mount Taylor and which is from San Francisco Peak. You make sure that the right one goes on the right side of the bundle.

Then at the bottom, before the whole thing is all tied up, a perfect white shell from the ocean is placed. It is shaped like a basket, and it is set at the bottom of the whole thing. Then the mirage stone is set at the center, and the little sacks are placed all around it. Then you fill in all around with other things, such as mirage stones, jewel offerings, bits of various types of vegetation that grow on the earth and all kinds of herbs. Mixed in with all this is the fur, or a little bit of hair or the hide, of all kinds of animals living on earth. That fills up this little shell basket that is underneath everything. The mirage stone stands on an inch or so of all these substances and then those other things are grouped around it.

The people who taught me used to say that the little shell basket resembles Mother Earth and all those materials in it are the things that are growing on top of the earth. Corn pollen is always in that bundle, too, among all the rest of the things.

This bundle is something you have to have to perform the Blessingway. Without it you cannot do Blessingway because that is the most essential property of the ceremony, right there. Not many Blessingway singers have bundles that are put together as carefully as mine was for me. A lot of times I have noticed that all some of them have is pollen, just pollen and nothing else.

There are special songs, Chief songs, that are sung during the time that they are making up that bundle for a new singer. Nobody knows them but me; my father taught me those songs. As far as I know, around here none of the Blessingway singers know those songs. I am the only one. Those particular songs are for tying up the Mountain Earth bundle. There is another reason that most Blessingway bundles are not as properly made as mine: these younger men just ask the older singers a few questions, but they do not stop long enough to find out the real answers; they just want to do it their own way. I know a lot of them who have this mountain earth, but it is not put together the way it should be.

1. Mitchell explains that he became a Blessingway singer so that he would have a source of income in his old age. Some cultures assume a religious vocation should have nothing to do with practical considerations about money or resources. Why does Mitchell not seem to share this assumption?

2. What are the traditional practices for burying the dead described here? What do attitudes toward these practices suggest about death and dying?

3. What is the significance of medicine bundles? How are they created and maintained?

Exemplar 1

From *The Hero Twins*

Jim Kristofic

The Hero Twins are the offspring of Holy People—Changing Woman and Jó'honaa'éí (the Sun). Together, they went on a quest to obtain magical weapons and slay a race of monsters called the *naayéé'* that was devouring humanity. In addition to their physical prowess and bravery, the Hero Twins show other ideal qualities such as respect for their mentors and faith in their advice. Jim Kristofic grew up on the Navajo Reservation in Arizona and works as a writer and oral historian. He published an English translation of the story of the Hero Twins so that others could learn the lessons from this tale that he had.

The stories of the Hero Twins of the Diné teach me many things over the years. When I was very small, they taught me that monsters existed. And that they could be beaten.

When I was a little older, they taught me that you can't defeat those monsters alone. Family and friends and wise mentors can lead you down good paths. As I matured, the stories taught me the importance of patience, persistence, bravery, and reverence. Through thinking, planning, action, and meditation, life could be balanced and enjoyed in harmony.

These stories still teach me these lessons today. And they've taught so many lessons to so many people—especially to the Diné.

It was a love for these stories and their lessons that made me want to bring them together in the form of a book. And I wanted that book to tell those stories in the Diné language for Diné readers of all ages.

There are many versions of the Hero Twins story. The stories can vary depending on the region of Navajo country.

So I consulted print versions by Dr. Washington Matthews, Navajo Community College Press, Rock Point Community School, Rough Rock Demonstration School, and Dr. Paul Zolbrod in order to understand what others had shown of these stories. These works have been accepted, overall, by Diné readers. I have tried to work within these lines.

In this way, I hope this book can tell this story—of the Hero Twins and *Yé'iitsoh*—in an accurate and respectful way without exposing too much of its sacredness. If it fails in this, the fault lies with me and me only.

Hágoónee',
Jim Kristofic

◆ ◆ ◆

Of a long time ago this story is told. After Changing Woman had been born with the help of First Man and First Woman, they and the last survivors of the Emergence People all traveled together.

They would sometimes think they were safe, and they would farm. But before the autumn harvest, the *naayéé'* would find them. They ran from the *naayéé'*. The *naayéé'* bit with teeth like knives.

They would eat them like wolves eat sheep who wander from the herd.

This is how the brothers came to be.

Changing Woman stood on a mountain and watched the Sun and thought it was handsome. She also admired a small waterfall that fell down into a pool on a mountain and thought it was handsome, also.

She became pregnant. After only eight days, the brothers were ready to be born, they say. *Haashch'ééłti'í*, the Talking God, and *Tó neinilí*, the Water Sprinkler, came to them on the peak of the mountain and helped the brothers emerge into the world.

During all of this, the *naayéé'* looked for the people all the time.

After four days, the two babies had already grown to the size of boys. Talking God and Water Sprinkler challenged them to a race around *Dził ná'ooditii*, the Traveler's Circle Mountain, they say.

The twins ran weakly like fat skunks. And because of this, Talking God and Water Sprinkler insulted and whipped the boys. They did this many times.

One day, *Níłch'i*, the Wind, spoke to the brothers.

"Do not give up, my grandsons. You can always grow stronger each day."

And so the boys trained harder.

The Holy People returned and they raced again. This time, the twins ran like tireless deer.

The Holy People blessed the brothers and hoped they would be moved to serve their people.

They were men now. Their mother gave the brothers bows and arrows and told them to hunt for food. But she warned them about wandering too far from the *hoghan*. But the brothers wandered too far because they wished to find their true father.

The spies of the *naayéé'* saw them and reported back to the monsters. They had seen the twins.

Now the *naayéé'* would come and eat up all the people like little pieces of corn.

The next morning, Changing Woman could not forget her fear. She made a corn-cake and set it on the ashes of the fire to bake.

Then she saw *Yé'iitsoh*, the Monster Giant. His armor glittered and his teeth gleamed. Changing Woman hid the brothers inside under a pile of firewood.

Changing Woman took the corncake out of the ashes. At that time, *Yé'iitsoh* pushed his head to the doorway.

"That is a nice cake you have made for me," he grunted. "But I'm looking for your boys to eat them."

"No," Changing Woman said. "Food that looks this good can't go into such an ugly mouth!"

Yé'iitsoh bellowed and pulled his head out of the door. And he walked away and said nothing else.

The brothers had not listened to their mother and they were ashamed. When the day ended, they left in order to find a way to help their people.

And they walked up the Traveler's Circle Mountain. They had met the Holy People here before.

They noticed a glint of a rainbow laying like a rope on the earth. They walked on it. And as they walked, they started flying faster than eagles. They were walking on *atiin diyinii*, the Holy Trail, created by the Holy People!

And then, after a long distance they landed on the edge of a canyon and spotted smoke swirling into the air. It came from a hole in a tall rock.

They walked inside to the home of Spider Woman. They asked her, "Who is our father? And what direction is our future?"

"Your father is *Jó'honaa'éí*," she said. "His home is in the sky. With his powerful weapons you can destroy the *naayéé'*. But the way to his house is dangerous. The *naayéé'* will try to stop you. *Jó'honaa'éí* will not say you are his sons. He will test you."

Spider Woman knew the brothers would face four dangerous enemies. And so she gave them the *naayéé' ats'os*, a sacred hoop made from feathers of the monster eagles in the East. She taught them how to use it with powerful singing.

And the brothers ran on the Holy Trail to find their father so they could help their people, they say.

That morning, in the white light of the dawn, the brothers faced the Crushing Rocks, who tried to smash them like two clapping hands.

In the blue light of the midday, they faced the Slashing Reeds, who tried to cut them to pieces.

In the yellow light of the afternoon, the faced the Giant Awl Cactuses that tried to pierce them with poisonous spines.

In the gray light of the sunset, the brothers faced the Boiling Dunes, who tried to shrivel them into ashes.

But each time the brothers anticipated them. They held out the sacred hoop and sang the powerful song.

Because the brothers believed in what the Holy People had told them, they overcame the *naayéé'*.

The brothers came to a glowing turquoise house on the shore of a large lake. The path to the door was blocked by two bears, a pair of large snakes, and a pair of tall tornados.

But the brothers anticipated them, and with the sacred hoop and the powerful song they passed by them.

Inside, two strong young men grabbed the brothers and rolled them into a blanket and put them up on a high shelf at the edge of the roof. They waited there until a giant entered. He carried a red shield. The shield burned so bright and so hot.

This man was *Jó'honaa'éí*, the Sun, the twins' father.

The Sun suspected the brothers were his enemies, and because of this he tried to destroy them.

He grabbed them by the ankles and threw them against a wall of sharp spikes. But the brothers used the chant of the *naayéé' ats'os* to shield themselves from the spikes.

"Is it true?" said *Jó'honaa'éí*. "These could be my sons."

The Sun filled his sweathouse with scorching steam.

But, actually, *Níłch'i*, the Wind, had dug an escape tunnel for the brothers. They crawled into this tunnel until the air cleared, and then they emerged unharmed.

"Is it true?" said *Jó'honaa'éí*. "These twins could be my sons."

Jó'honaa'éí then dressed the brothers in robes of white dawn, blue daylight, yellow twilight, and black darkness, and he loosened their hair so that it fell around their shoulders. Then he invited them into his house.

As they walked, *Níłch'i*, the Wind, whispered to the brothers, "Look down."

Wóóseek'idii, the Spiny Caterpillar, was crawling across the ground. *Wóóseek'idii* left behind two small streaks of blue spit.

The Wind said to them, "Take those two streaks of blue spit and put them in your mouths."

The Sun offered the twins his turquoise pipe. He had them smoke poisoned tobacco, but the spit protected the brothers from the poison.

"Is it true?" said *Jó'honaa'éí*. "These twins *must* be my sons."

Jó'honaa'éí asked, "Why have you come here?"

The twins said, "We have come because of the *naayéé'* stalking our people, like *Yé'iitsoh*."

Jó'honaa'éí gave them the tools to fight.

He gave to each brother a helmet and body armor of hard flint scales. He gave them these weapons: chain-lightning arrows, mighty sheet-lightning arrows, deadly sunbeam arrows, and killing rainbow arrows.

He gave them flint swords and stone knives to cut through the hard skin of the *naayéé'*.

Jó'honaa'éí said to them, "I will fire the first lightning arrow at the strongest of the *naayéé'*, *Yé'iitsoh*."

Jó'honaa'éí then led the brothers to the top of the sky and they saw the four sacred mountains. Also they also saw *Dził ná'ooditii*, the Traveler's Circle Mountain, again, where the Holy People had trained them to be men. They saw the home of their mother, whom they wanted to protect from the harassing *naayéé'*.

Jó'honaa'éí blessed them and spread a streak of lightning in front of them.

The two brothers stood on it and it descended like steps into the sky toward *Tsoodził*, the Blue Bead Mountain, and they ran down it towards *Yé'iitsoh*.

In front of the mountain, they met Holy Man and Holy Woman. They told the twins how they knew that over there somewhere is a place where *Yé'iitsoh* comes to drink.

The brothers ran and climbed a high, rocky cliff.

They could not see *Yé'iitsoh*.

They sat and waited and got so bored that the oldest brother fired a chain-lightning arrow and put a deep scar into a large rock near Blue Bead Mountain.

To this day it is still there.

The brothers knew the weapons were powerful.

They knew they could win the battle.

Soon they heard the sound of footsteps, like thunder rumbling inside a canyon.

And then the head of *Yé'iitsoh* looked over the top of Blue Bead Mountain. The mountains under him were like anthills.

When *Yé'iitsoh* took a step, he would cover as much ground as a man could walk between morning and noon!

The monster carried a basket full of prey that he had killed. He put it on the ground and drank from the lake. He kept swallowing and the water drained away after each huge gulp!

When he was done, he wiped his mouth with his forearm, which was as long as a small mountain. *Yé'iitsoh* saw the brothers and laughed. The cliff where the brothers crouched shook and swayed.

The brothers doubted they could win the battle.

Yé'iitsoh said, "You two look like you'll taste good and you'll fit right in my basket! You'll be small, but tasty!"

Then he laughed.

The older brother called back to *Yé'iitsoh*, "Even though we are small, we just might choke your throat if you try to swallow us."

Then *Níłch'i*, the Wind, spoke. "Beware! Beware!" He sent a rainbow and it swung under their feet.

Just then, *Yé'iitsoh* reached into his basket and pulled out a lightning arrow.

He hurled the lightning at the brothers and the brothers rose up on the rainbow as the arrow smashed the cliff into pieces.

Yé'iitsoh aimed to shoot the brothers out of the sky.

But a thunderbolt crashed down and smashed the side of the monster's head.

Thunder rumbled across the lake and made waves on the water.

It was *Jó'honaa'éí*. The Sun had fired the first shot into *Yé'iitsoh*'s head.

Yé'iitsoh stumbled but did not fall.

The older brother pulled back his bow and shot a chain-lightning arrow and it stuck into the monster.

The arrow exploded against *Yé'iitsoh*'s hard armor.

Yé'iitsoh swayed and bent his knees, but he remained standing.

He fired again. The monster's knees buckled and sand billowed into the sky.

The younger brother drew his bow and fired a chain-lightning arrow into the monster's chest.

Then *Yé'iitsoh* fell onto his hands. His head swayed like a tall pine tree in a strong wind.

He fell forward onto his face and his limbs stretched out flat and he never moved again.

The brothers cut off the head of *Yé'iitsoh* and his blood flowed across the valley in front of Blue Bead Mountain. These days, the red rocks are blackened by the blood in that area today.

The twins had cut away *Yé'iitsoh*'s life. They gave each other war names. The older brother was called *Naayéé' neizghání*—Monster Slayer. The younger brother was called *Na'ídígishí*—He Who Cuts Life Out of the Enemy.

After that killing, the twins prayed to their father, the Sun. They put the monster's arrows into the basket. They took them back to their mother. When Changing Woman saw her children return, they danced and sang in a beautiful way.

Haashch'ééłti'í, the Talking God, and *Tó neinilí*, the Water Sprinkler, sang around the mountain where the boys had learned to become men.

People today use this song that was given to them.

The brothers had also brought back *Yé'iitsoh*'s armor.

When the chain-lightning arrows struck him, they had smashed the armor and scattered it across the ground. The brothers gathered these pieces of flint and brought them back.

"Our people could use them for arrowheads and for knives," they said. "They could hunt and cut their food. This way, the evil of *Yé'iitsoh* can be used for something good."

But *Yé'iitsoh* was not the only monster.

Many other *naayéé'* still roamed. And they were still hungry . . .

Discussion Questions

1. One of the functions of myths is to explain why things are the way they are. What customs and natural phenomena are explained by this story?

2. Jim Kristofic states that as a child this story taught him that monsters are real and can be beaten. What are the *naayéé'*? Are they real creatures or metaphorical? How can you tell?

3. How do the Hero Twins model the relationship between human beings and the Holy People? What do they do for each other?

Exemplar 2

Departure of Changing Woman
FROM DINÉ BAHANE'

The Diné Bahane' is the Navajo creation myth describing how the Holy People emerged from the Earth and arranged the world as we know it. Changing Woman is one of the most beloved of the Holy People for her ability to transform ugliness into beauty and sickness into health. However, she no longer lives in the world of humans and resides in a house in the West created by her consort, the Sun. In this version of the story, translated by Paul Zolbrod, Changing Woman surprises the Sun by showing her independence, explaining that she owes him nothing.

It is also said that four more days passed, and that four more nights went by. Four times the sun rose and set, and four times the moon passed overhead.

And on the morning of the fifth day *Asdzáá nádleehé* the Changing Woman made her way to the summit of *Ch'óol'í'í* the Giant Spruce Mountain and sat down on a rock.

She recognized that spot well. It was where she had lain when she was all alone and wished for a consort. It was where she had first felt the warmth of the sun deep within her body.

And as she sat there recollecting, *Jó'honaa'éí* the Sun arrived and placed himself beside her.

He sought to embrace her.

But she struggled to free herself.

As she did so she said these words to him:

"What do you mean by molesting me so?" she said to him.

"I want no part of you!"

To which he gave her this reply:

"I mean simply that I want you for my own," he replied.

"I mean that I want you to come to the west and make a home for me there."

"But I wish to do no such thing," replied she.

"By what right do you make such a request of me?"

Said he then:

"Did I not give your sons the weapons they needed to slay *Naayéé'* the Alien Monsters? Have I not done a great deal for you and your people, in truth? In truth, shouldn't you reward me for what I have done?"

Answered she then:

"But I was not the one who asked for those weapons. It was not I who asked for your help. What you gave you gave of your own free will. I owe you no reward."

Following her words there was a distance of silence.

Then he tried to embrace her again, offering yet another reason for allowing himself to do so:

"When our son *Naayéé' neizghání* the Monster Slayer last visited me, he promised you to me."

And again she struggled to free herself, offering yet another objection:

"What do I care for promises made by someone else in my behalf? I make my own promises or else there are no promises to be made. I speak for myself or else I am not spoken for. I alone decide what I shall do or else I do nothing."

Hearing which words he sighed, stood up, took four paces apart from her, and then turned suddenly to face her.

And this is what he said to her:

"Please!" he said to her.

"Come with me to the west and make a home for me.

"I am lonely.

"Each day I labor long and hard alone in the sky. I have no one to talk with. I have no companion for my nights.

"What good is all that I do if I must endure my days and nights all alone? What use is male without female?

What use is female without male? What use are we two without one another?"

That is what *Jó'honaa'éí* the Sun said to *Asdzáá nádleehé* the Changing Woman.

She did not answer him at once, leaving another space of silence between his words and her reply.

Then at last she spoke. And this is what she said to him at last:

"You have a beautiful house in the east I am told," she said to him.

"I want just such a house in the west.

"I want it built floating on the shimmering water, away from the shore, so that when the Earth Surface People multiply they will not bother me with their quarrels.

"And I want all sorts of gems.

"I want white shell. I want blue shell. I want turquoise. I want haliotis. I want soapstone, agate, redstone, jet.

"Such things I want planted around my house so that I may enjoy their beauty.

"Since I wish to live there without my sister and without our sons, I will be lonely while you are gone each day. So I will want animals to keep me company.

"Give me elk. Give me buffalo. Give me deer. Give me long-tails. Give me mountain sheep, jackrabbits, prairie dogs, muskrats.

"Provide me with those things and I shall go with you to the west."

That is what *Asdzáá nádleehé* the Changing Woman said to *Jó'honaa'éí* the Sun. And this is how he replied:

"What do you mean by making such demands of me?" he replied.

"Why should I provide you with all of those things?"

This time she answered him quickly. And this is what she said to him:

"I will tell you why," she said to him.

"You are male and I am female.

"You are of the sky and I am of the earth.

"You are constant in your brightness, but I must change with the seasons.

"You move constantly at the very edge of heaven, while I must remain fixed in one place.

"Remember that I willingly let you send your rays into my body. Remember that I gave birth to your son, enduring pain to bring him into the world. Remember that I gave that child growth and protected him from harm. Remember that I taught him to serve his people unselfishly so that he would willingly fight the Alien Monsters.

"Remember, as different as we are, you and I, we are of one spirit. As dissimilar as we are, you and I, we are of equal worth. As unlike as you and I are, there must always be solidarity between the two of us. Unlike each other as you and I are, there can be no harmony in the universe as long as there is no harmony between us.

"If there is to be such harmony, my requests must matter to you. My needs are as important to me as yours are to you. My whims count as much as yours do. My fidelity to you is measured by your loyalty to me. My response to your needs is to reflect the way you respond to mine. There is to be nothing more coming from me to you than there is from you to me. There is to be nothing less."

That is what *Asdzáá nádleehé* the Changing Woman said to *Jó'honaa'éí* the Sun there on the summit of *Ch'óol'í'í* the Giant Spruce Mountain.

At first he gave no reply. He took time to weigh carefully all things that she had said.

Then, slowly, thoughtfully, he drew close to her.

Slowly and thoughtfully he placed his arm around her.

And this time she allowed him to do so.

Whereupon he promised her that all the things she wished for she would have. She would have a house in the west on the shimmering water. She would have gems whose beauty she could enjoy. She would have animals to keep her company. All that she wanted she would have.

So it is that she agreed; they would go to a place in the west where they would dwell together in the solid harmony of kinship.

✦ ✦ ✦

When *Asdzáá nádleehé* the Changing Woman was ready to depart for her new home in the west, *Hadahoniye' dine'é* the Mirage People and *Hadahoneestiin dine'é* the Ground Mist People were instructed to go with her. They were two groups of Holy People assembled to help her drive the animals that would keep her company.

She then bid farewell to her sister *Yoolgai asdzáá* and to their two sons *Naayéé' naizghání* and *Tó bájísh chíní*.

"I have finished with childbearing," she said to them.

"And I have finished rearing children.

"I shall leave now and dwell with your Father *Jó'honaa'éí nitaa'* the Sun.

"You are grown men now, and you have done much for your people and for the five-fingered Earth Surface People who will soon occupy this world. You need parents no longer, so I am no longer necessary here."

And so saying, she left them to go to her new home in the west.

She set forth with gods and animals accompanying her. Together they passed over the mountains at *Béésh lichíí'*, or Red Knife Summit as we would call it in the language of *Bilagáana* the White Man. There the herd trampled down the earth so that they formed a pass. That way the journey back and forth across the mountains would be easier.

They halted in the *Ch'ínlí* valley to celebrate the betrothal of *Asdzáá nádleehé* the Changing Woman to *Jó'honaa'éí* the Sun. Whereupon her hips widened and her breasts filled out. She grew more beautiful in her womanhood so that she and her husband would flourish in the company of one another.

Thereupon, also the animals began to increase rapidly. Soon the herd was so large that it trampled a deep pass over the summit of *Dzilijiin*, or Black Mountain as we would call it in the language of *Bilagáana*. So deep was the pass that its bottom was almost level with the surrounding plain.

There many of the buffalo broke loose from the main herd and drifted eastward to the country of the broad prairie. They never returned to *Asdzáá nádleehé* the

Changing Woman, and for all we know they roam the plains beyond the Great Stone Mountains to this very day.

Likewise the elks increased in numbers until many of them left the main herd and drifted north, never to return. Likewise antelope, deer, and other animals left the herd and drifted off. Ever since then they have populated the mountains and the valleys, the meadows and the plains. They dwell on the land in great numbers, testifying to the affection that was to grow between *Asdzáá nádleehé* the Changing Woman and *Jó'honaa'éí* the Sun.

The original herd of livestock remained with her, however, and she presides over a household rich with animals to this very day.

✦ ✦ ✦

Four days after they departed from the valley of *Ch'ínlí*, *Asdzáá nádleehé* and her retinue arrived at *Dook'o'oosłííd*, or San Francisco Mountain as we would call it in the language of the White Man.

Here they stopped to perform another ceremony. They laid *Asdzáá nádleehé* the Changing Woman across the very top of the mountain with her head to the west, because that is where she was to go to dwell with her husband. And they manipulated her body and stretched out her limbs. This ceremony she bid the people perform in the future for all Navajo maidens when the path of childhood becomes the trail of womanhood. Which is why the people perform the ritual of *kinaaldá* to this very day. To this very day they seek to mould the body of a maiden into the perfect form of *Asdzáá nádleehé* the Changing Woman, wife of *Jó'honaa'éí* the Sun.

What happened on the rest of the journey from *Dook'o'oosłííd*, where the San Francisco Peaks stand, to the great ocean in the west is not known. But it is known that *Asdzáá nádleehé* finally arrived there to dwell in her floating house beyond the shore. There she lives to this day. And there *Jó'honaa'éí* the Sun rejoins her each evening when his daily journey across the sky is completed.

Occasionally, however, he does not return. On dark stormy days when the wind blows and the sky is black with overcast clouds, he keeps to his home in the east and sends serpents of lightning to try to brighten the heavens. Often these serpents create great mischief in the absence of harmony between *Jó'honaa'éí* and *Asdzáá nádleehé*. The whole suffers when that conjugal solidarity is lost.

✦ ✦ ✦

After *Asdzáá nádleehé* the Changing Woman had departed to go with her husband *Jó'honaa'éí* the Sun, her son *Naayéé' neizghání* the Monster Slayer and his brother *Tó bájísh chíní* the Water Born went as they were bid by their father to *Tó aheedlí*, where two rivers come together in the valley of the San Juan.

There they made a dwelling for themselves, and there they live to this very day. There we may sometimes see their reflection when, after a summer rain which brings the rainbow, the mist rises from the water as the sky clears. The bright colors shimmer in the moist light and the forms of the monster-slaying twins materialize.

To this very day the Navajo people go there to pray. But they do not pray for rain at that place, and they do not pray for good crops. They do not pray for their livestock to flourish or for success in hunting. They pray only for victory over their enemies at that place. They go there to pray only when they recognize the need to restore order and harmony in the world, it is said.

All of these things happened a long, long time ago, it is said.

Discussion Questions

1. How does this story model the ideal relationship between husband and wife? What kinds of expectations and arrangements are acceptable and what kinds are not?

2. What kind of character is *Jó'honaa'éí* in this story? Does he seem to truly love Changing Woman or does he see her as a comfort to be possessed?

3. Changing Woman expresses a concern that the Earth Surface People (humans) will multiply and bother her with their quarrels. What does this suggest about the relationship between humans and the Holy People?

Controversy

Navajo Nation v. U.S. Forest Service

COURT OF APPEALS FOR THE NINTH CIRCUIT

Arizona's San Francisco Peaks are one of four mountains sacred to the Navajo. Legally, they are owned by the U.S. Forest Service. In 2002, a ski resort that operates under a Special Use Permit announced plans to expand its resort by pumping treated sewage water up the mountain to make artificial snow. Six native nations filed a lawsuit arguing that this violated the Religious Freedom Restoration Act (RFRA) because the sewage water would desecrate their sacred mountain. If the Forest Service allowed this, they argued, then the government was illegally burdening their religion. In 2008 the Ninth Circuit ruled in favor of the ski resort, arguing that their actions would not, in fact, burden Native American religion. In the excerpt below, Judge Carlos Bea lays out the argument for the Forest Service and Judge William Fletcher presents counterarguments in his dissent. At stake in this case are such issues as whether actions that damage the subjective experience of a religious practitioner can constitute a government burden on religion and whether the American legal system can understand Navajo religion well enough to assess such claims.

Opinion by Judge BEA; Dissent by Judge WILLIAM A. FLETCHER. BEA, Circuit Judge:

In this case, American Indians ask us to prohibit the federal government from allowing the use of artificial snow for skiing on a portion of a public mountain sacred in their religion. At the heart of their claim is the planned use of recycled wastewater, which contains 0.0001% human waste, to make artificial snow. The Plaintiffs claim the use of such snow on a sacred mountain desecrates the entire mountain, deprecates their religious ceremonies, and injures their religious sensibilities. We are called upon to decide whether this government-approved use of artificial snow on government-owned park land violates the Religious Freedom Restoration Act of 1993 ("RFRA"), 42 U.S.C. §§ 2000bb *et seq.*, the National Environmental Policy Act of 1969 ("NEPA"), 42 U.S.C. §§ 4321 *et seq.*, and the National Historic Preservation Act ("NHPA"), 16 U.S.C. §§ 470 *et seq.* We hold that it does not, and affirm the district court's denial of relief on all grounds.

◆ ◆ ◆

Plaintiff Indian tribes and their members consider the San Francisco Peaks in Northern Arizona to be sacred in their religion. They contend that the use of recycled wastewater to make artificial snow for skiing on the Snowbowl, a ski area that covers approximately one percent of the San Francisco Peaks, will spiritually contaminate the entire mountain and devalue their religious exercises. The district court found the Plaintiffs' beliefs to be sincere; there is no basis to challenge that finding. The district court also found, however, that there are no plants, springs, natural resources, shrines with religious significance, or religious ceremonies that would be physically affected by the use of such artificial snow. No plants would be destroyed or stunted; no springs polluted; no places of worship made inaccessible, or liturgy modified. The Plaintiffs continue to have virtually unlimited access to the mountain, including the ski area, for religious and cultural purposes. On the mountain, they continue to pray, conduct their religious ceremonies, and collect plants for religious use.

Thus, the sole effect of the artificial snow is on the Plaintiffs' subjective spiritual experience. That is, the presence of the artificial snow on the Peaks is offensive to the Plaintiffs' feelings about their religion and will decrease the spiritual fulfillment Plaintiffs get from practicing their religion on the mountain. Nevertheless, a government action that decreases the spirituality, the fervor, or the satisfaction with which a believer practices his religion is not what Congress has labeled a "substantial burden"—a term of art chosen by Congress to be defined by reference to Supreme Court precedent—on the free exercise of religion. Where, as here, there is no showing the government has coerced the Plaintiffs to act contrary to their religious beliefs under the threat of sanctions, or conditioned a governmental benefit upon conduct that would violate the Plaintiffs' religious beliefs, there is no "substantial burden" on the exercise of their religion.

Were it otherwise, any action the federal government were to take, including action on its own land, would be subject to the personalized oversight of millions of citizens. Each citizen would hold an individual veto to prohibit the government action solely because it offends his religious beliefs, sensibilities, or tastes, or fails to satisfy his religious desires. Further, giving one religious sect a veto over the use of public park land would deprive others of the right to use what is, by definition, land that belongs to everyone.

"[W]e are a cosmopolitan nation made up of people of almost every conceivable religious preference." *Braunfeld v. Brown*, 366 U.S. 599, 606, 81 S. Ct. 1144, 6 L. Ed. 2d 563 (1961). Our nation recognizes and protects the expression of a great range of religious beliefs. Nevertheless, respecting religious credos is one thing; requiring the government to change its conduct to avoid any perceived slight to them is quite another. No matter how much we might wish the government to conform its conduct to our religious preferences, act in ways that do not offend our religious sensibilities, and take no action that decreases our spiritual fulfillment, no government—let alone a government that presides over a nation with as many religions as the United States of America—could function were it required to do so. *Lyng v. Nw. Indian Cemetery Protective Ass'n*, 485 U.S. 439, 452, 108 S. Ct. 1319, 99 L. Ed. 2d 534 (1988).

✦ ✦ ✦

We affirm the district court's entry of judgment in favor of the Defendants on the RFRA claim, and the district court's grant of summary judgment to the Defendants on the NEPA and the NHPA claims.
AFFIRMED.

WILLIAM A. FLETCHER, Circuit Judge, dissenting, joined by Judge PREGERSON and Judge FISHER:

The en banc majority today holds that using treated sewage effluent to make artificial snow on the most sacred mountain of southwestern Indian tribes does not violate the Religious Freedom Restoration Act ("RFRA"). It also holds that a supposed pleading mistake prevents the tribes from arguing under the National Environmental Policy Act ("NEPA") that the Forest Service failed to consider the likelihood that children and others would ingest snow made from the effluent. I dissent from both holdings.

Religious Freedom Restoration Act

[D]ivers great learned men have been heretical, whilst they have sought
to fly up to the secrets of the Deity by the waxen wings of the senses.
—Sir Francis Bacon, *Of the Proficience and Advancement of
Learning, Divine and Human* (Book I, 1605).

The majority holds that spraying 1.5 million gallons per day of treated sewage effluent on the most sacred mountain of southwestern Indian tribes does not "substantially burden" their "exercise of religion" in violation of RFRA. According to the majority, "no plants, springs, natural resources, shrines with religious significance, or religious ceremonies . . . would be physically affected" by the use of the treated sewage effluent. According to the majority, the "sole effect" of the dumping of the treated sewage effluent is on the Indians' "subjective spiritual experience." The majority holds:

> [T]he presence of the artificial snow on the Peaks is offensive to the Plaintiffs' mental and emotional feelings about their religion and will decrease the spiritual fulfillment Plaintiffs get from practicing their religion on the mountain. Nevertheless, a government action that decreases the spirituality, the fervor, or the satisfaction with which a believer practices his religion is not what Congress has labeled a "substantial burden" . . . on the free exercise of religion. Where, as here, there is no showing the government has coerced the Plaintiffs to act contrary to their religious beliefs under the threat of sanctions, or conditioned a governmental benefit upon conduct that would violate the Plaintiffs' religious beliefs, there is no "substantial burden" on the exercise of their religion.

In so holding, the majority misstates the evidence below, misstates the law under RFRA, and misunderstands the very nature of religion.

✦ ✦ ✦

Misunderstanding of Religious Belief and Practice

In addition to misstating the law under RFRA, the majority misunderstands the nature of religious belief and practice. The majority concludes that spraying up to 1.5 million gallons of treated sewage effluent per day on Humphrey's Peak, the most sacred of the San Francisco Peaks, does not impose a "substantial burden" on the Indians' "exercise of religion." In so concluding, the majority emphasizes the lack of physical harm. According to the majority, "[T]here are no plants, springs, natural resources, shrines with religious significance, nor any religious ceremonies that would be physically affected" by using treated sewage effluent to make artificial snow. In the majority's view, the "sole effect" of using treated sewage effluent on Humphrey's Peak is on the Indians' "subjective spiritual experience."

The majority's emphasis on physical harm ignores the nature of religious belief and exercise, as well as the nature of the inquiry mandated by RFRA. The majority characterizes the Indians' religious belief and exercise as merely a "subjective spiritual experience." Though I would not choose precisely those words, they come close to describing what the majority thinks it is *not* describing—a genuine religious belief and exercise. Contrary to what the majority writes, and appears to think, religious exercise invariably, and centrally, involves a "subjective spiritual experience."

Religious belief concerns the human spirit and religious faith, not physical harm and scientific fact. Religious exercise sometimes involves physical things, but the physical or scientific character of these things is secondary to their spiritual and religious meaning. The centerpiece of religious belief and exercise is the "subjective" and the "spiritual." As William James wrote, religion may be defined as "the feelings, acts, and experiences of individual men [and women] in their solitude, so far as they apprehend themselves to stand in relation to whatever they may consider the divine." WILLIAM JAMES, THE VARIETIES OF RELIGIOUS EXPERIENCE: A STUDY IN HUMAN NATURE 31–32 (1929).

The majority's misunderstanding of the nature of religious belief and exercise as merely "subjective" is an excuse for refusing to accept the Indians' religion as worthy of protection under RFRA. According to undisputed evidence in the record, and the finding of the district court, the Indians in this case are sincere in their religious beliefs. The record makes clear that their religious beliefs and practice do not merely require the continued existence of certain plants and shrines. They require that these plants and shrines be spiritually pure, undesecrated by treated sewage effluent.

Perhaps the strength of the Indians' argument in this case could be seen more easily by the majority if another religion were at issue. For example, I do not think that the majority would accept that the burden on a Christian's exercise of religion would be insubstantial if the government permitted only treated sewage effluent for use as baptismal water, based on an argument that no physical harm would result and any adverse effect would merely be on the Christian's "subjective spiritual experience." Nor do I think the majority would accept such an argument for an orthodox Jew if the government permitted only non-Kosher food.

✦ ✦ ✦

Substantial Burden on the Indians' Exercise of Religion

The record in this case makes clear that the San Francisco Peaks are particularly sacred to the surrounding Indian tribes. Humphrey's Peak is the most sacred, or holy, of the Peaks. I accept as sincere the Indians' testimony about their religious beliefs and practices, and I accept as sincere their testimony that the Peaks, and in particular Humphrey's Peak, are not merely sacred but holy mountains.

✦ ✦ ✦

The Navajo

The Peaks are also of fundamental importance to the religious beliefs and practices of the Navajo. The district court found, "[T]he Peaks are considered . . . to be the 'Mother of the Navajo People,' their essence and their home. The whole of the Peaks is the holiest of shrines in the Navajo way of life." Considering the mountain "like family," the Navajo greet the Peaks daily with prayer songs, of which there are more than one hundred relating to the four mountains sacred to the Navajo. Witnesses described the Peaks as "our leader" and "very much an integral part of our life, our daily lives."

The Navajo creation story revolves around the Peaks. The mother of humanity, called the Changing Woman and compared by one witness to the Virgin Mary, resided on the Peaks and went through puberty there, an event which the people celebrated as a gift of new life. Following this celebration, called the *kinaalda*, the Changing Woman gave birth to twins, from whom the Navajo are descended. The Navajo believe that the Changing Woman's *kinaalda* gave them life, generation after generation. Young women today still celebrate their own *kinaalda* with a ceremony one witness compared to a Christian confirmation or a Jewish bat mitzvah. The ceremony sometimes involves water especially collected from the Peaks because of the Peaks' religious significance.

The Peaks are represented in the Navajo medicine bundles found in nearly every Navajo household. The medicine bundles are composed of stones, shells, herbs, and soil from each of four sacred mountains. One Navajo practitioner called the medicine bundles "our Bible," because they have "embedded" within them "the unwritten way of life for us, our songs, our ceremonies." The practitioner traced their origin to the Changing Woman: When her twins wanted to find their father, the Changing Woman instructed them to offer prayers to the Peaks and conduct ceremonies with medicine bundles. The Navajo believe that the medicine bundles are conduits for prayers; by praying to the Peaks with a medicine bundle containing soil from the Peaks, the prayer will be communicated to the mountain.

As their name suggests, medicine bundles are also used in Navajo healing ceremonies, as is medicine made with plants collected from the Peaks. Appellant Norris

Nez, a Navajo medicine man, testified that "like the western doctor has his black bag with needles and other medicine, this bundle has in there the things to apply medicine to a patient." Explaining why he loves the mountain as his mother, he testified, "She is holding medicine and things to make us well and healthy. We suckle from her and get well when we consider her our Mother." Nez testified that he collects many different plants from the Peaks to make medicine.

The Peaks play a role in every Navajo religious ceremony. The medicine bundle is placed to the west, facing the Peaks. In the Blessingway ceremony, called by one witness "the backbone of our ceremony" because it is performed at the conclusion of all ceremonies, the Navajo pray to the Peaks by name.

The purity of nature, including the Peaks, plays an important part in Navajo beliefs. Among other things, it affects how a medicine bundle described by one witness as "a living basket" is made. The making of a medicine bundle is preceded by a four-day purification process for the medicine man and the keeper of the bundle. By Navajo tradition, the medicine bundle should be made with leather from a buck that is ritually suffocated; the skin cannot be pierced by a weapon. Medicine bundles are "rejuvenated" every few years, by replacing the ingredients with others gathered on pilgrimages to the Peaks and three other sacred mountains.

The Navajo believe their role on earth is to take care of the land. They refer to themselves as *nochoka dine*, which one witness translated as "people of the earth" or "people put on the surface of the earth to take care of the lands." They believe that the Creator put them between four sacred mountains of which the westernmost is the Peaks, or *Do'ok'oos-liid* ("shining on top," referring to its snow), and that the Creator instructed them never to leave this homeland. Although the whole reservation is sacred to the Navajo, the mountains are the most sacred part. As noted previously, one witness drew an analogy to a church, with the area within the mountains as the part of the church where the people sit, and the Peaks as "our altar to the west."

As in Hopi religious practice, the Peaks are so sacred in Navajo beliefs that, according to Joe Shirley, Jr., President of the Navajo Nation, a person "cannot just voluntarily go up on this mountain at any time. It's the holiest of shrines in our way of life. You have to sacrifice. You have to sing certain songs before you even dwell for a little bit to gather herbs, to do offerings." After the requisite preparation, the Navajo go on pilgrimages to the Peaks to collect plants for ceremonial and medicinal use.

✦ ✦ ✦

The Burden Imposed by the Proposed
Snowbowl Expansion

Under the proposed expansion of the Snowbowl, up to 1.5 million gallons per day of treated sewage effluent would be sprayed on Humphrey's Peak from November through February. Depending on weather conditions, substantially more than 100 million gallons of effluent could be deposited over the course of the winter ski season.

The Indians claim that the use of treated sewage effluent to make artificial snow on the Peaks would substantially burden their exercise of religion. Because the Indians' religious beliefs and practices are not uniform, the precise burdens on religious exercise vary among the Appellants. Nevertheless, the burdens fall roughly into two categories: (1) the inability to perform a particular religious ceremony, because the ceremony requires collecting natural resources from the Peaks that would be too contaminated—physically, spiritually, or both—for sacramental use; and (2) the inability to maintain daily and annual religious practices comprising an entire way of life, because the practices require belief in the mountain's purity or a spiritual connection to the mountain that would be undermined by the contamination.

The first burden—the inability to perform religious ceremonies because of contaminated resources—has been acknowledged and described at length by the Forest Service. The FEIS [Final Environmental Impact Statement] summarizes: "Snowmaking and expansion of facilities, especially the use of reclaimed water, would contaminate the natural resources needed to perform the required ceremonies that have been, and continue to be, the basis for the cultural identity for many of these tribes." Further, "the use of reclaimed water is believed by the tribes to be impure and would have an irretrievable impact on the use of the soil, plants, and animals for medicinal and ceremonial purposes throughout the entire Peaks, as the whole mountain is regarded as a single, living entity."

Three Navajo practitioners' testimony at trial echoed the Forest Service's assessment in describing how the proposed action would prevent them from performing various ceremonies. Larry Foster, a Navajo practitioner who is training to become a medicine man, testified that "once water is tainted and if water comes from mortuaries or hospitals, for Navajo there's no words to say that that water can be reclaimed." He further testified that he objected to the current use of the Peaks as a ski area, but that using treated sewage effluent to make artificial snow on the Peaks would be "far more serious." He explained, "I can live with a scar as a human being. But if something is injected into my body that is foreign, a foreign object—and reclaimed water, in my opinion, could be water that's reclaimed through sewage, wastewater, comes from mortuaries, hospitals, there could be disease in the waters—and that would be like injecting me and my mother, my grandmother, the Peaks, with impurities, foreign matter that's not natural."

Foster testified that if treated sewage effluent were used on the Peaks he would no longer be able to go on the pilgrimages to the Peaks that are necessary to rejuvenate the medicine bundles, which are, in turn, a part of every Navajo healing ceremony. He explained:

> Your Honor, our way of life, our culture we live in—we live in the blessingway, in harmony. We try to walk in harmony, be in harmony with all of nature. And we go to all of the sacred mountains for protection. We go on a pilgrimage similar to Muslims going to Mecca. And we do this with so much love, commitment and respect. And if one mountain—and more in particularly with the San Francisco Peaks—which is our bundle mountain, or sacred, bundle mountain, were to be poisoned or given foreign materials that were not pure, it would create an imbalance—there would not be a place among the sacred mountains. We would not be able to go there to obtain herbs or medicines to do our ceremonies, because that mountain would then become impure. It would not be pure anymore. And it would be a devastation for our people.

Appellant Navajo medicine man Norris Nez testified that the proposed action would prevent him from practicing as a medicine man. He told the district court that the presence of treated sewage effluent would "ruin" his medicine, which he makes from plants collected from the Peaks. He also testified that he would be unable to perform the fundamental Blessingway ceremony, because "all [medicine] bundles will be affected and we will have nothing to use eventually."

Foster, Nez, and Navajo practitioner Steven Begay testified that because they believe the mountain is an indivisible living entity, the entire mountain would be contaminated even if the millions of gallons of treated sewage effluent are put onto only one area of the Peaks. According to Foster, Nez, and Begay, there would be contamination even on those parts of the Peaks where the effluent would not come into physical contact with particular plants or ceremonial areas. To them, the contamination is not literal in the sense that a scientist would use the term. Rather, the contamination represents the poisoning of a living being. In Foster's words, "[I]f someone were to get a prick or whatever from a contaminated needle, it doesn't matter what the percentage is, your whole body would then become contaminated. And that's what would happen to the mountain." In Nez's words, "All of it is holy. It is like a body. It is like our body. Every part of it is holy and sacred." In Begay's words, "All things that occur on the mountain are a part of the mountain, and so they will have connection to it. We don't separate the mountain."

The Hualapai also presented evidence that the proposed action would prevent them from performing particular religious ceremonies. Frank Mapatis, a Hualapai practitioner and spiritual leader who visits the Peaks approximately once a month to collect water for ceremonies and plants for medicine, testified that the use of treated sewage effluent would prevent him from performing Hualapai sweat lodge and healing ceremonies with the sacred water from the Peaks. Mapatis testified that he believes that the treated sewage effluent would seep into the ground and into the spring below the Snowbowl where he collects his sacred water, so that the spring water would be "contaminated" by having been "touched with death." Because contact between the living and the dead induces "ghost sickness," which involves hallucinations, using water touched with death in healing ceremonies "would be like malpractice." Further, Mapatis would become powerless to perform the healing ceremony for ghost sickness itself, because that ceremony requires water from the Peaks, the only medicine for illnesses of the upper body and head, like hallucinations.

The second burden the proposed action would impose—undermining the Indians' religious faith, practices, and way of life by desecrating the Peaks' purity—is also shown in the record. The Hopi presented evidence that the presence of treated sewage effluent on the Peaks would fundamentally undermine all of their religious practices because their way of life, or "beliefway," is largely based on the idea that the Peaks are a pure source of their rains and the home of the *Katsinam*.

Leigh Kuwanwisiwma, a Hopi religious practitioner and the director of the tribe's Cultural Preservation Office, explained the connection between contaminating the Peaks and undermining the Hopi religion:

> The spiritual covenant that the Hopi clans entered into with the Caretaker I refer to as Ma'saw, the spiritual person and the other d[ei]ties that reside—and the Katsina that reside in the Peaks started out with the mountains being in their purest form. They didn't have any real intrusion by humanity.
>
> The purity of the spirits, as best we can acknowledge the spiritual domain, we feel were content in receiving the Hopi clans. So when you begin to intrude on that in a manner that is really disrespectful to the Peaks and to the spiritual home of the Katsina, it affects the Hopi people. It affects the Hopi people, because as clans left and embarked on their migrations and later coming to the Hopi villages, we experienced still a mountain and peaks that were in their purest form as a place of worship to go to, to visit, to place our offerings, the tranquility, the sanctity that we left a long time ago was still there.

Antone Honanie, a Hopi practitioner, testified that he would have difficulty preparing for religious ceremonies, because treated sewage effluent is "something you can't get out of your mind when you're sitting there praying" to the mountain, "a place where everything is supposed to be pure." Emory Sekaquaptewa, a Hopi tribal member and research anthropologist, testified that the desecration of the mountain would cause *Katsinam* dance ceremonies to lose their religious value. They would "simply be a performance for performance['s] sake" rather than "a religious effort": "Hopi people are raised in this belief that the mountains are a revered place. And even though they begin with kind of a fantasy notion, this continues to grow into a more deeper spiritual sense of the mountain. So that any thing that interrupts this perception, as they hold it, would tend to undermine the integrity in which they hold the mountain."

Summarizing the Hopi's testimony, the district court wrote:

> The individual Hopi's practice of the Hopi way permeates every part and every day of the individual's life from birth to death. . . . The Hopi Plaintiffs testified that the proposed upgrades to the Snowbowl have affected and will continue to negatively affect the way they think about the Peaks, the Kachina and themselves when preparing for any religious activity involving the Peaks and the Kachina—from daily morning prayers to the regular calendar of religious dances that occur throughout the year. . . . The Hopi Plaintiffs also testified that this negative effect on the practitioners' frames of mind due to the continued and increased desecration of the home of the Kachinas will undermine the Hopi faith and the Hopi way. According to the Hopi, the Snowbowl upgrades will undermine the Hopi faith in daily ceremonies and undermine the Hopi faith in their Kachina ceremonies as well as their faith in the blessings of life that they depend on the Kachina to bring. . . .

The Havasupai presented evidence that the presence of treated sewage effluent on the Peaks would, by contaminating the Peaks, undermine their sweat lodge purification ceremonies and could lead to the end of the ceremonies. Rex Tilousi, Chairman of the Havasupai, testified that Havasupai religious stories teach that the water in Havasu Creek, which they use for their sweat ceremonies, flows from the Peaks, where the Havasupai believe life began. Although none of the three Havasupai witnesses stated that they would be completely unable to perform the sweat lodge ceremonies as a consequence of the impurity introduced by the treated sewage effluent, Roland Manakaja, a traditional practitioner, testified that the impurity would disrupt the ceremony:

> If I was to take the water to sprinkle the rocks to bring the breath of our ancestors—we believe the steam is the breath of our ancestors. And the rocks placed in the west signify where our ancestors go, the deceased. . . . Once the steam rises, like it does on the Peaks, the fog or the steam that comes off is creation. And once the steam comes off and it comes into our being, it purifies and cleanses us and we go to the level of trance. . . . It's going to impact mentally my spirituality. Every time I think about sprinkling that water on the rocks, I'm going to always think about this sewer that they're using to recharge the aquifer.

He further testified that he was "concerned" that the water's perceived impurity might cause the sweat lodge ceremony to die out altogether, if tribal members fear "breathing the organisms or the chemicals that may come off the steam."

The record supports the conclusion that the proposed use of treated sewage effluent on the San Francisco Peaks would impose a burden on the religious exercise of all four tribes discussed above—the Navajo, the Hopi, the Hualapai, and the Havasupai. However, on the record before us, that burden falls most heavily on the Navajo and the Hopi. The Forest Service itself wrote in the FEIS that the Peaks are the most sacred place of both the Navajo and the Hopi; that those tribes' religions have revolved around the Peaks for centuries; that their religious practices require pure natural resources from the Peaks; and that, because their religious beliefs dictate that the mountain be viewed as a whole living being, the treated sewage effluent would in their view contaminate the natural resources throughout the Peaks. Navajo Appellants presented evidence in the district court that, were the proposed action to go forward, contamination by the treated sewage effluent would prevent practitioners from making or rejuvenating medicine bundles, from making medicine, and from performing the Blessingway and healing ceremonies. Hopi Appellants presented evidence that, were the proposed action to go forward, contamination by the effluent would fundamentally undermine their entire system of belief and the associated practices of song, worship, and prayer, that depend on the purity of the Peaks, which is the source of rain and their livelihoods and the home of the *Katsinam* spirits.

In light of this showing, it is self-evident that the Snowbowl expansion prevents the Navajo and Hopi "from engaging in [religious] conduct or having a religious experience" and that this interference is "more than an inconvenience." *Bryant*, 46 F.3d at 949. The burden imposed on the religious practices of the Navajo and Hopi is certainly as substantial as the intrusion on confession deemed a "substantial burden" in *Mockaitis*, 104 F.3d at 1531, and the denial of a Halal or Kosher meat diet deemed a "substantial burden" in *Shakur*, 514 F.3d at 888–89. Thus, under RFRA, the Forest Service's approval of the Snowbowl expansion may only survive if it furthers a compelling governmental interest by the least restrictive means.

✦ ✦ ✦

Conclusion

I would therefore hold that the proposed expansion of the Arizona Snowbowl, which would entail spraying up to 1.5 million gallons per day of treated sewage effluent on the holiest of the San Francisco Peaks, violates RFRA. The expansion would impose a "substantial burden" on the Indians' "exercise of religion" and is not justified by a "compelling government interest."

Discussion Questions

1. In the majority opinion, Judge Bea lays out a simple argument: Because the Snowbowl project will only cover a small portion of a sacred mountain, no natural resources or shrines sacred to the Navajo will be physically affected; therefore, their objection is merely subjective and not a substantial burden on their religion. In his dissent, Judge Fletcher counters that this argument is illogical because subjective experiences are inherent to the nature of religion. Which side is right? Why?

2. Fletcher claims the majority is making "excuses" because they do not recognize the Navajo religion as worthy of government protection. He suggests that Judge Bea's arguments would not be accepted if Christians were expected, for example, to use treated sewage water for baptisms. Does Fletcher's claim seem plausible or not? If Navajo religion is subjected to a double standard, why is this the case?

3. Critics of the Religious Freedom Restoration Act sometimes complain that religious exemptions render American law meaningless. If the court had ruled that the government cannot do anything with public lands that would damage the way the Navajo experience their religion, would this set a dangerous precedent? Would this then invite other religious groups to impose restrictions on what can or cannot be done on public land, based on their subjective beliefs?

Atheism

Is atheism a religion? The answer to this question depends on how one defines religion as well as what sort of nonbelievers are being considered. Nonbelief runs a wide gamut from those who call themselves "spiritual but not religious" (SBNR) to secular humanists to "New Atheist" thinkers such as Richard Dawkins. Some nonbelievers simply regard God as an intellectual proposition that they find unpersuasive. Others are part of active communities that participate in weekly rituals, increasing their similarity to a religious tradition. Certainly it is possible to think about atheism *as if* it is a religion, using the four-part model applied to the other traditions in this book. The human problem is ignorance. The solution is knowledge. The techniques include reason, science, skepticism, and critical inquiry. The exemplars are freethinkers who dared to question the religious dogmas of their culture—some of whom were martyred for it.

The problem and solution in atheism are fairly self-explanatory and it is arguably more appropriate to learn about the techniques of atheism from a book on logic or the scientific method. Therefore we have included only writings from exemplars. While there were nonbelievers among the philosophers of ancient India and Greece, we have selected two twentieth-century figures who have exerted more influence on contemporary atheist movements and thought. Bertrand Russell (1872–1970) was a British philosopher whose 1927 essay "Why I Am Not a Christian" challenged the notion that religion is necessary to be a moral person. In fact, he turned this idea on its head and suggested that more religion leads to greater levels of cruelty and human misery. Madalyn Murray O'Hair (1919–1995), founder of the American Atheists, took much the same view. In an interview for *Playboy* magazine she explicitly rejected the claim that churches do more good than harm. And yet, in both these excerpts there is a suggestion that atheism is more than simply rejecting the idea of God. Both exemplars express a kind of faith in the human ability to solve problems and in human courage. Certainly both the exemplars had plenty of courage. Russell was repeatedly imprisoned for speaking out against war and O'Hair refused to be silent in the face of harassment and death threats.

Exemplar 1

Why I Am Not a Christian
Bertrand Russell

Bertrand Russell (1872–1970) was a British philosopher and an important proponent of atheism. He was also an activist who supported such causes as gay rights, reproductive rights, and access to contraception. He was imprisoned during both world wars for his outspoken pacifism. In 1950 he received the Nobel Prize in Literature. In a 1952 article called "Is There a God?" he presented the argument of "Russell's teapot" to show why the burden of proof falls on those making nonfalsifiable claims. Just as one cannot "prove" there is no God, neither can one prove there is not a teapot, orbiting the sun, and too small to detect with telescopes—yet no one would be expected to believe in the teapot. "Russell's teapot" anticipated arguments made by contemporary atheists who satirically claim that the world was created by a "Flying Spaghetti Monster."

The Emotional Factor

. . . I do not think that the real reason why people accept religion has anything to do with argumentation. They accept religion on emotional grounds. One is often told that it is a very wrong thing to attack religion, because religion makes men virtuous. So I am told; I have not noticed it. You know, of course, the parody of that argument in Samuel Butler's book, *Erewhon Revisited*. You will remember that in Erewhon there is a certain Higgs who arrives in a remote country, and after spending some time there he escapes from that country in a balloon. Twenty years later he comes back to that country and finds a new religion in which he is worshiped under the name of the "Sun Child," and it is said that he ascended into heaven. He finds that the Feast of the Ascension is about to be celebrated, and he hears Professors Hanky and Panky say to each other that they never set eyes on the man Higgs, and they hope they never will; but they are the high priests of the religion of the Sun Child. He is very indignant, and he comes up to them, and he says, "I am going to expose all this humbug and tell the people of Erewhon that it was only I, the man Higgs, and I went up in a balloon." He was told, "You must not do that, because all the morals of this country are bound round this myth, and if they once know that you did not ascend into heaven they will all become wicked"; and so he is persuaded of that and he goes quietly away.

That is the idea—that we should all be wicked if we did not hold to the Christian religion. It seems to me that the people who have held to it have been for the most part extremely wicked. You find this curious fact, that the more intense has been the religion of any period and the more profound has been the dogmatic belief, the greater has been the cruelty and the worse has been the state of affairs. In the so-called ages of faith, when men really did believe the Christian religion in all its completeness, there was the Inquisition, with its tortures; there were millions of unfortunate women burned as witches; and there was every kind of cruelty practiced upon all sorts of people in the name of religion.

You find as you look around the world that every single bit of progress in humane feeling, every improvement in the criminal law, every step toward the diminution of war, every step toward better treatment of the coloured races, or every mitigation of slavery, every moral progress that there has been in the world, has been consistently opposed by the organized churches of the world. I say quite deliberately that the Christian religion, as organized in its churches, has been and still is the principal enemy of moral progress in the world.

How the Churches Have Retarded Progress

You may think that I am going too far when I say that that is still so. I do not think that I am. Take one fact. You will bear with me if I mention it. It is not a pleasant fact, but the churches compel one to mention facts that are not pleasant. Supposing that in this world that we live in today an inexperienced girl is married to a syphilitic man; in that case the Catholic Church says, "This is an indissoluble sacrament. You must endure celibacy or stay together. And if you stay together, you must not use birth control to prevent the birth of syphilitic children." Nobody whose natural sympathies have not been warped by dogma, or whose moral nature was not absolutely dead to all sense of suffering, could maintain that it is right and proper that that state of things should continue.

That is only an example. There are a great many ways in which, at the present moment, the church, by its insistence upon what it chooses to call morality, inflicts upon all sorts of people undeserved and unnecessary suffering. And of course, as we know, it is in its major part an opponent still of progress and of improvement in all the ways that diminish suffering in the world, because it has chosen to label as morality a certain narrow set of rules of conduct which have nothing to do with human happiness; and when you say that this or that ought to be done because it would make for human happiness, they think that has nothing to do with the matter at all. "What has human happiness to do with morals? The object of morals is not to make people happy."

Fear, the Foundation of Religion

Religion is based, I think, primarily and mainly upon fear. It is partly the terror of the unknown and partly, as I have said, the wish to feel that you have a kind of elder brother who will stand by you in all your troubles and disputes. Fear is the basis of the whole thing—fear of the mysterious, fear of defeat, fear of death. Fear is the parent of cruelty, and therefore it is no wonder if cruelty and religion have gone hand in hand. It is because fear is at the basis of those two things. In this world we can now begin a little to understand things, and a little to master them by help of science, which has forced its way step by step against the Christian religion, against the churches, and against the opposition of all the old precepts. Science can help us to get over this craven fear in which mankind has lived for so many generations. Science can teach us, and I think our own hearts can teach us, no longer to look around for imaginary supports, no longer to invent allies in the sky, but rather to look to our own efforts here below to make this world a fit place to live in, instead of the sort of place that the churches in all these centuries have made it.

What We Must Do

We want to stand upon our own feet and look fair and square at the world—its good facts, its bad facts, its beauties, and its ugliness; see the world as it is and be not afraid of it. Conquer the world by intelligence and not merely by being slavishly subdued by the terror that comes from it. The whole conception of God is a conception derived from the ancient Oriental despotisms. It is a conception quite unworthy of free men. When you hear people in church debasing themselves and saying that they are miserable sinners, and all the rest of it, it seems contemptible and not worthy of self-respecting human beings. We ought to stand up and look the world frankly in the face. We ought to make the best we can of the world, and if it is not so good as we wish, after all it will still be better than what these others have made of it in all these ages. A good world needs knowledge, kindliness, and courage; it does not need a regretful hankering after the past or a fettering of the free intelligence by the words uttered long ago by ignorant men. It needs a fearless outlook and a free intelligence. It needs hope for the future, not looking back all the time toward a past that is dead, which we trust will be far surpassed by the future that our intelligence can create.

1. Russell rejects the claim that religion is necessary to be moral. In fact, he argues that religion causes people to be *less* moral. What evidence does Russell cite to make this claim? Does his argument seem plausible or not?

2. Russell claims that religion is primarily a way of coping with fear. Does this seem plausible? What about religious people who are afraid of hell or other forms of supernatural punishment that they would not have to fear if they rejected their religion?

3. Russell is clearly *against* Christianity. Is he *for* anything? If so, what?

Exemplar 2

Playboy Interview: Madalyn Murray

Atheist and feminist Madalyn Murray O'Hair (1919–1995) founded the American Atheists in 1963 and was once described as "the most hated woman in America." O'Hair sued Baltimore's public schools for compelling her son (also an atheist at the time) to participate in mandatory prayers and Bible readings. Her case was consolidated into *School District of Abington Township v. Schempp* (1963), in which the Supreme Court ruled that schools may not compel students to pray. Some conservatives still inaccurately describe this case as the moment the Supreme Court "kicked God out of the schools." In a 1965 interview with *Playboy* magazine, an unrepentant O'Hair describes the campaign of harassment her family experienced as well as her plans for further lawsuits. Although O'Hair was not diplomatic and her position on religion lacked nuance, one may still admire the intensity of her convictions. In 1995, she mysteriously disappeared along with her granddaughter and her other son, Jon. Their bodies were found buried on a Texas ranch in 2001.

Until June 17, 1963, she was dismissed by many people as a litigious, belligerent, loud-mouthed crank. On that day, however, the Supreme Court upheld her contention that prayer and Bible study should be outlawed in U.S. public schools, and Madalyn Murray became the country's best-known, and most-hated, atheist. She also became the churches' most formidable enemy when, undaunted, she promptly proceeded to launch another broadside at religion: a suit aimed at eliminating from tax exemption the churches' vast nationwide property holdings—a case which many lawyers concede she will probably win if it gets to the Supreme Court, and which, if she wins it, may be what one attorney has called "the biggest single blow ever suffered by organized religion in this country." Organized religion could hardly have an unlikelier nemesis.

Daughter of a Pittsburgh contractor, she studied law at Ohio Northern University and South Texas College, and served as a WAC officer-cryptographer on Eisenhower's staff during World War Two. A plain, plump, graying divorcee with two sons, she lived peacefully with her family in Baltimore—where she worked for 17 years as a psychiatric social worker—until her dismissal, within hours after she instituted her school-prayer suit, from a supervisory job in the city welfare department. Publishing a militant newsletter called The American Atheist, and organizing the Freethought Society of America, Inc. and Other Americans, Inc., legal-action atheist groups supported by contributions from their secret membership, she continued her anticlerical crusade at home and in an unprepossessing downtown office building, in which she and her sons soon became the targets for a three-year campaign of abusive mail, obscene telephone calls, bricks, beatings and death threats.

Finally, in June of last year, Mrs. Murray and her family fled Baltimore—where she and her son Bill, then 18, had just gone free on bail after being arraigned for assaulting several policemen during a fracas in front of her house—and flew to Hawaii for what she called "religious sanctuary from Christian persecution." In the intervening year, the governor of Hawaii has granted a request from the governor of Maryland to extradite Mrs. Murray and her son back to Baltimore for trial on the assault charges—which she claims were trumped up by the police as part of a Church-directed conspiracy to prevent her from pursuing her tax-the-churches suit. She had just petitioned the Hawaii Supreme Court for a reversal of the governor's decision when PLAYBOY called the embattled 46-year-old atheist (and onetime socialist) at her home in Honolulu with its request for an exclusive interview. Consenting readily, she invited us to meet her at Honolulu's Tripler Veterans' Hospital, where she was being treated for nerve injuries which she claims were inflicted by the beating she says she sustained at the hands of the police during the melee that precipitated her departure from Baltimore.

Our first two tape sessions took place at her hospital bedside, where she proceeded to hold forth on her various suits, trials and tribulations, on church and state, and on sex and marriage, with a pungent, four-letter vehemence undiminished by her bedridden condition. Our conversations continued some weeks later in the modest frame house which she shares with her mother, her brother and her 11-year-old son Garth on Honolulu's Spencer Street, where she confided that she would do "anything" rather than return to Maryland in compliance with the Hawaii Supreme Court's expected decision to permit her extradition.

No one can predict what the next chapter in the continuing melodrama of Madalyn Murray's life will be; but at this juncture, we feel that an exploration of her intransigent convictions, and of her continuing confrontations with the church, the law and the public, may shed some timely light on the issues involved in her private war on religion.

PLAYBOY: Why are you an atheist, Mrs. Murray?

MURRAY: Because religion is a crutch, and only the crippled need crutches. I can get around perfectly well on my own two feet, and so can everyone else with a backbone and a grain of common sense. One of the things I did during my 17 years as a psychiatric social worker was go around and find people with mental crutches, and every time I found one, I kicked those goddamn crutches until they flew. You know what happened? Every single one of those people have been able to walk without the crutches—better, in fact. Were they giving up anything intrinsically valuable? Just their irrational reliance upon superstitious and supernatural non-sense. Perhaps this sort of claptrap was good for the Stone Age, when people actu-ally believed that if they prayed for rain they would get it. But we're a grown-up world now, and it's time to put away childish things. But people don't, because most of them don't even know what atheism is. It's not a negation of anything. You don't have to negate what no one can prove exists. No, atheism is a very positive affirma-tion of man's ability to think for himself, to do for himself, to find answers to his own problems. I'm thrilled to feel that I can rely on myself totally and absolutely; that my children are being brought up so that when they meet a problem they can't cop out by foisting it off on God. Madalyn Murray's going to solve her own prob-lems, and nobody's going to intervene. It's about time the world got of off its knees and looked at itself in the mirror and said: "Well, we are men. Let's start acting like it."

PLAYBOY: What led you to become an atheist?

MURRAY: Well, it started when I was very young. People attain the age of intellec-tual discretion at different times in their lives—sometimes a little early and some-times a little late. I was about 12 or 13 years old when I reached this period. It was then that I was introduced to the Bible. We were living in Akron and I wasn't able to get to the library, so I had two things to read at home: a dictionary and a Bible. Well, I picked up the Bible and read it from cover to cover one weekend—just as if it were a novel—very rapidly, and I've never gotten over the shock of it. The mira-cles, the inconsistencies, the improbabilities, the impossibilities, the wretched history, the sordid sex, the sadism in it—the whole thing shocked me profoundly. I remember I looked in the kitchen at my mother and father and I thought: Can they really *believe* in all that? Of course, this was a superficial survey by a very young girl, but it left a traumatic impression. Later, when I started going to church, my first memories are of the minister getting up and accusing us of being full of sin, though he didn't say why; then they would pass the collection plate, and I got it in my mind that this had to do with purification of the soul, that we were being invited to buy expiation from our sins. So I gave it all up. It was too nonsensical.

A few years later, I went off to college, a good, middle-class, very proper college, where I studied with, and under, good, middle-class, very proper people; which is to say, the kind who regard sex as distasteful and religious doubts as unthinkable; the kind to whom it would never occur to scrutinize the mores of society, who absolutely and unquestioningly accept the social system.

PLAYBOY: What school was it?

MURRAY: Ashland College in Ashland, Ohio—a Brethren institution, where two years of Bible study are required for graduation. One year I studied the Old Testament and one year the New Testament. It was a good, sound, thorough, but completely biased evaluation of the Bible, and I was delighted with it, because it helped to document my doubts; it gave me a framework within which I could be critical. But I can't deny that I was an intellectual prostitute along the way many, many times. I can remember one examination where they said. "Describe the Devil," and in order to get 12 points on that question one had to say that the Devil was red and had a forked tail and cloven hoofs and fangs and horns on his head. So I merrily wrote this answer down and got my 12 points. I always got straight hundreds in Bible study. My independent study continued for 20 years after this. So I do know the Bible very well from a Protestant point of view—which is what, along with my reason, entitles me to refute it. You can't rationally reject something until you know all about it. But at this time, of course, my convictions hadn't yet crystallized intellectually. I didn't know where my doubts were leading me.

I recall that I had a terrible struggle finding anything antireligious in the school libraries. But many years later, the family returned to Pittsburgh and moved into a house where a woman had left a box of books containing 20 volumes on the history of the Inquisition.

It was then that I found out there was a word for people like me: "heretic." I was kind of delighted to find I had an identity. And then, as I grew a little bit older and got interested in law, I read that Clarence Darrow didn't believe in the Bible either. So I read everything he had ever written, all of his trials, everything—to search out the philosophy of his disbelief. But I couldn't find it. Then I went into the Army, and one day, in the middle of a bull session, somebody called me an atheist. Believe it or not, it was the first time I'd ever heard the word. It goes to show you how a person can grow up in America and have a college education and still not know a goddamned thing. Anyway, when I learned that there was such a thing as an atheist, I looked it up—and found out that the definition fitted me to a tee. Finally, at the age of 24, I found out who—and what—I was. Better late than never.

PLAYBOY: Do you think everyone should believe as you do—or rather, disbelieve?

MURRAY: I think this would be the best of all possible worlds if everybody were an atheist or an agnostic or a humanist—his or her own particular brand—but as for compelling people to this, absolutely not. That would be just as infamous as their imposing their Christianity on me. At no time have I ever said that people should be stripped of their right to the insanity of belief in God. If they want to practice this kind of irrationality, that's their business. It won't get them anywhere; it certainly won't make them happier or more compassionate human beings; but if they want to chew that particular cud, they're welcome to it.

PLAYBOY: Even as an atheist, would you concede that religion, at its best, can be and has been a constructive force, a source of strength and comfort for many people?

MURRAY: If you're talking about Christianity, absolutely not. I don't think the Church has ever contributed anything to anybody, anyplace, at any time.

PLAYBOY: How about the welfare and charity work to which many Catholic, Protestant and Jewish organizations dedicate themselves?

MURRAY: Oh, they love to point to their hospitals and orphanages—most of which are restricted, by the way. But what do these "good works" amount to? They're nothing but a sop to the clerical conscience, a crumb thrown to the populace, alleviating some of the miseries which the Church itself—particularly the Catholic Church—has helped to instigate and perpetuate. I can't pinpoint a period in history or a place in the universe where religion has actually helped the welfare of man. On the contrary, the history of the Church has been a history of divisiveness, repression and reaction. For almost 2000 years, Christianity has held mankind back in politics, in economics, in industry, in science, in philosophy, in culture. Anyone who has even a surface knowledge of the Middle Ages, when the Church held unchallenged sway, can recognize this. But if any one age could be singled out as the worst in the history of Christendom, it would be the administration of Pope Pius XII, the most reactionary head of the most reactionary single force in the world—a force that binds men's minds, a force that divides them, a force that chains them so that they are unable to think and act for themselves.

PLAYBOY: How do you feel about Pope John XXIII? Don't you think his humanitarian views, as enunciated in his *Pacem in Terris,* testify to the fact that enlightenment can flourish within the confines of the Church?

MURRAY: There are good, humanitarian people everywhere—occasionally even in the Church. But John was an amoeba of goodness in a sea of waste, mistakenly believing that the Holy See could or would really change in any fundamental way. He was a tragic figure, for he raised a false hope, cast a brief ray of light that was snuffed out when he died. With Pope Paul in the saddle, the Church is firmly back in the hands of archconservative reaction.

PLAYBOY: When you say that organized religion has contributed nothing to human welfare, do you include those many clergymen, such as Reverend Reeb, who have risked, and in some cases lost, their lives participating in civil rights demonstrations?

MURRAY: Of course not. Reverend Reeb, by the way, was a well-known atheist, a Unitarian, and was not even buried with a religious ceremony. But those priests, nuns and ministers who aren't afraid to stand up and be counted are very much in the minority. They're the exception that proves the rule. Archbishop Toolen of

Mobile-Birmingham has forbidden his priests to participate in Alabama civil rights demonstrations, and Cardinal McIntyre of California has punished priests in his diocese for getting involved in civil rights. These are the men who represent the Church mind—not the poor maverick priest who defies them by marching.

But the most heinous crime of the Church has been perpetrated not against churchmen but against churchgoers. With its poisonous concepts of sin and divine punishment, it's warped and brainwashed countless millions. It would be impossible to calculate the psychic damage this has inflicted on generations of children who might have grown up into healthy, happy, productive, zestful human beings but for the burden of antisexual fear and guilt ingrained in them by the Church. This alone is enough to condemn religion.

PLAYBOY: How do you feel about such Catholic canons as the vow of celibacy for priests, and the spiritual "marriage" of Catholic sisters to Christ?

MURRAY: Sick, sick, sick! You think *I've* got wild ideas about sex? Think of those poor old dried-up women lying there on their solitary pallets yearning for Christ to come to them in a vision some night and take their maidenheads. By the time they realize he's not coming, it's no longer a maidenhead; it's a poor, sorry tent that *nobody* would be able to pierce—even Jesus with his wooden staff. It's such a waste. I don't think *anybody* should be celibate—and that goes for priests as well as nuns. I don't even like to alter a cat. We should all live life to the fullest, and sex is a part of life.

PLAYBOY: As an atheist, do you also reject the idea of the virgin birth?

MURRAY: Even if I believed there was a real Jesus, I wouldn't fall for that line of hogwash. The "Virgin" Mary should get a posthumous medal for telling the biggest goddamn lie that was ever told. Anybody who believes that will believe that the moon is made out of green cheese. If she could get away with something like that, maybe I should have tried it myself. I'm sure she played around as much as I have, and certainly was capable of an orgasm. Let's face it: If a son of God was ever born, it was because of this wonderful sex act that Joseph and Mary enjoyed one night.

PLAYBOY: A moment ago, you said, "Even if I believed there was a real Jesus . . ." Are you saying that you don't believe that there was such a person as Christ, or are you denying his divinity?

MURRAY: I'm saying that there's absolutely no conclusive evidence that he ever really existed, even as a mortal. I don't believe he was a historical figure at all.

PLAYBOY: Do you dismiss all the Biblical records of his life?

MURRAY: Those so-called records were written by devout ecclesiasts who wanted to believe, and wanted others to believe, in the coming of a Messiah. Until someone *proves* otherwise, therefore, these stories must be considered nothing more than folk tales consisting in equal parts of legend and wish fulfillment. But there's never going to be any way of verifying them one way or the other. Scholars have found that references to Christ in Josephus were deliberately planted in the translation long after it was written, and the Latin references to Christ are not to a person of that name. In the Dead Sea Scrolls there *was* mention of a particular "teacher of righteousness" who had characteristics somewhat like those attributed to Christ, but it might easily have been someone else. About six years ago, *Life* magazine ran an article on the historicity of Jesus, and I was floored to find that they conceded the only evidence we have for his existence is in the Gospels. But don't take *Life*'s word for it. In his book *The Quest of the Historical Jesus,* the most definitive study that's ever been done on the subject, Albert Schweitzer admitted that there isn't a shred of conclusive proof that Christ ever lived, let alone was the son of God. He concludes that one must therefore accept both on faith. I *reject* both for the same reason.

PLAYBOY: Do you also reject the idea of a life hereafter on the same grounds?

MURRAY: Do you know anybody who's come back with a firsthand report on heaven? If you do, let me know. Until then, you'll pardon me if I don't buy it. If a humanist or an atheist or an agnostic says, "We'll bake you a pie," we can go right into the kitchen and bake it, and you can eat it an hour later. We don't promise you a pie in the sky by and by. It's charlatanry to promise people something that no one can be sure will ever be delivered. But it's even worse to offer people a reward, like children, for being good, and to threaten them with punishment if they're not. I'm reminded of the joke about Saint Peter sitting at the golden gate questioning a new arrival: "Well, my son, what good deeds have you done to get into heaven?" Well, the guy casts about for something to tell him and finally remembers that he gave five cents to a charwoman one night, and once he tipped a bootblack a nickel when he got his shoes shined, and another time he gave a beggar five shiny new pennies. And that's all he can think of that he's ever done for his fellow man. Well, Saint Peter looks at him and says, "Here's your fifteen cents back. You can go to hell."

That guy didn't know how lucky he was. I agree with Mark Twain, who wrote about the hereafter that there's no sex in it; you can't eat anything in it; there is absolutely nothing physical in it. You wouldn't have your brain, you wouldn't have any sensations, you wouldn't be able to enjoy anything—unless you're queer for hymn singing and harp playing. So who needs it? Speaking for myself, I'd rather go to hell.

PLAYBOY: Because of your success in persuading the Supreme Court to outlaw school prayer in public schools, many outraged Christians seem to feel that's just where you belong. What made you decide to pursue your suit in the face of this predictable indignation?

MURRAY: I was shamed into it by my son, Bill, who came to me in 1960—he was 14 then—and said: "Mother, you've been professing that you're an atheist for a long time now. Well, I don't believe in God either, but every day in school I'm forced to say prayers, and I feel like a hypocrite. Why should I be compelled to betray my beliefs?" I couldn't answer him. He quoted the old parable to me: "It is not by their words, but by their deeds that ye shall know them"—pointing out that if I was a true atheist, I would not permit the public schools of America to force him to read the Bible and say prayers against his will. He was right. Words divorced from action supporting them are meaningless and hypocritical. So we began the suit. And finally we won it. I knew it wasn't going to make me the most popular woman in Baltimore, but I sure as hell didn't anticipate the tidal wave of virulent, vindictive, murderous hatred that thundered down on top of me and my family in its wake.

PLAYBOY: Tell us about it.

MURRAY: God, where should I begin? Well, it started fairly predictably with economic reprisals. Now, I'd been a psychiatric social worker for 17 years, but within 24 hours after I started the case, I was fired from my job as a supervisor in the city public welfare department. And I was unable to find another one, because the moment I would go in anywhere in town and say that my name was Madalyn Murray, no matter what the job opening, I found the job filled; no matter how good my qualifications, they were never quite good enough. So my income was completely cut off. The second kind of reprisal was psychological. The first episode was with our mail, which began to arrive, if at all, slit open and empty—just empty envelopes. Except for the obscene and abusive letters from good Christians all over the country, calling me a bitch and a Lesbian and a Communist for instituting the school-prayer suit—they somehow arrived intact, and by the bushel-basketful. Hundreds of them actually threatened our lives; we had to turn a lot of them over to the FBI, because they were obviously written by psychopaths, and you couldn't be sure whether or not they were going to act on their very explicit threats. None did, but it didn't help us sleep any better at night.

Neither did the incredible anonymous phone calls we'd get at every hour of the day and night, which were more or less along the same lines as the letters. One of them was a particular gem. I was in the VA hospital in Baltimore, and I had just had a very critical operation; they didn't think I was going to make it. They had just wheeled me back to my bed after two days in the recovery room when this call came in for me, and somebody who wouldn't give his name told me very seriously and sympathetically that my father had just died and that I should be prepared to come home and take care of my mother. Well, I called home in a state of shock, and my mother answered, and I asked her about Father, and she said, "What are you talking about? He's sitting here at this moment eating bacon and eggs." Obviously, that call had been calculated to kill me, because whoever it was knew that I was at a low ebb there in the hospital.

Then they began to take more direct action. My Freethought Society office was broken into; our cars were vandalized repeatedly; every window in the house was broken more times than I can count, every flower in my garden trampled into the ground, all my maple trees uprooted; my property looked like a cyclone had hit it. This is the kind of thing that went on constantly, *constantly*, over a three-year period. But it was just child's play compared to the reprisals visited upon my son Bill. He'd go to school every day and hand in his homework, and a couple of days later many of his teachers would say to him, "You didn't hand in your homework." Or he'd take a test and about a week later many of his teachers would tell him, "You didn't hand in your test paper. You'll have to take the test again this afternoon." This was a dreadful reprisal to take against a 14-year-old boy. It got to the point where he had to make carbon copies of all his homework and all his tests to prove that he had submitted them. But that's nothing to what happened *after* school, both to him and to his little brother. Garth. I lost count of the times they came home bloodied and beaten up by gangs of teenage punks; five and six of them at a time would gang up on them and beat the living hell out of them. Many's the time I've stood them off myself to protect my sons, and these fine young Christians have spat in my face till spittle dripped down on my dress. Time and again we'd take them into magistrate's court armed with damning evidence and eyewitness testimony, but the little bastards were exonerated every time.

But I haven't told you the worst. The neighborhood children, of course, were forbidden by their parents to play with my little boy, Garth, so I finally got him a little kitten to play with. A couple of weeks later we found it on the porch with its neck wrung. And then late one night our house was attacked with stones and bricks by five or six young Christians, and my father got very upset and frightened. Well, the next day he dropped dead of a heart attack. The community knew very well that he had a heart condition, so I lay a murder to the city of Baltimore.

PLAYBOY: Sometime late in 1963, as we understand it, in the midst of all these harassments, your son Bill, then 18, started dating a 17-year-old Baltimore girl named Susan Abramovitz. In March of last year, according to court records, she left home because of family friction and moved in with you and your family, where she remained for several months. Then, on June 2, 1964, a petition filed by her parents was granted by the Baltimore Criminal Court, charging that you and your son "encouraged Susan to renounce her religion and become an atheist," and ordering you to give Susan into the care of her aunt and uncle, and charging you and Bill to refrain from all contact with Susan—in person, by phone or by letter—until further notice. When Susan subsequently ran off to New York in defiance of the court order, she was cited for contempt of court—along with you and Bill, who were sentenced *in absentia* to one year and six months, respectively, in the Baltimore city jail. Why did you defy the court order?

MURRAY: For the simple reason that by the time that contempt charge was filed, Bill and Susan were married, and he had become her legal guardian. Just for the record, though, I'd like to explain why I took Susan into my home in the first place. Her parents were making life hell for her with impossible restrictions and disciplines, and it finally came to a showdown. So when she asked to stay with us for a few days, I said yes, intending to straighten things out with her parents when both sides calmed down a bit. Well, I called them up a few days later to discuss it, but they were extremely rude and abusive to me, and said they didn't want her back anyway. What was I supposed to do? Kick her out in the street? I guess all the neighborhood talk made them change their minds, though, because the next thing I knew we had that court order slapped on us without a hearing. Well, those kids loved each other and weren't about to be separated by a court order, so they got married—with my blessings.

PLAYBOY: When was it that the police came to your house to take Susan into custody?

MURRAY: Eight days after the kids were married. She and Bill hadn't been home 15 minutes from their honeymoon when a police car pulled up in front of the house, and another behind the house—surrounding us. We got our tape recorder and turned it on and Bill and I went out to meet this cop, and I asked him, "What do you want?" He said, "I'm here to pick up Susan Abramovitz." Bill said, "There's no Susan Abramovitz here. There's a Susan Murray here." I said, "Do you have a pickup warrant?" He said, "No." "Then you have no jurisdiction here," I said. "If she puts her goddamned foot out into the street," he said, "I'm going to pick her up." I've got this on a tape recorder. So I said to him, "Look, this is a hostile neighborhood. We don't want trouble here. I'm going to take Susan to my office at 2502 North Calvert Street. You can come down there and talk to me. My attorney will be there. We will be glad to talk to the judge, the police, anybody else, but it's got to be in a neutral business district and not in a hostile neighborhood." And he said, "If you bring the goddamned girl out here, I'm going to lock her up."

Well, with police cars front and back, and him calling for more help—we had seen him put in an order for more squad cars—we decided to make a break for it, to get into the car and take off. Well, Susan and I made it to the car, but I looked back and saw the policemen stopping my son with a billy club raised, so that he couldn't follow us. So we took off. I said to Susan, "There's going to be trouble. I'm going to drop you off someplace and you sit there until I can come back."

So I drove her about five blocks away and left her on a neighbor's back porch and drove back. By the time I got back home, there were seven police cars in front of my house, two police cars behind my house, a minimum of 15 policemen on the front lawn, and a mob of at least 100 to 250 people milling around. And I walked through the melee there, and I said: "What's the matter? Is there a criminal at large?" Well, Bill was nowhere to be seen. I demanded to know where he was and the cops said he'd been taken off to jail. I found out later what had happened during the five minutes I was away taking Susan to safety. This cop who had raised his billy club on Bill started to give him a beating. Then another cop joined in, and in a few minutes, when the reinforcements arrived, there were four policemen there giving Bill a terrific beating.

PLAYBOY: According to the sworn testimony of those policemen and several eye-witnesses, Bill started the fight by shoving, then striking a patrolman in the nose and knocking off his glasses in an attempt to prevent him from intercepting Susan on her way out of the house.

MURRAY: Naturally they'd say that. The fact remains that there were *four* of them beating up on one 18-year-old boy.

PLAYBOY: Not according to their depositions.

MURRAY: You expect them to admit it? But wait till you hear what happened next. One of our neighbors saw the cops beating Bill and he rushed out and said, "Can I help?" and promptly waded in with the four cops.

PLAYBOY: Again, this is denied by eyewitnesses.

MURRAY: Well, my mother was an eyewitness, and she was watching all this through the screen door, and when the neighbor started in on Bill, she finally rushed out—she's a very frail 73 years old—and tried to beat him off with her scrawny, rheumatic little fists. Well, he turns and says to one of the policemen: "Get that fucking bitch off of me!" And the policeman just reaches out, taps Mother on the head once with his club, and she falls to the ground unconscious.

PLAYBOY: Again, this contradicts police testimony, which denies flatly that anyone struck her. According to the officer involved and several witnesses, she fainted in the midst of the struggle.

MURRAY: Well, she may be frail, but she isn't so old that she doesn't know the difference between a fainting spell and a rap on the head from a billy club. In any case, my brother, who has a bad heart, was watching all this from inside the house. He was afraid to get tangled up in it for fear he'd have a heart attack, but when he saw her get clubbed, he ran out and picked her up and carried her back inside and put her on the couch, which is where I found her, still unconscious, when I got back to the house. I also found two police officers in the house; they had broken the screen door open.

I said: "What are you doing in my house?" And they said: "It's none of your god-damn business." And I said: "Well, you get the hell out of here." And they said: "We'll get out of here when we goddamn well please." I said: "You'll get the hell out right now. Out!" And I took one of them firmly by the elbow and steered him to the door; to my astonishment, he went like a lamb. I had him halfway out the door when the bloodthirsty crowd outside spotted us, and one of the four policemen on the porch yelled, "Get that bitch out here!" And a second policeman snarled, "Yeah. Bring the bitch out!" Just like that, the cop I had by the elbow whirled and pounced on me like a bird of prey, and started to drag me out the front door. Well, I tried desperately to back up, and I had gotten back as far as the living room when the two policemen in there grabbed me and started pounding on me. I'll tell you, they gave me judo cuts; they kicked me in the kidneys with their knees; they really worked me over.

PLAYBOY: None of this gibes with the police version of what took place. They deny all of your allegations.

MURRAY: Of course they do. But I've got the bruises to prove it, buddy. I can assure you they weren't self-inflicted. I've never had a beating like that one. For the next 20 minutes I hung onto anything I could hang onto while they tried to drag me outside. I hung onto chairs. I hung onto the television set. I hung onto the door frame. I hung onto the doorknob. I hung onto the screen door. My fingernails were completely ripped off; they were just blood. Every single inch of the way I was breaking holds, grabbing onto anything, hanging on with my legs, with my hands. Finally they had me out on the front porch, and I locked my elbow through the iron banister outside, but they pulled me off of it and started rolling me across the lawn, pummeling me every inch of the way while that crowd just kept screaming: "Hit her again, hit her again, kill her, kill her, that bitch, hit her again, bitch, bitch, bitch, bitch, bitch!"

You'd think everybody had suddenly gone insane. And you should have seen the hatred, the blood lust in their faces as those cops beat and dragged me 30 feet across the lawn and onto the street. When they got me into the street, one of them put handcuffs on me and then dragged me up off the ground, bodily, by the cuffs. My arm was dangling there, the circulation in my hand completely cut off. Completely. My hand turned black. I hadn't landed a blow during the whole melee, but I was in such agony with those cuffs that I pulled back my leg and kicked that son of a bitch in the shins until his teeth rattled. Immediately, he yelled, "Witness, everybody—witness! Mrs. Murray has assaulted me." And that's the main charge against me today. That's why they want to extradite me to Maryland—because I kicked a poor, helpless little cop in the shins. Well, they decided they'd haul me off bodily to the paddy wagon, and by God, I decided I wasn't going to go without a struggle, handcuffed or not handcuffed, so when they tried to walk me off, I just lifted my feet up and threw them off balance.

One of them said, "You bitch, just wait until you get in that wagon." I thought. "Oh, oh, I'm in for it." So I stuck one foot between this guy's two legs on the left and one foot between the guy's two legs on the right, and I tripped them and they fell on their faces.

One of them said, "I'll grind your fucking face into the ground, you bitch!" And they dragged me up, and I stuck my feet in between them again, and down they went again. This is the other charge against me—that I assaulted two other officers by kicking them in order to trip them. Well, they threw me in that wagon and took me off to jail, where they kept me incommunicado for ten hours.

PLAYBOY: The police flatly deny this.

MURRAY: They're lying, as usual. The only way my attorney found out I was in jail was when he heard it on the radio, or otherwise he would never have come to our rescue. And I do mean rescue, because I found out when I got to jail that the police had taken my son into a cell and beaten him up. They dumped him on the floor and stomped on him while he was lying there.

PLAYBOY: How do you know this? Did you see it happen?

MURRAY: I was taken to the police station where my son was, and as I sat in the paddy wagon outside, I heard him being cursed and beaten. Bill told me all about it later. But he didn't have to, because when they brought him out of the prisoner lockup, he had a bootprint on the left side of his face; I saw it with my own eyes. He had another bootprint on the middle of his chest; and another one on the fly of his pants. The sons of bitches had kicked him in the genitals. When the judge brought him out to have him arraigned with me on those trumped-up assault charges, I said, "Judge, look at that boy's face." And I said to the newspaper reporters, "Look at the footmarks on him. Please note this." But not a word about it appeared in the newspapers.

PLAYBOY: Nor are there medical records of any injuries sustained by your son on this date, though he was examined by a doctor at his own request.

MURRAY: My son and I were taken to University Hospital and my mother was taken, unconscious for over three hours, to Union Memorial Hospital—that's a pretty long faint! UPI has a picture of me, printed in *The Washington Post,* swathed in bandages as the police forced me into the paddy wagon again after I was released from the hospital. It's interesting to hear now that there are no hospital records. But then, a lot of things seem to happen in Baltimore for which there are no records. I know it's only my word against theirs, and that my word wouldn't be worth two cents in a Baltimore court of law. But I know I'm telling the truth, and they know they're lying.

Anyway, we put up bail and finally went home. Well, you talk about terror; somebody tried to break into our house three times that night. We got my old German Luger out, and we found the old shells to it and filled it up. And we called our attorney out there, Joe Wase, who brought out a private detective with him—but too late, unfortunately, to catch them in the act. You know who they were? Men in navy-blue pants and short-sleeved white shirts. We caught one of them in a flashlight beam and I saw a badge with the word "Lieutenant" on it. Two others we saw with badges on. So we knew that the police were trying to get into our house. Not openly, but surreptitiously. The light in our back yard was put out, and the street light had a stone hurled through it. And our dog was silenced by a piece of wood rammed into his jaws. We had that tape recording in the house, incriminating the cops in a clear case of illegal entry, and they wanted it back.

PLAYBOY: As you no doubt know, Mrs. Murray, tape recordings cannot be used as evidence in court, so it seems doubtful that the police would risk violating the law to obtain this one. In any case, do you have any witnesses, apart from your own family, willing to swear that the housebreakers were policemen?

MURRAY: No; as I said, my lawyer and the private detective got there too late. So I must be making this all up—right?

PLAYBOY: We didn't mean to imply any such thing. But you understand, don't you, that police spokesmen have flatly denied these charges?

MURRAY: I understand all too well. Anyway, shall I go on with my version—the true version—of what happened?

PLAYBOY: By all means.

MURRAY: Well, after that night we lived in fear of our lives. The beating we'd gotten and the three attacks on the house were just a sample of things to come if we were foolish enough to stick around like sitting ducks. Even if we weren't murdered in our beds before the trial, I knew that if they got us into a courtroom, we'd get at least 200 years—plus 60 days extra for every time we breathed, blinked or raised our eyebrows.

[According to the Baltimore state's attorney's office, there are a total of ten criminal assault charges against Mrs. Murray and her son—carrying maximum sentences, if they are convicted on all counts, of ten years for each of them.]

MURRAY: Anyway, after another sleepless night, I decided that we'd have to take our chances with the law and get the hell out of Baltimore. I thought of seeking asylum in Canada or Australia or England, but I didn't want to leave the United States, because for better or worse I'm an American, and this is my land; so I decided to fight it out on home ground, and finally we hit upon Hawaii, because of the liberal atmosphere created by its racial admixture, and because of its relatively large population of Buddhists, who are largely nontheistic, and might therefore be more tolerant of our views. So we packed up all the worldly possessions we could carry with us and took the next flight to Hawaii from Washington.

PLAYBOY: How many were in your party?

MURRAY: Six of us—mother, my brother, my two sons, Bill's wife and me. And I can tell you, it took just about every cent we had to our name just to pay the plane fare. When we arrived, we had about $15 left among us. We were really in pitiful shape. But we were together, and we were alive, and this was all that mattered.

PLAYBOY: How did you find a place to stay?

MURRAY: Well, we were just floored by the kindness of the people here. The minister of the Unitarian Church in Honolulu invited us over to his office the day we arrived and told us to make it our headquarters while we looked for a permanent residence. When we couldn't find a place for about a week, he let us live in the church; that's ironic, isn't it? But it points up the vastly different intellectual atmosphere that prevails here in Hawaii. Anyway, we rustled up some mattresses and put them on the floor and slept there, cooked there and ate there until we found a home. I was overwhelmed by the number of calls we got from people offering to rent us houses, to take us out to dinner, to drive us around house hunting. Everyone was just indescribably kind. Finally we moved into a house offered to us for an incredible $125 a month by a man who feels that the separation of church and state is a valid constitutional issue which should be fought for. And we've found us a brilliant lawyer to help us fight extradition back to Maryland—which the Catholic governor of Hawaii has already granted. We've appealed the case to the state supreme court, which is considering its decision now.

PLAYBOY: If the court upholds the governor's decision, what will you do?

MURRAY: Well, whatever happens, I won't go back to Maryland, because I'd never get out again. Even if I managed to stay alive long enough to stand trial, I'd "accidentally" fall in my cell and fracture my skull or something. As a last resort, if I found I had no other alternative to returning, I would seriously consider suicide. I don't say this with any emotion. It's just that I'd much rather blow my own brains out than have it done for me in a Baltimore jail cell. You think I'm being paranoiac? I know them. There've been people found mysteriously dead in those Baltimore police cells before, and I don't intend to be one of them.

PLAYBOY: Well, you haven't been extradited yet. Meanwhile, where are you getting the money to pay your landlord and your lawyer?

MURRAY: It's been a terrific struggle, because we had to leave my Freethought Society offset printing plant and all of my office equipment behind when we fled Maryland, and my headquarters there has since been taken over by a group of so-called atheists who have denounced me, deposed me as president and installed themselves as the board of directors, treasurer, secretary, managing editor and general manager of the organization. I mean they've just taken over the entire operation, which I founded and built up and ran, lock, stock and barrel. But we've managed to establish sort of a government in exile here, after a fashion; we're turning out our newsletter again, and the contributions are beginning to trickle in, now that our members know where to find us—enough to live on, but only barely enough to fight extradition, and not nearly enough to keep our tax-the-churches suit alive. We desperately need funds if this case is going to stand a chance of reaching the Supreme Court—which is the only place we'll win it.

PLAYBOY: Considering the repercussions of the school-prayer case, why did you decide to take on the tax-the-churches suit?

MURRAY: Once involved in the school-prayer fight, I rapidly became aware of, and appalled by, the political and economic power of the Church in America—all based on the violation of one of our nation's canon laws: the separation of church and state. The churches rose to power on the income from tax-free property. What earthly—or heavenly—right have they got to enjoy a privilege denied to everyone else, even including nonprofit organizations? None! My contention is that with the churches exempted from property taxation, you and I have to pay that much more in taxes—about $140 a year per family, according to a recent survey—to make up for what they're not contributing. If this exemption were rescinded, our property taxes would be substantially lowered, and those who rent houses and apartments would consequently be able to pass along this savings in the form of lowered rents. It could have a profoundly salubrious effect on the entire economy. I decided that if nobody else was going to do anything to rectify this colossal inequity, I'd have to do it myself. So I instituted a suit against the city of Baltimore demanding that the city assessor be specifically ordered to assess the Church for its vast property holdings in the city, and that the city tax collector then be instructed to collect the taxes once the assessment has been made.

PLAYBOY: Have you made any estimate of approximately how many annual tax dollars the churches will have to pay if you win your suit?

MURRAY: On a nationwide basis, I would guess that the various churches would have to pay annually an amount at least equal to the national debt. But it's impossible for me to make an exact estimate, because the churches hide their wealth in every way they can—deliberate falsification as to the value of property, registering it under phony names in order to obscure the fact that the Church owns the property. In Baltimore alone, I know that the Roman Catholic Church alone would have to pay taxes of almost $3,000,000 a year. This is why the Roman Catholic Church has become a codefendant with the city in the suit—an unprecedented occurrence in a case of this nature. I'm going after them where they live—in their pocketbooks—and they're fighting for their lives. They have a tremendous amount at stake—more than any other church, because they're the biggest property owners and they've dabbled in business more than any other church. More than any other church, they've been greedy about grabbing up land and property—not just in Baltimore, but all over the country. According to a Catholic priest writing in *The Wall Street Journal*, the assets and real-estate holdings of the Church "exceed those of Standard Oil, A.T.&T. and U. S. Steel combined." I'd make an educated guess that 20 to 25 percent of the taxable property in the U. S. is Church-owned. In a recent book, *Church Wealth and Business Income,* it was estimated that this property—all of it tax-exempt—is worth upwards of 80 billion dollars. I know that's a fantastic, unbelievable figure, but there's every reason to believe that it's on the conservative side; and this amount is increasing yearly at a geometric rate. They're moving into everything—gas stations, banks, television stations, supermarket chains, hotels, steel mills, resort areas, farms, wine factories, warehouses, bottling works, printing plants, schools, theaters—everything you could conceivably think of that has nothing to do with religion, they are moving into big. They're even coming in as stockholders in the big oil companies, and the Bank of America is almost entirely owned by the Catholic Church. And mind you—they don't pay a penny in taxes on any of it, even on the income from rentals. The Roman Catholic Knights of Columbus, for example, pays *no* income tax on any of its vast rental revenue— which comes from such sources as the land on which Yankee Stadium stands.

Almost every constitutional authority has spoken on this issue, and the overwhelming consensus is that we will *win* if we can get it to the U. S. Supreme Court. But we won't unless thousands of people help me raise the money to pay the legal fees—at least $40,000.

PLAYBOY: You've been quoted as saying that the Catholic Church in Baltimore was behind a conspiracy to have you and your family jailed on some pretext so that you would be unable to pursue this suit, and that this is why you were subjected to a "campaign of extralegal harassment" by the police, the courts and the citizens of Baltimore. Do you really believe that?

MURRAY: I can't think of any other plausible explanation for this vendetta. But quite apart from the Church's financial self-interest in getting me out of the way, Baltimore is an overwhelmingly Catholic city and, like most good Christians, they felt we ought to be punished for our unorthodox views. Intolerance has always been one of the cornerstones of Christianity—the glorious heritage of the Inquisition. It's no coincidence that most of my abusive mail—sentencing me to exquisite Oriental tortures and relegating me to hell-fire and damnation—comes from self-admitted Catholics.

PLAYBOY: Are you still receiving that kind of mail here in Hawaii?

MURRAY: For some reason, the letters we've been getting here have been just a little bit more rational; I wonder what's happened to our lunatic fringe. I kind of miss them.

PLAYBOY: Is it true that you received a letter in Baltimore composed only of the word "Kill" clipped from dozens of magazines and newspapers, and pasted onto a sheet of paper in the style of a blackmail note?

MURRAY: Absolutely. It was from a man who had written to me over a period of about two years. He started out in his first letter with something innocuous like: "You're a damn fool!" But each successive letter got more and more violent, until he came to the point where he was very explicit in his threats. We turned that whole series of letters over to the FBI. One of the things this guy said he was going to do to me was put a gun up my ass and blow the crap out between my eyes. Nice? But that's mild compared to some of them. I've gotten literally thousands in the same vein. Someday I'd like to publish a book of these mash notes. It would be an extraordinary document. I'd call it *Letters from Christians.*

PLAYBOY: Would you include the photograph of yourself which you received smeared with feces?

MURRAY: That would be the frontispiece. This was a picture of my mother and me coming out of the United States Supreme Court, with fecal matter smeared across our faces. They wrapped it in wax paper so that when I received it I'd get the full impact of the message. Though I haven't gotten anything quite that original lately, there's still never a dull moment in my mailbox. Here's a dilly that came in the other day. I'll read it aloud, if I may:

I dreamed that Mrs. Murray died
And no one but the Devil cried.
He had plenty more work for her to do;
And people like her were very few.
Well, it was a blow that would last him long;
He couldn't find anyone else so very wrong.
But no one in the city cried;
Most all were glad that she had died,
And thought it was a shame that fate was slow
And death had not snatched her long ago.
The churches all looked on in awe and wondered why
She could change a law.
In death her face looked like a stone;
So cold, so hard in life it had grown;
They had dressed her like a fashion show;
Expensively dressed and no place to go;
There was no service at the grave;
Her soul was gone too late to save.
It is a shame she went to hell;
But at least down there she cannot yell;
And rant and rave about the prayers.
How could she creep in unawares and
Change the routine of our schools?
We have always had our religious rules;
I wonder if she is allowed to pass the golden gate.
Can't Saint Peter see her heart of hate?

Beautiful, isn't it? Kind of gets you right here. That's from one of my most faithful correspondents: "Anonymous." And here's another one, signed "I Pity You." Unusual name, don't you think? I have so many people pitying me and praying for me that I'll probably be the only atheist that gets into heaven.

Here's another—this one from a sophomore in the State University of New York, College of Oswego. He says:

> I'd like to refer you to Hugh Hefner, author of *The Playboy Philosophy*, which appears in PLAYBOY magazine. He is doing an excellent job of revealing to the masses the religious and superstitious background of many of our laws, pointing out the clear stupidity of these laws in the light of reason. More power to both of you.

How about that? We occasionally get an intelligent letter like this one mixed with the rest, but most of them are like this gem:

How would you like to die of cancer? Or be blind the rest of your miserable haunted life? Filled with such fear you have to get a police dog. Ha. You are so filled with hate you will poison yourself to death. You are making a screwball out of your none-too-bright dopey-looking son, you big crude brawling peasant. Time will fix you but good. Leprosy is too good for you. Shame on you. You aren't a mother or even a woman, you are a no-good thing.

Isn't that delightful? But that's nothing compared to some of the goodies I keep in this box labeled NUT MAIL. Shall I read you excerpts from a random sampling?

PLAYBOY: Please.

MURRAY: You asked for it. Here goes: "You should be shot!" . . . "Why don't you go peddle your slop in Russia?" . . . "YOU WICKID ANAMAL" . . . I will KILL you!" . . . "Commie, Commie, Commie!" . . . "Somebody is going to put a bullet through your fat ass, you scum, you masculine Lesbian bitch!" . . . "You will be killed before too long. Or maybe your pretty little baby boy. The queer-looking bastard. You are a bitch and your son is a bastard" . . . "Slut! Slut! Slut! Bitch slut from the Devil!" That'll give you the general idea. Oh—just one more; I love this one: "May Jesus, who you so vigorously deny, change you into a Paul."

Isn't that lovely? Christine Jorgensen had to go to Sweden for an operation, but me they'll fix with faith—painlessly and for nothing. I hate to disappoint them, but I'm not the least bit interested in being a man. I'm perfectly satisfied with the female role.

PLAYBOY: What *is* the proper female role, in your opinion?

MURRAY: Well, as a militant feminist, I believe in complete equality with men: intellectual, professional, economic, social and sexual; they're all equally essential, and they're all equally lacking in American society today.

PLAYBOY: According to many sociologists, American women have never enjoyed greater freedom and equality, sexually and otherwise, than they do today.

MURRAY: Let's distinguish between freedom and equality. The modern American woman may be more liberated sexually than her mother was, but I don't think she enjoys a bit more sexual equality. The American male continues to use her sexually for one thing: a means to the end of his own ejaculation. It doesn't seem to occur to him that she might be a worth-while end in herself, or to see to it that *she* has a proper sexual release. And, to him, sex appeal is directly proportional to the immensity of a woman's tits. I'm not saying that all American men are this way, but nine out of ten are breast-fixated, wham-bam-thank-you-ma'am cretins who just don't give a damn about anyone's gratification but their own.

If you're talking about intellectual and social equality for women, we're not much better off. We're just beginning to break the ice. America is still very much a male-dominated society. Most American men feel threatened sexually unless they're taller than the female, more intellectual, better educated, better paid and higher placed statuswise in the business world. They've got to be the authority, the final word. They say they're looking for a girl just like the girl who married dear old dad, but what they really want, and usually get, is an empty-headed little chick who's very young and very physical—and very submissive. Well, I just can't see either a man or a woman in a dependency position, because from this sort of relationship flows a feeling of superiority on one side and inferiority on the other, and that's a form of slow poison. As I see it, men wouldn't want somebody inferior to them unless they felt inadequate themselves. They're intimidated by a mature woman.

PLAYBOY: Like yourself?

MURRAY: Yes, as a matter of fact. I think I actually *frighten* men. I think I scare the hell out of them time after time. It's going to take a pretty big man to tame this shrew. I need somebody who can at least stand up to me and slug it out, toe to toe. I don't mean a physical battle. I mean a man who would lay me, and when he was done, I'd say: "Oh, brother, I've been *laid*." Or if we had an argument, he would stand up and engage in intellectual combat and not go off and mope in the corner, or take reprisals, or go to drink. I want somebody who's whole and wholesome and has as much zest for living as I have. But I haven't found *one* who fills the bill; you can't hardly find them kind no more. And I know many women my size, psychologically and intellectually, who have the same problem. Most women don't, of course, because they don't make the same demands, because they're not fully women—which is to say, alive and constantly growing. I haven't had an enduring love relationship, because I'm growing constantly, and at a brisk rate. I'm changing constantly and enlarging my viewpoints, and I've simply never met a man who could keep pace. So men finally bore me. They get in a rut. I saw one of my ex-lovers ten years later and was shocked to realize he had not moved an inch intellectually or emotionally from his position of a decade before.

PLAYBOY: How many lovers have you had, if you don't mind our asking?

MURRAY: You've got a hell of a nerve, but I don't really mind. I've had—if you count my marriage as an affair, which I would like to do rather than count it as a marriage, because I'm not proud of having been married—I've had five affairs, all of them real wingdings. I've enjoyed every goddamned minute of them, but sooner or later I've outgrown every one of them, and when I did I got fed up and threw them out. If they can't keep up with me, the hell with them.

PLAYBOY: Suppose a man were to get fed up with you first. What then?

MURRAY: Well, then *he* should be the one to pick up and leave. No hard feelings. I don't feel that people should glom onto other people. I feel that relationships should be nice and easy and convenient and happy and not strictured with legality or jealousy.

PLAYBOY: When you say "not strictured with legality," are you saying that you don't think people ought to get married?

MURRAY: Well, I've found that most people who are bound together legally would be a damn sight happier together—or apart—if they were released from the contract. A man–woman relationship is physical and emotional, not legal. Legality can't create love if it isn't there, or preserve it if it's dying, but it can *destroy* love by making it compulsory. You don't need a marriage license to live with someone, to have the security of a home, to rear any number of children, to have years of companionship; it's not illegal. But the moment you want to screw somebody, you have to get a license from the state to use your genital organs—or run the risk of being charged with any number of crimes carrying sentences up to and including death. So sex is really the only sensible reason for getting married. But I'd suggest pulling down the shades instead. In the long run, it's cheaper—and more fun.

PLAYBOY: How do you feel about the heritage of puritanical sexual guilt which many social scientists assert precipitates early marriages in this country?

MURRAY: It's shit for the birds. When will we grow up? Sex is where you find it. I say take it and enjoy it. Give and receive freely, without fear, without guilt and without contractual obligations.

PLAYBOY: Starting at what age?

MURRAY: Let nature decide. When a cow is biologically ready to have sex relations, she mates with the nearest well-hung bull. When a flower is ready to scatter its seed, it pollinates. It's the same way throughout nature—except with man, who tries to postpone consummation of his sex drive, unsuccessfully, for the most part, for six or eight years after he reaches puberty. By the time it's considered socially acceptable to start screwing, most of us are sexually constipated, and this is often an incurable condition. I think young people should be able to have their first sexual love affair whenever they feel like it. In the case of most girls, this would be around 13 or 14; with most boys, around 15 or 16.

PLAYBOY: What about VD and pregnancy?

MURRAY: They should be taught about sex, sex hygiene and contraceptive methods starting in the sixth grade, and whenever they want to try it, they should be allowed to go at it without supervision or restriction—in their parents' bedroom, on the grass in a park, in a motel; it doesn't matter, as long as the setting is private and pleasant. If we did all this, our kids would grow up into happier, healthier human beings. But we won't, of course. It would make too much sense.

PLAYBOY: Would you call yourself an advocate of free love?

MURRAY: I'd describe myself as a sexual libertarian—but I'm not a libertine. "To each his own" is my motto. If anybody wants to engage in any kind of sexual activity with any consenting partner, that is their business. I don't feel that I can sit in judgment on them, or that society can sit in judgment on them. Anybody can do anything they damn well please, as long as the relationship isn't exploitive. And I don't feel that legality should have anything to do with it. There are certain bodily functions of mine which I will not allow to be supervised. One of these is eating.

Nobody's going to license me to do this. Another one is bodily disposals. I will defecate and urinate when I damn well please and as the spirit—and the physical necessity—moves me. And my sex life is peculiarly my own. I will engage in sexual activity with a consenting male any time and any place I damn well please.

PLAYBOY: Do you have any immediate plans along these lines?

MURRAY: It's none of your business, but as a matter of fact, I do. I've been completely without a sex life for about five years now—ever since I began the school-prayer suit—and if you don't think that's a hardship for a hot-blooded woman in her prime, just try it. I'm taking applications for stud service at this address—care of Good and Haffner, Attorneys, 1010 Standard Building, Cleveland 13, Ohio—as well as contributions for our tax-the-churches suit. Please enclose photograph, vital statistics, and a check for the lawsuit.

PLAYBOY: Are there any particular qualifications you're looking for?

MURRAY: No, I just want a man—a real, two-balled masculine guy—and there aren't many of them around, believe me. But I do want somebody my own age, and somebody who has brains enough to keep me interested and to earn enough money to support me in the style to which I've become accustomed. And I want a big man physically as well as intellectually. I want a man with the thigh muscles to give me a good frolic in the sack, the kind who'll tear hell out of a thick steak, and yet who can go to the ballet with me and discuss Hegelian dialectic and know what the hell he's talking about. I want a strong man, but a gentle one. And, most unlikely of all, but most essential, I want a man with a capacity for love—to give it generously and accept it joyously. I also want somebody who, when I say, "Let's call it quits," won't hang on; who'll say, "All right, it was fun while it lasted. So long and good luck."

PLAYBOY: Have you ever known a man like that?

MURRAY: No, but there was one who came close, and I loved him madly for some time. I don't think anybody in the world thought he was gentle, but he was gentle with *me*. And he treated me like a woman, which is all I really ask or want. I felt *handled* by him, and this is a good feeling. But, unfortunately, he never outgrew his particular intellectual commitment, so I outgrew *him*. He was an engineer and he was almost totally involved in his work; engineers have a very limited education and background, I think. You need to move into the broader humanities in order to become a total person. But I loved him very much.

PLAYBOY: Was he the one you loved most?

MURRAY: I think so. He's a damned Dago. That's a term of affection.

PLAYBOY: Of the men you've had affairs with, how many others were foreigners?

MURRAY: None of them. But they were of different extractions. This particular guy was of Italian parentage; another had English blood; one was a real upper-class Bostonian; one had a Russian background, and one was Irish; he was the one that was best in bed. Did you know that we ladies have bull sessions like this among ourselves, and we talk about which of you fellows are good stud service and which ones aren't? If you boys knew what you sound like when you and your bedroom manners are dissected by a bunch of WACs, it would curl your hair, because we talk about exactly the same things you do among yourselves—and just as graphically.

PLAYBOY: You served as a WAC in Italy and North Africa during World War Two, didn't you?

MURRAY: Yes, and we were outnumbered by men five hundred to one, so you can see why we were preoccupied with sex. There was a good deal of everything going on—fornication, masturbation, homosexuality, promiscuity, you name it. We were near the front lines, and there was a gluttonous feeling of "eat, drink and make merry, for tomorrow we die" in the air; it was kind of a last-gasp clutching at straws, at almost anything to relieve the strain.

PLAYBOY: Did you participate?

MURRAY: No, I was still pretty much of a puritan when I got into the Army, believe it or not, and when I saw these girls shacking up every night with a different GI, I thought, "How horrible. They're nothing but prostitutes." And I wouldn't even talk to them. But I began to get a lot more tolerant and understanding after a few months, and pretty soon I started an affair myself, and I slept with this one guy the whole time I was in the Army; nobody else. I've never been a one-night-stander. Say, I wonder why I'm telling you all this. I know I'm being indiscreet, because this kind of thing could be used against me nationwide; it'll just add fuel to the fire, which is already hot enough for me. But you know something? It just so happens that I don't give a damn. I'm going to be damned anyway. If they haven't destroyed me yet, I'd say I'm indestructible.

Five years ago, before I opened Pandora's box by starting the school-prayer case, I was doing all right financially; I had my health, a good job, a nice brick Colonial home, beautiful furniture, three cars, we were a happy, close-knit, well-adjusted family. Well, brother, look at me now, as the saying goes: Here I am in a termite-ridden bungalow in Hawaii, my savings are gone, my job is gone, my health is gone—thanks to the beating I got in Baltimore, which has lost me almost all the use of two fingers in my right hand. I'm bothered by a continuous low-grade pain in that same hand and arm, which distracts me from my work and keeps me awake nights. My Baltimore home is in jeopardy; I may lose it. I've lost my furniture and my cars. My brother can't find a job, though he's been looking for work ever since we arrived here; so he's just a nice, educated bum at this point. I've lost my father by a heart attack, and my son Bill has broken down emotionally to the extent that he's under psychiatric care. My aged mother is with me, and she can't even be buried next to Dad, whose grave is back in Baltimore. And my son and I are living under the Damoclean sword of imminent extradition back to Maryland, where we are certain to be convicted and sentenced to several years in the state penitentiary for assault—a crime which we not only didn't commit, but which was perpetrated against *us*. So my life and the life of my family has been completely disrupted in absolutely every way. But it's been worth it. It's uncovered a vast cesspool of illegitimate economic and political power in which the Church is immersed right up to its ears, and I intend to dive in head-first and pull it out of there dripping wet for all the world to see—no matter how long it takes, no matter whose feet get stepped on in the process, no matter how much it costs, no matter how great the personal sacrifice.

PLAYBOY: It sounds as if you intend to make this cause your *raison d'être*.

MURRAY: No, this crusade to separate church and state is only one expression of my *raison d'être*. I'm an atheist, but I'm also an anarchist, and a feminist, and an integrationist, and an internationalist—and all the other "ists" that people seem to find so horrible these days. I embrace all of them.

Long ago, when I was a very young girl, I said that I wanted to go everywhere, see everything, taste everything, hear everything, touch everything, try everything before I died. Well, I've been a model, I've been a waitress, I've been a hairdresser, I've been a stenographer, I've been a lawyer, I've been an aerodynamics engineer, I've been a social worker. I've been an advertising manager, I've been a WAC. There isn't anything you can name that a woman can do that I haven't done. Before they put me under, I'm going to get involved in everything there is to get involved in. That's what I want from life. I don't intend to stand by and be a spectator. I want to be right in there in the midst of it, right up to my nose—totally involved in the community, in the world, in the stream of history, in the human image. I want to drink life to the dregs, to enlarge myself to the absolute limits of my being—and to strive for a society in which everyone—regardless of race, creed, color and especially religious conviction—has the same exhilarating *raison d'être,* and the same opportunity to fulfill it. In other words, to paraphrase Jack Kennedy and John Paul Jones, from this day forward, let the word go forth, to friend and foe alike: I have not yet begun to fight.

Discussion Questions

1. What does Murray mean when she states, "Atheism is not a negation"?

2. Why, according to Murray, is it important for atheists to study the Bible?

3. Although Murray did not believe in God, she uses the adjective "goddamned" four times in this excerpt. What does this say about how religion shapes the way people talk or even think in addition to how they believe?

Credits

Introduction

Russell T. McCutcheon: "What is the Academic Study of Religion?" Reprinted by permission of the author.

Joseph P. Laycock and Natasha L. Mikles: "Name it and Disclaim it: A Tool for Better Discussion in Religious Studies," *Bulletin for the Study of Religion* 47:3–4 (2018), pp. 18–23. © 2018 Equinox Publishing Ltd. Reprinted with permission.

Hinduism

Patrick Olivelle (translator): Excerpts Chapter 7: "Katha Upanishad" from *The Early Upanishads: Annotated Text and Translation* (New York: Oxford University Press, 2018). © 2018 Patrick Olivelle. Reproduced with permission of the Licensor through PLSclear.

Mirabai: Excerpts from *Songs of the Saints of India* (New York: Oxford University Press, 1988), translated by J. S. Hawley & Mark Juergensmeyer. © 1988 by Oxford University Press. Reproduced with permission of the Licensor through PLSclear. Introductions to each poem from Wendy Doniger, edited by Jane Dammen McAuliffe, from *The Norton Anthology of World Religions*, edited by Jack Miles, et al. Copyright © 2015 by W. W. Norton & Company, Inc. Used by permission of W. W. Norton & Company, Inc.

Chandrima Chakraborty: "Narendra Modi's victory speech delivers visions of a Hindu nationalist ascetic," from The Conversation, May 26, 2019. Chandrima Chakraborty, Professor of English and Cultural Studies, McMaster University

Buddhism

Ṭhānissaro Bhikkhu (translator): *Poems of the Elders: An Anthology from the THERAGĀTHĀ and THERĪGĀTHĀ*, translated by Ṭhānissaro Bhikkhu (Geoffrey DeGraff). Copyright © 2015. Ṭhānissaro Bhikkhu. Reprinted by permission of Metta Forest Monastery.

John Ross Carter and Mahinda Palihawadana (translators): Excerpts from *The Dhammapada* (New York: Oxford University Press, 1987), translated by John Ross Carter and Mahinda Palihawadana. © 1987 by Oxford University Press. Reproduced with permission of the Licensor through PLSclear.

Glen Dudbridge (translator): Adaptation from *The Legend of Miaoshan* (New York: Oxford University Press, 2004). © 1978, 2004 by Glen Dudbridge. Reproduced with permission of the Licensor through PLSclear.

Thich Nhat Hanh: "Interbeing" and "Roses and Garbage" reprinted from *The Other Shore: A New Translation of the Heart Sutra with Commentaries* (2017) by Thich Nhat Hahn with permission of Parallax Press, Berkeley, CA, parallax.org.

Hannah Beech: "The Face of Buddhist Terror," from *Time Magazine*, July 1, 2013 © 2013 Time, Inc. All rights reserved. Used under license.

Sikhism

Jagmeet Singh: *Love and Courage: My Story of Family, Resilience, and Overcoming the Unexpected* (New York: Simon & Schuster, 2019). © 2019 by Jagmeet Singh. Reprinted by permission of Simon & Schuster Canada.

Harbani Ahuja: "A Revolution Called Love," by Harbani Ahuja. Reprinted by permission of She Writes Press from Meeta Kaur (ed.), *Her Name is Kaur: Sikh American Women Write about Love, Courage, and Faith* (Berkeley, CA: She Writes Press, 2014), pp. 278–282.

Judaism

David Goldstein (translator): "Lament on the Devastation of the Land of Israel" (1012) from *Hebrew Poems from Spain* (Oxford: The Littman Library of Jewish Civilization, 2007). © Berenice Goldstein 1965. Reproduced with permission of the Licensor through PLSclear.

Dan Ben-Amos and Jerome R. Mintz (translators): Excerpts from *In Praise of the Baal Shem Tov*, edited and translated by Dan Ben-Amos and Jerome R. Mintz. Reprinted with permission.

Stewart Ain: "Pulpit of Color," by Stewart Ain. Originally published in *The Jewish Week*, May 20, 2009. Reprinted by permission of *The Jewish Week*.

Yochi Rappeport: "Well-behaved women seldom make history," by Yochi Rappeport. Originally published in *The Jerusalem Post*, March 5, 2020. Reprinted by permission of *The Jerusalem Post* and the author.

Christianity

Augustine: Excerpts from *The City of God Against the Pagans* (Cambridge: Cambridge University Press,

1998), edited and translated by R. W. Dyson. © 1998 Cambridge University Press. Reproduced with permission of the Licensor through PLSclear.

Martin Luther: *The Freedom of a Christian* (1520) reprinted by permission of Augsburg Fortress Press from *Luther: Selected Political Writings* (Philadelphia: Fortress Press, 1974), edited by J.M. Porter, translated by W. W. Lambert, revised by Harold J. Grimm, pp. 25–31, 33–34.

Desmond Tutu: December 1984 Nobel Lecture: "Apartheid's Final Solution" © The Nobel Foundation 1984. Reprinted with permission.

Dorothy Day: Excerpts from *The Duty of Delight. The Diaries of Dorothy Day.* Edited by Robert Ellsberg. Marquette University Press © 2008 Milwaukee, Wisconsin, USA. Used by permission of the publisher. All rights reserved. www.marquette.edu/mupress

Islam

Malcolm X: April 20, 1964 from "Letters from Abroad" from *Malcolm X Speaks.* Copyright © 1965, 1989 by Betty Shabazz and Pathfinder Press. Reprinted by permission.

Sahih Al-Bukhari: "The Story of the Night Journey" from *The Early Years of Islam,* translated by Muhammad Asad. Reprinted by permission of The Book Foundation.

Abu 'Abd ar-Rahman as-Sulami: Reprinted with permission from Fons Vitae Publishing from *Early Sufi Women: Dhikr an-Niswa al Muta abbidat as-Sufiyyat* (Fons Vitae, 1999), by Abu 'Abd ar-Rahman as-Sulami, edited by Rkia Elaroui Cornell.

Fatima Mernissi: Excerpts from *The Veil and the Male Elite* by Fatima Mernissi, © Fatima Mernissi 1991. By Permission of Edite Kroll Literary Agency Inc.

Confucianism

James Legge (translator): Excerpts from *Shu Ching: Book of History: A Modernized edition of the translations of James Legge* (George Allen & Unwin, 1972), edited by Clae Waltham.

Confucius: Excerpts from "The Analects of Confucius" from *Chinese Religion: An Anthology of Sources* (Oxford University Press, 1995), edited by Deborah Sommer. © 1995 Oxford University Press. Reproduced with permission of the Licensor through PLSclear.

Wing-tsit Chan (translator): "Inquiry on the Great Learning" from *A Source Book in Chinese Philosophy* (Princeton: Princeton University Press, 1963), edited and translated by Wing-tsit Chan. Reprinted by permission of Princeton University Press.

Yu Dan: From *Confucius From the Heart: Ancient Wisdom for Today's World* by Yu Dan, translated by Esther Tyldesley. Copyright © Translation copyright (c) 2009 by Macmillan Publishers Ltd. originally published in China (c) 2006 by Zhonghua Book Company. Reprinted with the permission of Atria Books, a division of Simon & Schuster, Inc. All rights reserved. And by permission of Pan Macmillan.

Tu Wei-ming: "The Confucian Way of Being Religious." Reprinted by permission from *Centrality and Commonality: An Essay on Confucian Religiousness: A Revised and Enlarged Edition of Centrality and Commonality: An Essay on Chung-yung,* edited by Tu Wei-ming, the State University of New York Press ©1989, State University of New York. All rights reserved.

Daoism

Charles Q. Wu (translator): Excerpt from *Thus Spoke Laozi: A New Translation with Commentaries of Daodejing* (Honolulu: University of Hawaii Press, 2016), translated by Charles Q. Wu, pp. 124–125. Reprinted by permission of the Foreign Language Teaching and Research Publishing Co., Ltd.

Chuang Zu (Zhuangzi): "The Secret of Caring" and "Free and Easy Wandering" from *Chuang Tzu: Basic Writings,* translated by Burton Watson. Copyright © 1964 Columbia University Press. Reprinted with permission of the publisher.

Eva Wong (translator): From *Seven Taoist Masters: A Folk Novel of China,* translated by Eva Wong, © 1990 by Eva Wong. Reprinted by arrangement with The Permissions Company, LLC on behalf of Shambhala Publications Inc., Boulder, Colorado, shambhala.com.

Seth Faison: "In Beijing: A Roar of Silent Protestors," from *The New York Times,* April 27, 1999. © 1999 New York Times. All rights reserved. Used under license.

Navajo

Vincent Werito: "Understanding Hózhǫ́ to Achieve Critical Consciousness." From *Diné Perspectives: Revitalizing and Reclaiming Navajo Thought,* edited by Lloyd L. Lee. © 2014 The Arizona Board of Regents. Reprinted by permission of the University of Arizona Press.

Frank Mitchell: "Learning the Blessingway," from *Navajo Blessingway Singer: The Autobiography of Frank Mitchell 1881–1967* by Frank Mitchell. © 1977 The Arizona Board of Regents. Reprinted by permission of the University of Arizona Press.

Jim Kristofic: From *Hero Twins* by Jim Kristofic. Copyright © 2015 University of New Mexico Press. Reprinted with permission.

Paul Zolbrod (ed.): From *Diné Bahane: The Navajo Creation Story* by Paul Zolbrod. Copyright © 1984 University of New Mexico Press. Reprinted with permission.

Atheism

Bertrand Russell: From *Why I Am Not a Christian* by Bertrand Russell, edited by Paul Edwards. Copyright © 1957 & 1985 George Allen & Unwin, Ltd. Reprinted with the permission of Touchstone, a division of Simon & Schuster, Inc. All rights reserved. And by permission of Taylor & Francis Books ltd.

Madalyn Murray: The *Playboy* Interview of Madalyn Murray from the October 1965 issue of *Playboy* magazine. Archival *Playboy* magazine material. Copyright © 1965 by *Playboy.* Used with permission. All rights reserved.